P9-CCP-299

10 STUPID THINGS COUPLES DO TO MESS UP THEIR RELATIONSHIPS

Also by Dr. Laura Schlessinger

10 STUPID THINGS COUPLES DO TO MESS UP THEIR RELATIONSHIPS

Dr. Laura Schlessinger

Cliff Street Books
An Imprint of HarperCollins*Publishers*

HarperCollins books may be purchased for educational, business, or sales promotional use. For information please write: Special Markets Department, HarperCollins Publishers, Inc., 10 East 53rd Street, New York, NY 10022.

FIRST EDITION

Designed by William Ruoto

Library of Congress Cataloging-in-Publication Data

Schlessinger, Laura.
Ten stupid things couples do to mess up their relationships
/ Laura Schlessinger.
p. cm.
ISBN 0-06-028066-2
1. Man-woman relationships. 2. Marriage. I. Title.
HQ801.S4367 2001
306.7—dc21
2001028761

01 02 03 04 05 ❖/QWF 10 9 8 7 6 5 4 3 2 1

To Deryk and Lew,
who make both the lows
and highs worthwhile.

Acknowledgments

I am grateful for those who stood by me in times of pain and turmoil, including family, friends, colleagues, and my listening audience.

Thank you to my Chief of Staff, Keven Bellows; the President of Premiere Radio, Kraig Kitchen; and the special folks who work with me on my radio program, Cornelia Koehl, Michelle Anton, DeWayne McDaniel, and Dan Galanti. My radio program is the engine for my foundation for abused and neglected children (The "My Stuff" bag program), and Janine Holmes is the conductor of that train of mercy.

I am fortunate to have friends of substance and loyalty, without whom life would be a more difficult trial. I especially want to acknowledge Rabbi Moshe Bryski and the entire Chabad network for keeping me connected to my Judaism—sometimes in spite of myself.

My editor and publisher, Diane Reverand (aka The Reverend Diane) has been with me through six books. I respect her so much that I am quadruply enthralled when a sentence doesn't get the red pencil treatment.

I thank Hashem. In spite of the fact that the mission sometimes seems too big a burden, I am grateful for the gifts and for the opportunity to do something of value. I hope I live up to Hashem's expectations.

—Dr. Laura C. Schlessinger
April 2001

Contents

Introduction

Ten Stupid Things Women Do to Mess Up Their Lives was published in 1994, and *Ten Stupid Things Men Do to Mess Up Their Lives* hit the bookstores in 1997. It is now January 2001, and by my estimation, things have only gotten worse. It is my observation, from talking to tens of thousands of men, women, and children over a span of a quarter century on my syndicated radio program, that these last few decades of the millennium have been horrendously destructive to the ability of men and women to relate, commit, and enjoy building and being a family.

This book is not about documenting the ugly and relentless attacks on the healthy expression of the unique qualities of masculinity and femininity, marriage, family, and parenting; I've passionately done that in *Parenthood by Proxy* (later published in paperback as *Stupid Things Parents Do to Mess Up Their Kids*). This book is about the problems men and women face in finding "peace in love" in an American society that is anything but conducive to spiritual bonding and the joyful mutual commitment to obligations which are, as

1

everyone ultimately admits on his deathbed, the very foundation of a meaningful life.

American society is best defined by the nature of its children and young adults. Our children believe that chastity is defined by oral and anal intercourse—as long as there is no vaginal penetration. (Thank you, President Clinton.)

Our children believe that commitment is temporary at best, so why marry at all—just shack up. (Thank you to many of their parents.)

Our children believe that relationships are not for them to cherish, but, as slaves, to serve them; and when the relationship just doesn't "feel good" anymore—move on. (A thank you to their parents who leave "to find themselves" or for "true happiness"—generally in somebody else's undershorts.)

Our children believe that children are not very important. If they were, why would parents leave, marry someone else, make new children, and not see them anymore? If children were important, why would their mommy and daddy only see them just before bedtime? If they were important, how come they don't even know who their daddy is?

Our children don't know what they're supposed to do with respect to being a man or a woman, a husband or wife, a mother or father. There are no definitions and no scripts; not for healthy behaviors, anyway. There is hostility to anything masculine and there is victimization mentality about anything feminine; no one really needs to be married; parents are replaceable by hired help and technology.

Our children don't know how to face a future with all these uncertainties and chaos typifying our society. The focal point for the current confusion, resentment, and stupid behaviors of people today in their relationships with the opposite sex are the new *norms*, which are devastating.

Sexual intimacy doesn't have to mean anything.

Commitment is dependent upon your current feelings or circumstances.

It's not only okay, but necessary for you to be sexually experimental, including a variety of techniques, partners, and genders. College campuses like Penn State U. and the State University of New York at Albany now have student activities, under the guise of health, which promote S&M and other vulgar displays. In other words, nothing you do is wrong, your actions cannot be judged; people need to be free to express themselves in the basest of ways.

I think we've lived and played with these notions long enough to determine whether or not this experiment is a success or a failure. Results are in. This experiment is a failure. The reason is simple. Human beings have needs—not only temporary curiosities and desires—they have needs. The profound human need for the consistency and safety of a loving, bonded relationship is not met with the free-for-all mentality that promises only the moment, not tomorrow.

Recently on my program, I had a call that so neatly clarifies this truth. A young woman in her early twenties talked to me about the pain of two betrayals. She is visiting the United States from Australia on a three-month "educational experience." Her boyfriend of three years just e-mailed her that he's already in someone else's bed and body. Her comment to me, "Well, that's okay, but my friends are still hanging out with him." Can you believe that! The "love of her life" just started "doing" someone else during her brief absence, and all she says is, "okay," but the real pain is the lost loyalty of her friends?

First of all, I told her she was in denial to merely accept that her boyfriend didn't care enough about her and their relationship to sustain himself through his "inner sexual pressures." I explained that when young men experience free and easy sex without commitment, just for the feeling of it, that it is a spigot not easily turned off. Fidelity is about commitment to a person and to an ideal—one absent from their lives. She admitted this to be so.

I then answered her question about whether or not she was being unreasonable to presume that her friends would be loyal to her because "he did her wrong." I responded, "Yes, you're being unreasonable." She was really shocked here. I explained it this way: "You and he had no commitment. You expect your friends to react to your relationship as though you had one, and he had breached a vow. There was no vow, no promise, no covenant, no commitment. There was only familiarity and sex. There is no foundation for your friends to have to choose. They are living in exactly the same way as the two of you and realize that they want the freedom he took."

So, here it is. This young woman wanted to feel loved, cherished, valued, and special. She wanted to be in a safe, loving, warm commitment. Yet, she did nothing to ensure that because none of that is the *norm* any longer. She wanted to feel supported by her community when the sanctity of her unsanctified relationship was broken. That support is not there. In other words, today's societal norms *do not* provide for or create or support romance and a place for valued, safe, and truly intimate relations.

Men and women of all ages, religions, educations, ethnicities, socioeconomic realities, backgrounds, and experiences call me every day about their problems in life. It has become more and more clear that the core issue for almost all of these problems is a basic lack of moral standards by which important decisions are made. Why are these people astonished when it doesn't work out "right"?

For example, let's look at "courtship." That's a term most people don't even know, much less use in their lexicon or life. Courtship used to be a special time for people to get to know one another. It had rules, chaperones, support, and advice. Courtship provided an opportunity for men and women to develop a friendship, an understanding, a true knowledge of one another. It was a time of flirtatiousness and of chivalry, it was also a time to discuss religion, work, children, families, homes, philosophy, and to see how the respective families could function together. Courtship was about taking time to learn about another in enough depth to decide whether or not to become intimate.

Courtship is gone—instant "intimacy" is in. "Hooking-up" is the catchword of the day. That means having sex before you actually even know the person's middle name. Hooking-up and shacking-up are not about being in love with the ideals, goals, and promises historically inherent in such proximity. Hooking-up and shacking-up are about having without true giving. And when it stops giving, don't worry, just go someplace else and hook-up and shack-up all over again, and again, and again.

Eventually, they call my show. They're wondering what went wrong. They're hurt or angry, and definitely confused. They feel what one would expect from losing a loved one, yet have trouble admitting that their own behaviors created the loss. Hook-ups and shack-ups have no depth, no promise, no attachment, no contentment, no meaning. They do not demonstrate assumed value of the participants.

The saddest calls come from women and men who, after years of shacking-up (and maybe a baby or two), want to marry, only to find the other person enjoys this perpetual state of uncertainty.

The most annoying calls come from men and women who, after years of shacking-up, decide that this really isn't "the one," and it's time to move on. They call about whether or not they should keep seeing the others' children and wonder whether or not this is going to hurt the kids. I'll admit, I go crazy. It flabbergasts me to this day how cavalier people are with the psyche, feelings, and well-being of children.

When folks start out a call telling me about shacking-up with somebody with kids, I ask them directly if they think this teaches children something positive and hopeful for their futures. They almost always say, "No," but continue on as if those children don't matter, only their own feelings do.

Next to the chaotic, amoral, ultraliberal, current social *norms* that currently dictate our behaviors, hyperindividuality is the worst problem people have in relating to one another. Basically, if anything goes, and I'm not obligated by G-d to people in any way which doesn't serve me, then what I want/need/desire/do at the moment is my life's philosophy. If everybody lives that way then no one lives for anyone else, and none of us are safe from each other's whim or mood.

Welcome to modern America.

Twenty years ago, I would likely hear women callers complain about not being able to find a man who would commit. Now that's a rare call. Today, I more generally hear from men not being able to find a woman serious about marriage, family, and mothering. And, it would seem, it's getting more and more difficult for a man to find a woman he can respect.

Herb, one of my listeners, wrote in June of 2000.

"I was listening to your radio program when I heard you say something to the effect that you still believed in chivalry and that modern men don't see it in the same way as in the past, because the feminist movement paints that behavior negatively.

"But there is another side to this. In a modern world where a substantial number of particularly young women behave as boorishly, vulgarly, and sluttily as uncouth men do, falling on one's sword is not a logical reaction from men. The concept of even acknowledging, not to mention protecting, a woman's honor is about as foreign as the lunar landscape. What honor? Where?"

One "very concerned mom and grandmom" wrote in on the same day:

"What have these women become over the last forty to fifty years? Personally I think they're all brain-dead when it comes to their well-being, self-respect, children, etc. They have sex outside of marriage without thinking of consequences. It's the in thing. The feminist movement believed this would bring women on an even level with men. . . . Real men respect women who respect themselves. The feminists have encouraged women to give it away for free. Guess who ends up getting 'screwed' again!! (excuse the pun). And, in the process, they hurt innocent children, families, etc."

I receive thousands of letters from young men and women in their twenties and thirties trying desperately to untangle themselves from the nonsense they've been sold by a popular culture which cares nothing about people's true spiritual needs. Young women, who are born-again-virgins, want some meaning to their physical intimacy. Young men and women, who profess to hold virginity dear until their wedding nights, are mocked and dismissed by their peers, teachers, and other adults. Young women who, after having children and taking the six weeks of maternity leave, realize that they have to take career leave in order to properly parent and bond with their children. And young men don't know where to look for that old-fashioned girl with values.

Karl, one of my listeners, weighed in at this point.

"It seems that the feminist movement has done a marvelous job in alienating cooperative and warm relationship dynamics between men and women. A majority of American women now have fallen victim to the doctrine that devalues fatherhood, equal relationship dynamics, and a devaluation of men in general. This doctrine promotes single motherhood and that a/the father is not a necessity, actually a hindrance to actualization. Materialism and career-egocentrism are central to a woman's happiness and

that is all that matters. And yes! Dr. Laura, . . . children have become a 'cool fad' like SUVs and other yuppiedom possessions.

"Unfortunately, this is the prevailing atmosphere in the dating scene for those of us in our thirties and forties. But not to be dissuaded, there is hope for those of us men who long for a cohesive family that is based on love, devotion, and family values.

"If the fruit of a tree is poisoned, go to another tree. In my professional travels, I met a delightful and wonderful woman nearly my age. She is what we polite, well-mannered, loving, communicative, devoted, and supportive American guys are longing for. She is brilliant and talented, yet is interested in a warm family with two parents and knows that one parent alone does not work in raising children, or for the fabric of society as a whole. Plus, she appreciates my holding the door for her, and having a warm and balanced relationship. We plan to have children not dumped off to day care and we both know that our larger family will be important.

"So to all the chivalrous and sincere men out there, there are plenty of loving women around, stick to your principles. Don't give up."

I know what you're thinking . . . that I am blaming women alone for this current social mess. I do put more emphasis on women, because I see them as the ones with the ultimate power. What women don't allow, men can't and won't do. I learned this from my now deceased father. The notion inspired my first book, *Ten Stupid Things Women Do to Mess Up Their Lives.* He and I argued about responsibility, and he made the point that the upward or downward trend of the morals and morale of a culture was dependent upon what women did and permitted. He believed that men, rejected by women, would not continue the behavior that got them rejected in the first place. From womb (mother) to vagina (sex), he said, men are judged and approved of by women. Men behave badly when women accept it—simple as that.

In my then feminist mode, I argued bitterly with his point

of view, angry that he was blaming women for men's bad behavior. Now, I have come to see that he wasn't blaming, he was explaining, and he was right.

The feminist movement has become hostile to heterosexual relationships in general, marriage, mothering, modesty, and religious values in particular. Young women are surrounded by this liberal muck and are stumbling around "relationships" grateful for the morning-after pill and the abortion pill to get them out of one jam after another. Years later, I get the letters of shame and regret.

One sixteen-year-old girl called my program recently to "confess." She'd been at a party at a friend's house with drinks provided by her friend's parents, and had been making out. I asked her about whether her parents knew or would have approved.

"No," she said.

"So after getting sloshed on the booze, you started necking with him in the open, where others could see? Not very dignified, was it?"

"Well, we were a little off to the side."

"Then what happened?"

"He started to take me up the stairs to go into one of the bedrooms and have . . ."

"Is this a guy you're going steady with, or something?"

"No."

"Is this a guy your parents have met?"

"No."

"This is just a guy at school who happened to be at the party getting looped and touchy-body with you?"

"Yes."

"Did you end up having sex upstairs?"

"No, my friend's mother saw us going upstairs and said we couldn't use those rooms and sent us back downstairs. We started to neck again."

"What's your question for me?"

"Well, I feel bad about what I did and I want to know what I should say to him when I see him at school."

The so-called old-fashioned rules usually included parents who were responsible with their own kids and those of others. When adults are permissive about drugs, alcohol, and sex, children feel empowered by what is ultimately an inappropriate expectation. This teenager certainly did, as peer pressure extended to irresponsible adults.

I commented to her about how easy it is to do one stupid thing after each added stupid thing: drinking . . . necking . . . intercourse, and how this could have landed her in an abortion clinic, an adoption center, a welfare office, a STD clinic, or a counseling office. I suggested she tell the guy, "I made a mistake, I am ashamed, and I won't be doing that again."

I also told her to tell her parents.

My point is that our children lack direction, because we adults have lost direction. And the lost adults get older and older. One of the more frequent subjects callers seem to be struggling with is errant "grandparents." Can you believe it? Young married couples with children call me wondering what to do with their shacking-up and/or affair-leading parents: "Should we let them see the kids?" or "Should their 'honey' be introduced to the kids?" or "How do we work family holidays?" and so forth. Man 'o man, it's just all falling apart. The role models are dropping. Age is not bringing wisdom anymore. Decency is under attack from everywhere!

Yet, ultimately, people come to understand what they need is a warm, happy, secure nest. Susan wrote to my website (www.drlaura.com) that it is the truth from the past that brings us back to what is good and true about life and love:

"I met my prospective husband in July and married him in Sep-

tember. My mother had always told me, 'Be sure you know a man through all four seasons before you marry him,' and boy was she right! Three months is nowhere near long enough to discover someone's character. My (now ex-) husband claimed to have left some very nasty habits behind him when we started dating, but, as I said, three months isn't long enough to see the truth. Within two weeks of our wedding, he returned to using marijuana, which he had claimed to have quit for good. A little over a year later, two months after the birth of our son, he returned to using heroin, which he claimed he had been clean from for quite a few years. Apparently marriage and fatherhood were too much for him to cope with and the only coping tools he knew were drugs.

"I am sadder and wiser. My wonderful second husband and I knew each other for several years before we even started dating, both of us believing that a good friendship is a good basis for a good marriage. Through friendship we were able to really get to know each other's character, long before that tricky little devil, lust, got in the way of our clear judgment. Dr. Laura, I teach both my sons (ten and twenty-two) that anything truly important for a long-term, successful marriage can be learned through good solid friendship, even before a first kiss takes place. That's when you can still think with your brains instead of your libido. I also tell them, 'Know someone through all four seasons before you marry them.' Hmmmm . . . where have I heard that before?"

Grateful for the contributions of my twenty million listeners—via calls, e-mail, faxes, and letters—I offer this book as a guide for those fateful four seasons.

Dr. Laura Schlessinger
January, 2001

1

Stupid Secrets

*"Dr. Laura, when, if ever, should I tell a woman
I'm dating that I used to own and run a whorehouse?"*

Believe it or not, that was a recent question from a caller on my syndicated radio program. Though this specific question may stimulate snickers and outright laughs, the basic question is an important one: What, if any, information from your past are you obligated to reveal during dating, engagement, and marriage? And what if the past is only last week? And on the flip side, is there any danger in "the whole truth, and nothing but the truth"?

Is Everything Private a Secret?

The first issue to think about when deciding "what to tell" is to be able to distinguish between *secrecy* and *privacy*. This is not a small issue or insignificant distinction at all. I recently asked my listening audience their opinions and experiences with secrecy and privacy in intimate relationships and got the largest and most immediate response I ever received to an on-air question. Here are some of those responses:

➤ "Privacy is something you 'give' someone out of respect. Secrecy is something you 'withhold' from another."

➤ "Privacy is when you want to go to the bathroom or pick your nose without your spouse looking—or try to buy them a gift without their knowing. Secrecy is when you feel guilty about something that you can't tell your spouse."

➤ "For spouses to be secretive, they would also have to be separative. Secrecy builds lack of trust, reservation, guarded intimacy of the heart, and resentment—all of which lead to bitterness. Private is personal only to the individual and should not include anything that affects in any way both parties or the family."

➤ "In my opinion, privacy in marriage is your own personal space. In this, there is trust and respect. The other partner is aware of this space and respects it without intrusion. We all need a little private time to ourselves, otherwise we go nuts! I think secrecy is destructive in marriage—it is a lack of trust and respect. This is something the other partner is unaware of, and in essence, it is a lie."

➤ "Privacy is something we value within ourselves. It is something we decide a little at a time to share. My thoughts are private and I will choose to share bits and pieces. Secrets are wrong if they promote dishonesty, distrust, and compromise morals and integrity."

➤ "Privacy is having some quality time or spiritual time alone. I think secrecy in a marriage could be a form of deceit."

➤ "Privacy is the withholding of information concerning yourself, the disclosure of which would be of no benefit to the partner, and which you do not wish to share. Secrecy, on the other hand, is the withholding of information that may have an effect on the well-being of the partner. This effect may be financial, spiritual, physical, or mental. Privacy is acceptable. Secrecy is not, unless it protects the partner from harm."

➤ "Privacy is using the bathroom (especially when smell is involved), plucking your eyebrows, picking your nose, popping zits . . . all the ugly little things that are bad enough doing yourself let alone being involved with your spouse. Secrecy is not telling your spouse about a special surprise for them . . . definitely not something which would hurt the marriage or the spouse."

Whenever I receive a call about "telling" something to an intimate, the issue of what is private and what is secret is always the first part of the discussion. I not only want people to have integrity in their treatment of others, but it is vitally important for their well-being that they have compassion for themselves and maintain reasonable dignity. Too many folks seem to believe that they have to filet themselves wide open on the cutting board of their new relationships in order truly to be cleansed. These are the folks who have no sense of personal privacy at all. Others are filled with so much self-disgust that they want to hold everything in for fear that there is no forgiveness and no moving on. These are the folks for whom absolutely everything becomes a secret.

Being able to accept one's limitations, historical warts, and problems while being willing to risk truly being known by another is a definite sign of positive mental and emotional health, without which, quality relationships are not possible.

Fear of Privacy

There are flawed and sad elements in everyone's life and there are people with profound insecurities. These are the people who have to know everything you're doing, saying, thinking, reading, writing, and with whom. If they don't have this constant reassurance of information (their attempt to control the world and make themselves safe), they immediately imagine the worst and exaggerate and misinterpret everything and anything—leaving a wake of arguments and frustration.

Our cultural environment propels otherwise reasonably secure and well-meaning people to question the sincerity and fidelity of their dates, fiancés, and spouses like never before in history. Why? The answer is as simple as it is destructive:

➤   The general societal approval of out-of-wedlock sex has led to an epidemic of experimentation, casual sex, promiscuity, and a diminished "meaning" of physical intimacy. This produces a long line of prior lovers, who are still present at work, in the community, or in families—or who just can't let go.

➤   Pop-psych has called much of infidelity and promiscuity and perversion a *disease*. Men and women are ignoring their families to have internet affairs because of an *addiction*. Men and women are cavorting with extrarelational dalliances because of an *addiction*. This puts the victim of bad, selfish behavior in the position of being unsympathetic to their philandering partner's illness. Oh, puhlease!

➤   Our culture has supported the moment-to-moment quest of immediate satisfaction and gratification by making divorce no-fault and by saying shacking-up is equivalent to marriage. This puts people into positions that historically would have offered security (marital vows and social pressure), but now the social pressure is for individuality at the expense of vows, spouses, children, marriage, and community.

➤   The family courts do not support the sanctity of marriage, nor do they recognize the absolute needs and welfare of children. Spouses can up and leave for virtually no good reason, take the children three thousand miles away, shack-up with one or more new sex partners, and still retain status as good parents.

Rome is burning and most people are getting scalded—yet there are no alarms being sounded—just faint fiddling. It is no wonder that there is an increase in fear and cynicism about making a commitment.

Putting these extraordinary pressures aside for a moment, the fact remains that where there is no trust there will be no respect, and where there is no respect there will be no ultimate security for the relationship. Where there is so much insecurity in one person, the healthy, necessary, and natural line between privacy and secrecy will be squashed as the unhealthy partner will interpret reasonable privacy as a dangerous attempt at keeping evil secrets.

On the other hand, insecure people, so fearful of judgment or rejection or losing control, make absolutely everything private in a kind of desperate attempt to hold themselves together. In other words, they make everything a secret as a way of hiding, ducking, avoiding hurt.

One listener wrote in with her firsthand experience with a spouse who had such fears.

"Even though we wed too young, we made it through very rough years and hung in, based on our learning of this key element, privacy vs secrecy. At the beginning, my husband had huge

issues with privacy and felt very invaded, since he was no longer able to keep everything about himself to himself. He has learned to let go and let me in. I have learned that some things should be private, because telling the truth about absolutely everything can be quite destructive. For instance, my husband is the only sexual partner I have ever had. Before we met, my husband did have other partners. So, he has chosen to be secretive about the particulars since telling me will not be productive to OUR relationship and will most likely bring about a twinge or two.

"Learning that there is room for privacy without it being considered a destructive secret has made all the difference in our marriage. He feels secure, now that he has shared so much of himself with me, and I feel much more secure since I realize there is no need for me to know all."

Wow! What an accomplishment for them both. He changed by trusting her with his secrets, becoming secure in her affection and acceptance of his basic, true self; she changed by trusting his love without needing perpetual details which she now could allow him to keep private. That's the balance everyone should strive for.

People must be able to keep a sense of self as well as share their lives.

Keep It to Yourself!

There are times on my radio program when I yell directly at the caller, "What were you thinking!?! Why would you tell them that?!" I just can't believe it when, for example, a question will come in like:

"Dr. Laura, I'm looking to get some insight from you. I had a girlfriend when I was around eighteen years old. Now I am married with a beautiful ten-month-old son. Recently I became unhappy in my

marriage for an unknown reason. I got back in touch with my ex-girlfriend. I very quickly became depressed. I finally told my wife that I missed my ex-girlfriend. And it has understandingly hurt our relationship. I have told her that I am over it now, but she still brings it up when she gets mad. I was on the internet checking my e-mail today and I found a message from my ex-girlfriend asking me to give her a call. I don't know what I should do. I love my wife and son, but I don't know why I still have feelings for my ex-girlfriend. I don't know whether it is her friendship I miss or if I still love her."

He told his wife about his fantasies for another, real-life woman? Oy! This is definitely the realm of private. When we treat our spouse like our shrink or confessor we make a huge mistake that is often impossible to repair, even if the relationship continues. This is a time when we go to a real shrink or to real clergy. It's a time where we struggle with the natural impulse to avoid the difficult (marriage, mortgage, children, bills, busted water heaters) and escape to the easy (new or old sex/fantasy partners).

Such private struggles are the struggles of all human beings. These struggles enter the realm of destructive secrets when we return that call or e-mail.

As one listener wrote:

"Privacy deals with thoughts or ideas that are personal. Often situations that occur in nightly dreams are better not shared. Recounting laundry lists of ex-boyfriends is unnecessary and private. Ideas that take shape, but are just ideas, that might not be productive to the marital relationship are private. Privacy ends when thoughts, situations, or ideas are acted upon and impact the relationship and could damage the marriage.

"Frankly, I don't want to know what went on in his life when we went to separate colleges before we were married. Moreover, I'm sure he doesn't want to know my thoughts when I'm premenstrual or when I had the dream about the sexy stranger. We share

our future goals, funny jokes, most thoughts, our daily lives, and most importantly, our love for each other. I think we both stay away from situations that we would have to keep secret."

If that last comment isn't perfect! I'm suddenly remembering the caller who said he had a wonderful Harley motorcycle. His wife, whom he loved dearly, had no interest in bikes. One day he put an extra helmet on the back of his bike to use whenever he gave a ride to a pretty, young, female coworker who was thrilled at getting motorcycle rides. He called because his wife was upset. She noticed the extra helmet when he got home, and he told her what it was for. She was hurt and angry. He wanted to know if he was out of line. I suggested that unless he were suicidal, stupid, or disingenuous, it was inappropriate for him to spend vibrating bike time with a single woman while he was, and wanted to stay, a happily married man. I reminded him that he wouldn't have kept it a secret if he had really believed it was acceptable.

After the Fact

Sadly, sometimes there are predicaments and situations that can't be remedied and the truth or information has to be revealed. Other times, what seems like an obvious secret should be made known, because there's time left for an important lesson to be learned so that history won't repeat itself.

One young woman wrote to me wondering about keeping something a secret or making every effort to make sure the "involved" party was informed.

"I had been seeing my boyfriend for a year and a half. Two weeks before my eighteenth birthday I got pregnant. My parents and I decided that the best thing was to have an abortion. So ten days after my birthday, I had an abortion.

"He was totally against abortions. So, he does not know I had an abortion. I told him I was not pregnant. Am I obligated to tell him eventually? I feel it is my personal business, between my parents and myself. I know if I ever told him I had an abortion, he would be so upset. Should I tell him or keep it a secret?"

The truth is that this is not an issue between the young woman and her parents. It is an issue between her, the father of the child, the terminated child, and G-d. Her parents expedited the termination and preserved her secret, but there is more to the story.

If this were ten years or so after the event, my answer would be not to impose pure ugliness and hurt on someone who has gone on with their life. This situation is in the present, and this boy-man must know that unmarried, unprotected sex resulted in his first child being eliminated. While the young woman has the power to make the decision about terminating the life of her child, he has the responsibility to behave in a way that would never endanger his potential offspring. He needs to know, in my opinion, because he needs to learn something which will direct him to make better choices in the future.

The Right to Choose

When it comes to people having informed consent, I'm very pro-choice; that is, people need to take the time to learn enough about their potential partner, making a true choice— not just a response to fantasies, hopes, dreams, desires, or desperation. It takes a certain amount of maturity to slow down to do that, and the honesty of the other person willing to reveal important issues and factors that might "break the deal." Of course, since no one wants rejection, it's easy to understand why people fake it or keep secrets that shouldn't *don't. We all need to grow up and see that the universe does not revolve around only us."*

I'm sure that as you read April's letter, you thought to yourself, "Well, yeah, that's obvious—so what's the big deal?" I agree. The idea should be obvious. Too bad the practicing of it seems to be so troublesome to so many. The problem doesn't lie in any epidemic of genetic mutations that have produced self-centered, inconsiderate, selfish, self-protecting-through-hostility, insensitive, frightened, or confused people who don't know how to "become one." There have always been some folks with personality styles incompatible with healthy intimacy. But there is something new under the sun: the societal emphasis on individuality and the determination toward SELF-fulfillment, SELF-actualization, and PERSONAL happiness, as separate from obligations, commitments, and sacrifice.

As one of my listeners realized:

"Trying to be 'my own woman' has hurt my relationship. I found that the more I became my 'own' self, the less I was part of 'our' life. I started thinking more about individual needs instead of family needs. I was lucky enough to have a husband who brought me back to reality. Now, I have my 'own sense of individuality' within my family."

Jim, another listener, came to the same conclusion:

"I am man enough to give up my 'rights' and 'individualism' for the benefit of my family. It works because I think of them first and their needs before I think of myself. And, when they see that in me, they give up their rights for my sake. It's a win-win situation.

"But, know this, I can't do this on my own, but through the power of God alone can anyone think of another before they think of themselves. In our own power, we are too selfish and self-centered."

Jim's letter points out a highly contested issue in our society today: Can one be "good" or "moral" without G-d? Senator Joseph Lieberman, while running for Vice-President in be kept. Ultimately, secrets are revealed—and it's rarely a happy ending.

One listener wrote:

"My husband chose not to tell me that he had a mental break-down and was in a state mental hospital six years before we met. Needless to say, it all came out. After almost three years of marriage, we had a baby. During my pregnancy I watched him change and become someone I didn't know. He said he didn't tell me about it prior to our marriage, because he thought I would leave him.

"Shortly before our baby's birth, he injured himself on the job on purpose, the same job he was begging me to let him quit even though our baby was due within weeks. Oftentimes he would only get out of bed minutes before I came home. I spent two months with him maxing credit cards, gambling it all away, buying a truck with payments higher than our rent, and getting into physical confrontations with drug dealers.

"My husband was finally diagnosed by a counselor as manic-depressive. When he was hospitalized, I found out several secrets and things he had done since day one. We were forced to file bankruptcy, and I had to go to work. Needless to say, this has wrecked our marriage. I've spent enough time praying to God for the strength to forgive him for his lies and what I feel was his betrayal—praying for the strength to honor my vows and keep our home intact for my children.

"He never told me, because he was afraid I wouldn't marry him. Maybe I wouldn't have, but I wish he had given me the chance and respect to make that decision."

If he had been willing to share that secret, it would have built trust, because it would have demonstrated his willingness to face truth and reality with her, not operate against her. If he had been up-front about his problems, she likely would have helped him on his journey toward functioning better with medication and therapy. Instead, he and his family (who bear some responsibility here) tried to protect him from hurt, not considering how he would hurt his wife and children, and that he would end up abandoned and rejected and in ever-growing psychiatric distress.

Bad secret.

Another woman had a similar experience with problematic secrets of her husband.

"I have been married to my husband now for twelve years and we have a nine-year-old son. I met my husband and we clicked immediately and things moved very fast. He gave me a ring after two weeks of dating, but we did wait for eight months to marry.

"I thought I knew everything about him. I had talked with his parents and siblings and became part of the family very fast. After we were married I started seeing a side of him that I had no idea existed.

"First of all he would spend many, many hours on the computer. Then I noticed some feminine things about him. He would, supposedly as a joke, ask me to put makeup on him. He would put on my clothes and pretend that he was playing it as funny. It went away, or so I thought, for a few years, and we had our son after two years of marriage.

"He was traveling with his job and staying in hotels where he dressed like a woman and went out in public. I decided to leave. I came back because my father said to give it another try.

"It has put a lot of distance between us. My son loves his dad dearly and doesn't know any of this. The thing that really got to me about this is that his parents and siblings knew and never said a word to me! I have sat and cried and wondered why I was kept in the dark. How could anyone keep something like this from someone that would affect them the rest of their life?"

The answer is selfishness, plain and simple. Their collusion with her husband to keep this secret from her suggests that this man's parents and siblings probably are ashamed and somewhat in denial; that's when if you don't look at it, don't see it, and don't speak about it, you can pretend it no longer exists. Her husband is more willing to give in to this compulsion than seek treatment. These emotions and motivations were dealt with selfishly as he and his family wanted everything to appear normal, at the expense of this woman and her children, if need be.

The ultimate moral to this story is that there is *always* something wrong when impulsiveness (love at first sight, engagement at first date, sex at first lust) and instant intimacy present themselves. The romantic, childlike part of ourselves always loves such made-in-heaven or soul-mate moments. But, reason and patience and a willingness to get "real" must prevail. There are always going to be predators; most of the time the victims are volunteers; innocent vulnerability is a definite liability.

Getting to Know You

Self-interest is normal and natural. Self-interest at the expense of truth and the welfare of others is just plain evil. One of the reasons I nag people via my radio program to take time, at least two years of getting to know someone, before taking steps which minimize or eliminate objectivity (intimate sex, shacking-up, marriage) is because it takes time to get past reasonable, much less unreasonable, attempts to put one's best foot forward and not to reveal information or traits which might jettison us out of someone else's heart and life.

My experience with callers concerning secrets in dating is that they are more upset about the lack of openness, the deceit, and manipulation than they usually are about the issues being hidden. Sometimes that makes sense—sometimes it doesn't. I am disheartened by what some people are willing to tolerate just to be able to say to themselves that they have somebody.

It is obviously self-defeating to tell lies or mislead a potential loved ones about yourself. If they stay in your life and "love you," they're not really loving *you*—just the pretend you. Your goal of really being loved for yourself is never really met. You haven't really won anything.

One listener wrote me about how her boyfriend's deceit was a deal-breaker:

"He and I had been together for seven years. Partly as a result of becoming a listener to your show, I was no longer content to be a forty-year-old part-time shack-up honey. I told him I was uncomfortable with this arrangement and wanted to become engaged. He proposed to me in August, 2000, and presented me with a lovely ring. Intuitively, I sensed there was more behind the ring than he was telling me. He was vague about where it had come from, and elusive when I asked. I didn't want to be rude or seem ungrateful or materialistic, so I let the matter drop—even though I wondered why he had selected a ring that I never would have picked for myself.

"Three months later the truth came out. When he decided to propose to me, he asked his mother if she had a ring he could give me. She gave him an old pendant she had inherited from an aunt, which he made into a ring. The irony is that receiving a ring that had been in his family (whom I adore) would have been the best engagement present he could have given me.

"Before you think I'm being petty—the fact that he had not been forthright about the origins of the ring, had carried this secret for three months without fessing up, and moreover went on and on about how much he spent on it turned me right off. I gave the ring back to him and told him that I would only start our married life off on a note of complete honesty.

"The deal-breaker was when I found out that he had sucked his family in on the secret—asking them not to let on. His mother told me she had urged him to tell the truth, but his fear of either

looking like he couldn't afford a ring—or his unwillingness to actually spend the money—clouded his judgment and made a liar of him, a fool of me, and dupes of his family.

"I learned more about his character than ever at this point. He turned the whole thing around to make me somehow at fault: I would have thought him cheap, nothing is good enough for me, I'm making a mountain out of a molehill, etc. Everything but take responsibility.

"Though I am disappointed to no longer be engaged—I am grateful that his character was revealed to me before it was too late. Well, actually, after seven years I have had ample opportunity to see other signs of weak character—walking in on him in bed with another woman, giving me half-burned-down candles in a Ziploc bag for my birthday, smoking pot with the boys—but I chose not to see that. This was the last straw, because I realized I need and want a husband with a healthy relationship to money, truth, and integrity.

"While privacy should be respected, there is no room for secrecy. As we say in Al-Anon, you're only as sick as your secrets."

There it is—some folks are just more sensitive to the concept of secrets than they are to infidelity, disdain, drug abuse, cheapness, lack of respect, regard, or love. It's as though the devil they find out they don't know is not as acceptable as the devil they do know.

Here's where some laws of physics do apply to human relations. Once an object is in motion, it tends to stay in motion unless confronted by equal or opposite force. Well, the same goes for some people. Once they're in a relationship, being sexually intimate, shacking-up, or having sent out the invitations, they're loathe to use their best judgment and withdraw from an obviously bad situation. There is denial and there are excuses and there are the promises and there are the hopes that it will all just miraculously get better or spontaneously work out.

That equal or opposite force quite often is the rude awakening that occurs after ugly secrets are found out.

One listener had been in a relationship for three months when she became suspicious, because her questions about financial topics were not answered. She called in a private investigator. She found out that he had been married one more time than he had admitted to. It turns out he was financially responsible for three ex-wives.

"He said if he told me the truth that I might reject him. I told him I can deal with the truth easier than a lie. He was not completely honest about his financial integrity either. My trust has been broken and I feel like there is probably more I don't know and don't know when to believe him. It is very important to be honest when building and laying down the foundations of a relationship. I was lied to to cover up past and present mistakes, so I feel misled about the person I thought I was in love with. I was on top of the world when I didn't know about the lies and now I feel at the bottom of the barrel, but I am glad I know."

The secret is out: People who hide and manipulate truth in order to get or keep someone in their lives do not love that person, they just want that person. Love for another person consists mainly of caring about their well-being and welfare. Unfortunately, the victim of the lies too often takes an inappropriately sympathetic approach because the deceiver gets all pathetic and pleads fear of rejection. The victim too often gets mushy and forgiving and "feels their pain." Instead, the victim should be running for the hills. Forgive the deceiver if you want, but steer clear of them. Forgiveness does not mean you have to continue to put yourself at risk—nor are you obligated to struggle with the other person's issues. Better the deceiver learns from a true rejection and grows into a better human being for the future.

Me, me, me is the main motive for lying and keeping

secrets to get and keep someone. It isn't love, love, love or relationship, relationship, relationship—so don't kid yourself and don't be beguiled. One listener wrote about her one-year involvement with a man who had been involved with another woman when they met. My listener told him in no uncertain terms that she would not see him if he were so involved. One month later, he informed her that his prior relationship had been resolved. She later found out that this was a lie. He had been sexually intimate with both of them, with neither of them aware of the other. When my listener caught him, he said that it was easier for him to lie to keep her in the relationship than risk losing her while he was still "working through his issues" with the other woman.

She responded to him with:

"So, let me get this straight. You lied to me to keep me in the relationship. And you lied to her to keep me in the relationship. And you were intimate with her to keep me in the relationship? How perplexing. What, did you do a handspring from the bed one night and cry, 'Eureka! I've got it! I will be intimate with both of them and this will sure win X's love for me?!'"

She then went on to tell him that his secret was not only stupid and deceitful, but that it was playing with two people's lives. His attempt to keep her lost her, and his deceit was cruel and reprehensible.

I was gratified that she was an exception to Newton's First Law of Motion—she used human good sense. What people do IS who they are.

The Past Is Right Here, Right Now

There isn't one person reading this page, there isn't one person existing on the face of the earth, for that matter, who doesn't have stuff they'd rather keep in the past. Who wants to dredge up and have to explain some of the bad and dumb things they once did for which they now have guilt, shame, or embarrassment? More horribly, who wants to relive the pain of vicious victimization or unwittingly struggle with a serious psychiatric problem? It's true that some people just won't understand; some will judge; some will be repelled; some will be rejecting.

As I've said earlier in this Chapter, what good does it do you to be "loved" and "accepted" when you know there's more to the story?

When we get to know someone new, and it seems to be getting "serious," are we obligated to tell all? Is each new relationship experience a forced confession? How many times are you expected to reveal deeply private concerns before it begins feeling as if you're volunteering for psychological/emotional rapes? How much depth of detail is necessary? At what point in the relationship should you open up this much? At what point in the relationship do you take this risk? These are vitally important issues. Let me use some listener examples to answer these questions.

Unfortunately, sexual abuse (molestation or child rape) is a frequent "secret." Here's what one listener wrote with respect to talking to a prospective partner about sexual abuse:

"It was not very smart to go into a relationship with someone when you haven't dealt with this issue (sexual abuse) yourself. You think you can hide and pretend it never happened, but in reality lots of things are centered around what happened to you. You can't be your true self and be comfortable. You always feel as if you are hiding something, and you present signals you are not even aware of, like feeling guilty or uncomfortable with holding hands or kissing.

"You are afraid you will be rejected because you are 'used.' You are afraid someone may think you are weird or not normal. You didn't ask for these things to happen to you, and when you realize

that and get help with related issues, you don't feel like you are hiding something from someone you love."

The calls I get on my radio program are not only from women wondering about whether, how, when to talk to their boyfriends or husbands about their experience being molested as a child, they are from women who found out too late that their husbands were molested and were still suffering with the guilt, filled with shame, afraid of intimacy, confused about their sexuality and about having children—lest they do to others what was done to them. Additionally, the calls come in from men, loving and protective of their girlfriends and wives, but now angry, frustrated, and confused about what to do when there is a sudden revelation about their partners' molestation, and a clearer explanation of such strange behaviors as moods and negative issues about sex.

We all realize that withholding of this information isn't done to be mean—it's an issue of self-protection. The unknowing partner is still deceived, and disallowed to make a choice about what they wish to take on and deal with in their married lives, and the partner is not given the opportunity to work with the secret holder to make things better.

I've had callers say, "I don't really need to talk about it—I'm fine with it and it doesn't impact my life at all in any way." My answer is generally, "Then it would be wonderful for you to share how resilient you are. That's a positive quality that would make you valuable in a marriage!"

The answer to that is silence.

I don't think it's at all correct, much less necessary, to bare your soul, psyche, and history when you're casually dating. I believe that people do this compulsively when their history has become their sick identity. Then, it's kind of a provocation, a test, a manipulation, an immature game.

When it seems clear that this person is a likely "keeper," it's important to talk about the more profound issues that have forged and challenged your life. After all, what we all are today is largely a response to all we've gone through. And, don't kid yourself, it shows. It shows in the reactions you have to things today. It shows in the effort it takes to conceal. It shows.

Waiting until after marriage is not fair and not the way to build a secure foundation. As one listener wrote:

"I kept this horrible, sick secret from my husband and his family, praying that no one would ever find out my deep and harrowing shame. Finally, after three years of marriage, my conscience could take no more. I knew that in order to protect my marriage and my sanity I had to be honest with him at all costs. We were both exercising in the workout/computer room; I finally got up the courage to let him know everything. He forgave me for not telling him before he married me. But it took a long time for him to be able to trust me again.

"The lesson of this is that I should have told him the truth in the first place. Yes, there was a chance that he would dump me.

"I was finally able to find someone who accepted me as I was— and by not being honest with him from the beginning, I almost lost it all. As it was, he did forgive me and we will be married for nine years as of February 2001."

Are you thinking, "How dare he or anyone else get on his high horse and claim injury, just because he didn't know something?" Think about it some more. When you commit to someone, don't you want to feel that you are the one person in the world he or she can trust, rely on, come to, be open with? Of course. Add to that the fact that secrets of the magnitude of molestation are corrosive to the individual hoarding them as well as to the openness, comfort level, and teamwork of the marriage.

Punch line: Secrets about the past always have an impact today. You can minimize the negative effect of the past on the present and future by dealing with problems therapeutically and spiritually (that means opening up to a professional or clergy), and by letting your beloved in. This way your partner can understand you better (and can deal with some of your behavioral characteristics without taking them so personally) and can be helpful in supporting your ongoing growth.

Rejection Is a Good Thing!

So far, I've only given you happy endings, but sometimes a sad ending is its own happy ending. One listener wrote of learning that lesson:

"I was nineteen at the time and dating what I knew would be my future husband. I had a secret that was haunting me, and I really wanted to tell him before we were married. I posed the question like this: 'I have a deep dark secret. I'll tell you my secret if you tell me your deep dark secret.'

"He told me, 'No.' I took that as, well, I tried, and he can't say later that I didn't.

"He was a virgin at thirty-three and he knew I wasn't but what he didn't know is that I had lost my virginity through incest. Well, eight years later I told him anyway. The words he told me which hurt the most, and I wanted to avoid were, 'I would have never married you if I knew about the incest.'

"The secret was stupid because in my mature nineteen-year-old mind I thought that he was the man for me—that this deep secret wouldn't affect my relationship/marriage, but it did."

This is exactly the point I make to so many callers: If this (wo)man can't deal with such truths, how do you expect to be able to count on this person with the challenges of life in the future: illness, finances, children, and natural disasters . . . ? Unfortunately, we think too much in the box of mirrored walls: "It's just about me," we whine and worry.

Wrong! It's also about him (her) and his (her) character, compassion, and strength, and it's about you two as a team, handling problems together.

Dealing with these secrets is an important way to find out if this is "the one." Too bad the usual approach is mainly based on romance and orgasms. Too much of more significance is missed.

Another listener confirmed this. She wrote:

"When I was in college, I was raped, became pregnant, and gave the baby boy up for adoption. I did not tell my boyfriend, who eventually became my husband, because I was afraid he would look on me as damaged merchandise. Had I done so, his reaction to the information would have been the testimony of how HE really was. Therefore, I would NOT have married him. It wasn't until after the wedding that his true selfishness came to light."

You really come to know people when you deal with the difficulties, not just the fun stuff. Remember that.

Secrets Keep You Stuck

In addition to finding out if the two of you can really take on life together, there is still the important issue of personal growth and change. The profound impact of our past unfortunate experiences often follows us through life as we "defend" against the pain and the truth. Here's what one man had to say to confirm that:

"The stupid secret that I hid from my ex-wife was in the end the reason for our divorce. My ex-wife attributed my outgoing and sociable personality to a kind heart. The reality was that it was a front for much insecurity and behavior that was directly connected to sexual and psychological abuse in my childhood and early teenage years.

"My ex-wife was almost 100 percent right in separating several times and then leaving, for my behavior was grossly disrespectful and wrong. Examples are: flirtation with women as a way to regain the manhood that I believed was 'taken' from me, harsh criticism of my wife, and misplaced loyalty to a dysfunctional family and 'mother.'

"I fought the separation, but with time embraced my time alone in a rooming house. For one year, I read books on the subject of child molestation and abuse, and emotional incest. Listening to your radio program, and Rush Limbaugh's, I heard the philosophies which were later the catalyst for the changes I made to my character. The abuses would no longer have a stronghold on my mind.

"In retrospect, if I had told her about the abuse in my younger years, all the bad moments could have been avoided. Now I work on releasing the guilt from a failed marriage, so that I'm open to relationships as God intends and work on my character every day.

"If there is a message for men and women who are abused it is this: You must deal with it—not keep it a secret from those you love and who love you. You must deal with it, it is the only path to freedom—or else you continue to reinforce the power the abuser once had."

Another listener learned the hard way about how secrets keep you stuck. She met a young man in church and married him some eight months later. These short courtships generally are an attempt to "make something be" rather than "allow things to evolve." There's generally immaturity and insecurity involved.

What she hid from him, her secret, was that she was bulimic and had struggled with depression.

"I didn't intentionally try to fool him, because I kept thinking I would get better and stop doing those things to my body. I wasn't even honest with myself. I think a big mistake we made was we were not honest and open in our conversations when dating, and were just blinded by the 'lusty' side of attraction.

"After we were married for about a year he slowly found out what a mess I was inside myself. We fought a lot and ignored each other a lot, and he felt that I had deceived him.

"Now we have been married over five years. I did get medicine for my ongoing depression, and I stopped the bulimia one year ago. We are yet to have a romantic relationship—it is more of a partnership.

"I think the moral of the story is, wait to get married. Be friends first. Talk a lot. Talk about your faults and insecurities more openly. I put on a facade for my husband before we were married, that I was 'perky and perfect,' but I was not. I had problems.

"We are still married and will stay married—we both believe very strongly in working things out and staying together, but the journey has not been fun at all. But I think as things improve, and as we both grow and mature over the years, things will work out."

To Know My Journey Is to Know Me

I can't tell you how many callers, ashamed of some past action or behaviors, suffer forever because they can't forgive themselves. Part two of that lack of forgiveness is a terrible fear of being hated or rejected by a loved one as part of that perpetual punishment.

I remind these callers that true repentance means that they have taken responsibility, experienced true remorse, done what's possible to repair, and are committed to not repeating. Once these 4 R's have been accomplished they are to move on!

It is so difficult for some people to give themselves points for progress—to realize that they have changed, would never repeat the "bad thing," and that they have the right to be happy and be respected for their courageous journey.

One listener wrote about making such a journey:

"Had I kept secret a long past abortion from my pro-life boyfriend, only to have it surface after several years of marriage, it could have been catastrophic. I told him about it, and how much I truly regretted it. He was able to understand that I was no longer that person who was so stupid and irresponsible. He told me that he loved me. We now have two beautiful boys and have been married seven-plus years."

Virginity: Private or Secret?

Considering the impact of the sexual revolution of the 1960s and the impact of condoms being handed out in public school classrooms in the 1990s, there wouldn't seem to be much necessity to discuss virginity. Happily, there is, since it's making a comeback as a virtue and as a protection against unwanted pregnancies, abortions, sexually transmitted diseases, low self-esteem brought on by meaningless intimacies, and an ultimately empty feeling.

One listener had converted to the Mormon religion after years of secular free sex.

"In the Mormon community, when you marry you assume you are marrying a virgin, because you are taught from a very young age to abstain from unmarried sex. I knew in my heart that if my future husband did not know about my past it would be unfair to him, and he could not make a clear choice about whether he should marry me. With all my strength and fear of losing him, I told him. He loved me anyway, and my sharing my secret brought us closer to one another."

And you thought sex was the ultimate in intimacy.

But, here is the important point. What do you tell? How many? What positions? This is where people get into trouble. Clarifying where you've been in your thinking and being is a way of getting close. Giving details is what you do when you're selling your story to some disgusting tabloid newspaper sold in grocery stores.

One listener had this very question:

"Do I have to tell my husband the truth about how many sexual partners I had before we met? I told him five because I thought it was an easy number to maintain in my lie, but the truth is that it is more like ten. I told him this lie to keep from looking like a slut.

"In my younger years I made some choices in order to be accepted, and later I came to realize that in fact I was only alienating myself from everyone and everything that was valuable. Should I now tell my husband the truth and risk hurting him? He may not be very understanding as he has only had one partner prior to me, and his values are very old-fashioned."

Okay, here's the answer. He needs to know everything from "In my younger years . . ." to ". . . valuable." That is what will tell him about you. That's what he really needs to know: that you were lost and suffering and used sexuality to try to be found and achieve peace. You've grown from that into the wonderful woman you are. This is what's valuable about your story for him. This is what should not be a secret. The number of guys is private—keep it that way. It doesn't add to the story, it takes away from it.

If It Ain't About Sex, It's About Money

It's probably true that the two biggest secret categories are about sexuality and finances. As one listener wrote:

"I have read a million times that finances are one of the main reasons for relationship troubles. I am a twenty-four-year-old female, on the verge of getting married. My boyfriend does not know yet, but I have a horrible, horrible credit record from when I

was eighteen to twenty-two. I know I should tell him. But I have never needed to. I have a car, and we currently rent a house. It's going to come up and be a problem when we want to buy a house. I live in dread that an old creditor will find me and reveal everything, perhaps on the answering machine or something.

"I carry this secret around like a big, black, dead weight in my gut. I know this is something that will highly impact him in the future; once we are married our 'credit rating' will be as one. . . . He thinks that I am just as responsible with my money as he is. I am okay now but that's because no one will give me credit so that I have no current debt—just a bad old debt record."

It is really stupid and useless to imagine you are going to keep secret something that is public record. All you do is add deceit to what was a problem to be handled. Since this young woman has "changed her irresponsible ways," she has a positive story to tell. And that's the key in telling the other person your deep, dark, ugly, yukkies: Find the positive story.

I'll give you another example that seemed hopeless. Another listener wrote:

"Not telling my husband about the incredible debt I had incurred before our marriage led to many problems that entangled the entire family. Avoiding my debt, instead of sharing with him my problem, made him angry and bitter—especially after our tax refunds were being withheld in order to pay for my debt.

"He said it would have been better to come clean from the beginning. Now, the refunds that should be going to the family savings for kids' activities and family holidays are going to pay my debt.

"So—no secrets when it could impact the family in a negative manner. You're not just lying to yourself and your spouse—your kids suffer too."

So, what could have been the positive story? How 'bout this: "Honey, I've been living with one set of priorities, but now that I've met you, that's all changed. I used to think about having stuff in the moment as a way to feel good about myself and bring happiness to my life. So, I spent too much money and worked up a debt. Now, since I've met you, I see that love, commitment, family obligations—you know, caring and living for others—is the right way to feel good about life and to be truly happy. Problem is, that I have debt from my stupid way of thinking. I want very much to marry you and have your children. I want you to trust and respect me—so, I'm going to take the necessary time to pay off these debts before we marry so that you can trust my intent and maturity."

I bet that would work!

Secrets Are Often the Symptom

When there are sad and serious problems in a relationship, secrets are sometimes the means by which people try to hide from that truth. Instead of facing the problems, getting help, trying to change, or realizing the sick futility of their predicament, people will use the glue of secrets to shore up the dam. It ultimately doesn't work.

As one listener wrote:

"I know a person who has to sneak stuff into their own house. Perhaps it is clothing, or a new CD, movie, or even a book. They keep it a secret instead of facing the fact that their relationship must be unhealthy, not allowing them to be an individual with responsibilities, rights, respect, and discipline. Secrets usually are kept to avoid a confrontation."

Clearly, this is not a relationship of loving, equally sharing, caring adults. This is a relationship of fear and domination—deceit and manipulation. Not much chance for improvement, repair, or relief when the truth is hidden. Secrets in this case replace dealing with truth and reality.

Another listener came to understand how she shifted into secrets to protect a fragile relationship:

"After having come out of some pretty serious problems in our marriage, I guess I took for granted that things were okay again. So, one day as I was doing the checkbook and paying the weekly bills, I realized an error I had made to the tune of $200. I then took the same amount from our savings to make up for the deficit. I planned not to tell my husband, because I didn't want him to know I goofed and I wanted to avoid a fight. When he inquired about the savings account one day, I lied and said it was the amount it had been for a long time.

"This morning he found the savings book and saw what I did. He demanded an explanation. But, as I gave him my reason, I began to see just how stupid it sounded."

When you're working on improving a relationship, making sure you look good or don't get caught making errors or seem always to be right, are not the means to a healthy, loving relationship. First of all, they're all about you—not about him or her or us! Keeping secrets about mistakes in judgment or action is a form of lying and can do serious damage to the relationship by hurting your credibility and trustworthiness. Probably one of the most important elements of a relationship is the confidence you have in the other person's fundamental intent never to hurt you or the relationship.

In order to gain that credibility and trust, you must never give your spouse an indication that you would be deceptive to avoid a confrontation, keep out of trouble, be held accountable, look bad, be wrong, or not be in control. The "us" has to be more important than that.

On the flip side, instead of making sure you look good, it does little for the long-term health of a relationship to protect your spouse from him or herself. One listener was, unfortunately, doing just that.

"My husband is very touchy about making sure bills are paid

on time; this would not be an issue except that he also wants to overspend on things that are not necessary to survive. As a result, I have been keeping an $800 credit card debt (in my name only) a secret and trying desperately to get it paid off without calling attention to it. The $800 was accumulated here and there to pay utility bills, etc., it was not used for unnecessary spending. It was a result of his using the checking account to buy tools, leaving us short on the bill money. He would always get mad if I stated that we couldn't afford something and demand to know why, leaving me to sometimes say, 'Yes, honey, go ahead—we have a little extra money this week,' when we don't, and then use the credit card to pay for the phone or electricity.

"*I hate to have any secrets between us.*"

If she had called my radio program, I would have told her to put the finances in his hands. She needs to get him one of those electronic checkbooks, so that he can know exactly what groceries, utilities, and so forth really cost. This way, he's being the petulant child, not caring about what there is, just about what he wants. The secret makes her live in fear and keeps him childlike.

Secrets Keep You Alone

The saddest aspect of secrets in a marriage is that you are alone with your fears and problems. Obviously, that is counterproductive to intimacy. One listener wrote about her marriage. She described a year's courtship and engagement filled with agreements on such important issues as religion, family, work, and monetary priorities. While her husband was completing his final year at the university, she became pregnant. That's when everything seemed to unravel. She found large sums of money were missing from their savings account, he had gotten failing grades at school, and then faked that he was going to school at all. Instead, he hung out at the mall, leaving her home with the twins.

Though she was determined to divorce him, they went into Christian counseling first.

"Building back trust takes a lot of work, and there are still some awkward feelings which I do not hesitate to tell him about! My husband had one terrible secret: He could not handle the pressures of going to school, working, and my difficult pregnancy. His mistake was covering up the fears with lies. Lies begat more lies and so on. This destroyed trust . . . one of the most cherished things in a marriage. We have worked hard to rebuild our marriage. I sense that he did not feel like he could tell me he was under pressure. He knows and regrets what he did. People can learn a lot from our story. He withheld information from me thinking that the truth would destroy our relationship. It was not the truth, but the secrets that almost destroyed our relationship."

Whether your spouse is the best-looking, smartest, most successful, most fun, sexiest, most agreeable person you'd ever hope for or not, that person has vowed to face life with you. That is the counterpoint to being alone. We are each distinct, separately contained entities. It takes a leap of faith to touch and care about another person and to allow them, invite that person to take care of you. It means lowering your pride and ego, and raising your arms in an embrace of trust.

We all deal with adversity better when we deal with it together with our loved ones. None of us is loved for being perfect—if we are loved, it's for compassion, vulnerability, kindness, thoughtfulness, humor, sensitivity, and trustworthiness. It is never better to have some stupid secret pop up—it is always better to swallow pride, admit the truth, and work it through together. What makes all relationships strong is standing up together against some outside threat or challenge.

One listener summed it up:

"I kept my feelings secret from him. I allowed him to think everything was fine with me when it wasn't. When I realized I was hating him, I got scared. Once I stopped keeping my feelings a secret EVERYTHING started to change in our relationship. With hard work and faith we are still married heading into our fifteenth year. We both realize what damage an unspoken secret can cause."

We cannot love when we do not trust. We cannot be close when we hide. For the most part, secrets have little place in intimacy. Intimacy and secrets are like poles of magnets—they repel each other.

Good Secrets

All this said, there are times when truth becomes cruel and destructive. Perhaps we could call these "good secrets." For example, you should never tell your spouse that you're turned off because of receding hairlines, ripples in thighs, sagging, postpartum breasts, crow's feet, graying hair, slower gait, a few extra age pounds, and so forth. We all need to age gracefully and accept the aging and imperfections of our loved ones graciously.

You also should never tell your spouse that you've had sexy feelings about anyone real. Instead, you should remove yourself from that temptation and hike up your attention and affection with your spouse. It's amazing how being more attentive gets more back in return than just fantasizing in anger does.

To the ire of some listeners, I have told some callers that they might consider taking to their graves the secret of a brief dalliance, IF AND ONLY IF they were truly repentant; the impact of full disclosure on the marriage and family might be terminal and the children only stand to suffer. If the behavior is repetitive or long-standing, I generally recommend not keeping that a secret, since it implies more of a serious character failing than an "event."

When the Secret Is You!

One of the more unusual responses I received from my radio listeners on the subject of secrets was from a woman who had recently been introduced to a fellow to whom she was very sexually attracted; when asked, admitted that he had a girlfriend. They ran into each other a month later.

"I had no intention of having sex with him knowing that he had a girlfriend. However, that night, as we were lying in bed, we ended up having sex. It has now been four weeks, and he says he doesn't plan to be with his girlfriend forever and doesn't want to ever marry her, but he hides me from her, and I can't stand it that I am a secret.

"Is it good for me to be involved with him?

"If I stop seeing him, do you think he will give up his girlfriend?

"Do you think he would be good for me if he did this?"

I guess she thinks being a secret sex toy is a compliment and the beginning of a beautiful relationship. Well, here are my answers: No. Who cares? Not likely.

This letter makes the point that sometimes the worst secrets are the truths we keep from ourselves. It's generally downhill from there.

2

Stupid Egotism

"How many egocentric folks does it take to screw in a lightbulb?

One.

She just holds the lightbulb up to the fixture and waits for the world to revolve around her!"

—APRIL, A LISTENER

That quote was April's *P.S.* The first part of her letter was a blunt confession of the main problem with egocentrism in a relationship; basically, that it's an oxymoron:

"Being an Aries, I have a big, inflated ego which I have to keep in check. Now I am married and I love it more than anything, but when I was younger I had the 'everyone for him/herself' mentality, which is egocentric thinking. I now know that EACH PERSON IN THE RELATIONSHIP NEEDS TO BE BRINGING SOMETHING WORTHWHILE AND SPECIAL TO THAT RELATIONSHIP. WE HAVE TO THINK OF OUR FAMILY MEMBERS AND BE AWARE OF ACTING IN THE BEST INTERESTS OF THE FAMILY/RELA-TIONSHIP . . . EVEN IN THE DAYS OF EXTREME PMS!

"If we are egocentric in our relationship we are being stupid because nobody wants to be with someone like that! Do you? I

2000, got caught in that maelstrom when his religious Orthodoxy at once won him a title of "very moral and having profound character," and an attack (from his own side) that he'd better not be saying that religiosity and morality had to go hand in hand. Whew! Make up your mind!

The reality is that secularism is pragmatic and spirituality is transcendent. Our society has become one in which collective values and virtues are secondary to individual and self-proclaimed group claims, protests, angers, irrationality, radicalism, intimidation, and outright terrorism. In other words, special interest groups will say or do whatever it takes to satisfy their agenda, regardless of fairness, goodness, or truth. Those individuals who stand for traditional (religious) values are scoffed at, demonized, and marginalized.

The result of all this societal transformation is a population that is frankly egotistical. Historically, one would more likely hear, "Ask what you can do for your country," today the slogans are, "Yeah, but when do I get mine? You can't make me! I'm entitled! But I want it!"

G-d Is Dead—Long Live ME!

Lately I've been reading a lot of nonsense published in the mainstream press about how believing in and respecting "G-d's Commandments" is unnecessary to compassion and morality. As proof, we are given the actions of animals. One example I read recently was how ants will sacrifice themselves by forming a bridge of their bodies over water to allow other ants to live. You actually believe the ants sit around and philosophize about the morality of sacrificing the few for the many? Of course not! Their behavior is built into their genetic wiring—it's called "instinct." Instinct isn't reasoned, it is reflexive.

When you see adult male brown bears moving into an area with mother bears and their cubs, killing the young, and mating with the females, you're not viewing sociopathic behavior. You're witnessing the genetically hard-wired, instinctive behavior to make the new male's genes go forward, not those of their competitors.

When you see a human firefighter, rush into a burning, collapsing building to rescue someone else's children, you are not seeing instinct (that would be to run away!), you are seeing commitment, compassion, responsibility, heroism . . . and . . . maybe the rush of the thrill of facing danger. Interviews with heroes usually give little information other than that the person was taught it was the right thing to do. That's morality. That's uniquely human, and definitely tied into the spiritual quest to be more than our animal instincts.

Family Values . . . Yucch!

The predominantly liberal press has a field day with the notion of "family values." Instead of a respect for a construct that connects, supports, nurtures, loves, and motivates each one of us, this institution is the object of perpetual derision and condemned as an exploitation and domination of women, a Victorian kill-joy of sexual pleasure, and an unrealistic and oppressive brake on the natural tendency toward polygamy.

The loss of the respect for obligation to family has inevitably produced a self-centered population struggling to find something by which to make life meaningful.

What I have witnessed growing over these years is not a celebration of freedom, but a sadness, loneliness, and confusion as the promised land turns out to be of sour milk and fetid honey.

Family values are about sex, marriage, and children. Let's take these issues one at a time.

Sex

The sexual revolution promised sex free of commitment and responsibilities, promiscuity without judgment, and intercourse without conception (the birth control pill with an abortion chaser)—just self-centered pleasure seeking. The feminist movement taught us that this was all a good thing. When women, it said, are freed from the shackles of morality, modesty, and marriage, then orgasms would be more frequent and more explosive. What actually happened was the loss of courtship, romance, chivalry, falling in love, commitment, and marriage. It does not appear that most women are particularly happy that the price for this liberation was so profound and personally devastating.

Sex has become a kind of sport for both men and women. Where once, a pregnancy precipitated assuming responsibilities, today men easily walk away as women are left with their freedoms of abortions and unmarried parenthood. It is ironic that there is still such an emphasis on criticizing deadbeat dads for walking away, when an aborting mother is not seen as a deadbeat mom, though her decision actually brings death upon the scene. What's the big deal about deadbeat dads when women can get sperm from a bank or an unsuspecting sexual partner and, like many movie and TV celebrities, just be a "single mom" with no criticism? Sounds like woman are speaking out of two sides of their mouths.

And what about "safe" sex? There isn't any. The epitome of intimacy, the union of men and women in pleasure and procreation is anything but safe because it is a leap of trust. Forget the STDs, abortions, and the unfortunate illegitimate children, and think of the repetitive hurts of "serial monogamy" and the ultimate loneliness and emptiness that follow sex without context.

Marriage

At best, marriage is now seen as a fragile promise. The young people I talk to are afraid of "commitment" because they have seen so little of it from their parents and peers. How can we expect young people to give their hearts and be willing to trust and love, when their own lives have been traumatized, sometimes by multiple losses of family cohesion and stability as their parents marry, divorce, shack-up, move on, again and again?

Consequently, these frightened but lonely, needy, and somewhat hopeful young adults are shacking-up. Contrary to their hope of finding the right one through this trial period, the statistics show elevated depression and anxiety, infidelity, violence, and a greater rate of breakup inside or out of a marital relationship. Unfortunately, too many children are born into these even more fragile relationships, only to suffer the loss and hurt along with their parents.

In the past, callers to my radio program who were contemplating divorce, did so out of great angst; alcoholism, abuse, affairs were the triggers. Nowadays, divorces seem more and more to come out of a sense of entitlement for perpetual glee and satisfaction on all grounds.

The most surprising trend is looking at marriage as barely a home base for one's individual endeavors. A number of women, for example, have called my program proclaiming their spouses "controlling" because the husbands were not overjoyed at their leaving the country for months or years to complete some course of study or take on some "once in a lifetime" job opportunity. What?

Another example of callers who make it clear that marriage will not stand in the way of their personal endeavors is the man who wondered if it would be okay to place their several-month-old child with their in-laws for a year and a half or two so that they could get on developing their careers. What?

Marriage used to be about folks finally learning that the greatest value in life is to be a part of something greater than yourself: family and children. Marriage today is about having some company, for as long as you like it, while you get on with your life. Pure egotism.

Children

There is hardly a more profound teacher about generosity, selflessness, bonding, mission, compassion, or love than parenting. For most of us, life becomes more serious and meaningful when we become responsible to others.

Even this has been thwarted by a "me" and "career" and "acquisition" oriented society which falsifies reality (thanks to certain agendized sociological and psychological groups) in order to tell parents that their children do not need them other than to earn money and be happy. Full-time, evening-time, sick-time, vacation-time, anytime childcare is promoted as a boon to individual, adult freedom. There have even been "studies" purporting that mothers at home with their children hurt their children intellectually and socially. How low can a movement go to justify itself? Obviously, very low.

The responsibilities of, and participation in, marriage, marital sex, and child rearing are how an individual not only

lives for others, but lives for the future of others and humanity. Obviously, that is the opposite of the narcissism, the
demand for immediate pleasures, accomplishments, and sat-
isfactions which predominates today.

Feminism

"I was sorry to hear that Barbara Hall would be giving a love
interest to Maxine of *Judging Amy*. Maxine is an independent
and self-sufficient woman. There are lots of ways for her to
continue to be self-actualized on her own . . . a hobby, or
other pursuits in which she can help society. I thought feminism had progressed beyond the age-old theory that women
need to have a man. . . ." Jan Winning, West Hills, California
(*The New York Times*, Letter to the Editor, April 9, 2000).

What saddens me the most, in addition to the fact that
this was written by someone in my neck of the woods, is that
it is an attempt to deny a basic biopsychological reality of
healthy, normal women: They desire and enjoy bonding
with a man. Hobbies, work, and other pursuits are a wonderful, creative, and necessary aspect of any human's life, man
or woman, but the drive for connection is normal, natural,
and important too. It makes me mad that feminists would
deny this undeniable reality and, in so doing, cause substantial harm to so many women.

*"I am . . . a reformed feminist. I am twenty-two years old . . .
and once thought that I could basically do whatever I wanted in a
relationship because I was a strong, young woman. I didn't want
to do something special for my 'man.' I would often be
defensive . . . because I was filled with this BS feminist nonsense,
and I did not want to have to cook a dinner or have a relationship
with him. But now I see that you should do things for your partner
to make them happy. I cannot stand it when I see these women on*

talk shows who do not work and say they feel like slaves because their husbands want them to clean and cook for them after the man is out working all day . . . it is crazy. You have to make certain sacrifices in a relationship, but doing your part isn't a sacrifice, it's just how things are supposed to be."

Wow! Now, that's an important revelation for the feminists. ". . . doing your part isn't a sacrifice, it's just how things are supposed to be." It's an issue of teamwork—not oppression against ovaries. I also consider myself a "reformed feminist." Having been at University in the 1960s, I was "enlightened" to believe that marriage and mothering were conspiracies to eliminate my power, worth, and voice. I carefully watched every word, nuance, attitude, suggestion, expectation, reaction, and behavior for proof that "he" was trying to dominate or disrespect me as a woman.

At the same time, I wore pretty clothes and makeup, expected to be asked out by the man, waited for him to open the door and pay the check, and played coy at the door after a date. How crazy-making was I? Looking back, though, the point is that there was a disconnect between social pressures and natural tendencies. I have learned in the many years since this time that femininity, modesty, and domesticity are not horrors, nor are they the assassins of freedom and individuality. They are elements special to life, values, and relationships. They are not "instead," they are "in addition to."

As one listener wrote:

"I grew up with a feminist mentality that no man would rule me. I am just now beginning to realize how this has put undue pressure on my marriage. I think the biggest problem comes by 'straddling the fence.' There have been times when I want to play the damsel and my husband the knight: 'Save me, dear husband,' one moment and 'How dare you expect anything of me,' the next. I have been arrogant and pompous at times."

Having a feminist mantra of distrust of the masculine and disdain for the feminine has been at the crux of a lot of confusion and dismay for women who guiltily like the idea that woman is different from man.

I received this letter from one of my listeners:

"The first year of our relationship was hell. I was trying to be myself, a strong and independent woman. I rarely asked him for permission to do things or spend money, especially if I thought it was okay myself. I am somewhat masculine in that I like to do hard work and wear jeans and T-shirts most of the time. I rarely wear makeup or perfume or jewelry. Well, apparently that is not what he wanted. He would get upset that I didn't dress up more often, that I didn't ask him about big decisions I made, that I refused to play the 'weaker sex,' and that I was working at a man's job (I was an assistant for a horse vet, which required heavy lifting and hard work). It really floored me at first that this man actually WANTED a woman like that.

"I am the daughter and granddaughter of a pastor. . . . I knew that the Bible says to submit yourself unto your husband, but I didn't understand at first what that means. It DOESN'T MEAN 'LET YOUR HUSBAND WALK ALL OVER YOU,' it just means consider him first, and let him be the leader in family decisions. I learned that the compromising that is marriage isn't just going to a Mexican restaurant when you are in the mood for Chinese. It is compromising your life and yourself because you love someone. Sometimes I would purposefully ask my husband to lift something heavy, all the while thinking I could do it myself, because it makes him feel needed. Sometimes I dress up just for him because it makes him feel wanted.

"I haven't given up my SELF for him (I still plan to be a vet and work with horses on my own ranch). I've merely modified myself in exchange for a deeper love and peace in the household. I think it is worth it."

Frankly, in my feminist years I would have had a fit over

this letter because she appears to have given in, she is pretending for his ego, she has caved in to sexist roles. How foolish I was to ignore the realities of man and woman—the subtle means by which men and women relate in order to please and connect.

During the late 1970s and 1980s I found myself, as a licensed Marriage, Family, and Child Therapist, counseling many couples struggling with how to relate in this new society. Whether they were dating or married, it often came down to an important piece of advice: To men (women) I would say, treat her like a woman(man), not just like a brain, a human being, a buddy, a partner, a neuter. The astonishment and resistance was huge! Nonetheless, I stayed with the program of reminding people that IQ and extraordinary talents notwithstanding, we are ultimately male or female, with a brain and endocrine system organized in unique, somewhat polarized ways, which require respect and attention.

Without acknowledging and responding to the masculine and feminine in each other, with the respect, admiration, and attention these aspects deserve, I saw that marital partners would be more demanding, less patient and understanding, and less solicitous and thoughtful—in other words, more egocentric. When I emphasized with them that they both needed to express what was uniquely male/female, it opened up part of their relationship previously ignored or inappropriately devalued. They both would become kinder to each other.

Why is it that women can complain about a man not expressing his emotions and talking and sharing with her so that she can feel involved and useful but a man cannot with equal respect complain about her not needing him for the trouble-shooting and problem solving and protecting and providing that is more typically in the male personality? Feminism, of course, and the desire to feminize men.

Here's an example of that short-sighted hostility:

"I remember as if it were yesterday his statement that I didn't really need him because I could change the oil in the car, mow the lawn, and build a deck. It was like a baseball bat to the brain— the revelation that he did not understand emotional needs . . . but only those other needs of defined male/female roles."

Well, how 'bout that she didn't understand the physical and practical needs? Why is it this competition rather than cooperation? Fortunately, this next listener "got it":

"I was raised to be 'independent.' 'You can accomplish anything you set your mind to. Don't rely on others to make yourself happy.' Being 'betrayed' by an adult from when I was nine to fifteen years of age, and being on survival mode for those years, has contributed to my 'independent' quality.

"After an argument the other night . . . his last line of the fight was . . . 'You don't need me, you don't rely on me for anything. . . . You do whatever you want without thinking of me.'

"He was right. This has been troubling me because I so much love this man and he puts me and our son above everything else in his life. . . . Well, it does do damage to have that mind-set of 'being my own woman.' It is alienating my husband, making him doubt his own ability to be a husband."

Early on in my therapy career, I was taught various techniques for dealing with controlling people. First, I was made to appreciate the fear that went into the need to control: fear of loss of self, security, love, change. The issue of control, therefore, was neurotically centered.

Then feminism put a whole new spin on control: It's something that happens automatically in a relationship with a man, and if you don't control everything in your life yourself, then you are pathetic, neurotic, powerless, and vulnerable to the whims of a despot spelled "h-u-s-b-a-n-d." Whew! How confusing. Here, I'll make it simple: If men control, they're bad; if women control, they're good. There. Now you're clear, right?

As another listener learned, it's not "right":

"My husband and I got married when I was twenty-four and discovered I was pregnant. I told him upon our 'agreement' to get married that I was going to continue to work . . . and we were going to keep everything 'separate and equal.' I had my own checking account and he had his own. We even filed separate tax returns. There was no way I was going to be 'dependent' on any man. After our little girl was born I came to the realization there was NO way I could go back to work and leave her with a sitter or a day care. I didn't come right out and tell my husband . . . how could I admit this 'weakness' and then on top of that be 'dependent' on him. So, instead, I got resentful and angry . . . hated him for existing. I hated the fact that I wouldn't have my own money and I wouldn't have any power in the relationship because I wasn't contributing financially to the household.

"I was going to be a mom and dependent on a man . . . everything I was indoctrinated against. I went back to college and took up another degree . . . you see I needed a job where I could make good money, take care of my baby, and not be dependent on my husband. During nursing school I spent less time with my husband and daughter.

"Today I truly believe God had different plans. It was during my drive to and from nursing school that I discovered the Dr. Laura show. My priorities changed. I realized that my behavior and attitude toward my husband wasn't God directed—I was going to break up my marriage and take my daughter away from her daddy in the name of my independence . . . because of my stupid pride.

"I love my husband . . . I love my children . . . and I am loving being 'dependent' on him. I pray that I can be a better example for my daughter and son. I have turned into the woman that my friends and I were trying to liberate during our rallies in college . . . and I am so very glad."

Many women are angry at the bill of goods the boomer generation and the 1960s and 1970s sold them. *"They really screwed with our heads. Let women be what they want and respect them for their choices,"* is what one exasperated listener wrote. It is a paradox, that the very folks, the feminists, who espouse CHOICE, CHOICE, AND MORE CHOICE, only mean, as with most radical groups, their style of choice and then demean all others.

A major eastern women's college, for example, permitted a radical group to yank references to the high marriage rate of successful graduates from their recruitment brochure. Why? They said it was discriminatory against those who preferred not to marry men and sexist in its obvious reassurance to parents that their daughter's education would not undermine their ability or desire to marry. It struck me as awful that "choice" did not include what has been a normal, natural and desirable, and G-d commanded activity since humans walked the earth: the bonding of men and women in holy matrimony, creating the stability and love in which to raise children. Tsk, tsk—how insulting can we be?

I Want to Be Alone . . . Move Over

I am struck at how the totality of liberalization of sex, cohabitation, and childbearing have caused massive confusion and devastation in personal relationships by emphasizing the "me" over the "we."

This is probably one of the most frequent issues to come up on my radio program as callers grapple with what they should be allowed to do in spite of being married and what they're spouses shouldn't be doing because they're married!

"Single while married," is a recurrent problem because our ego-loving society doesn't seem to put any reasonable demand on people, no limits, no boundaries. Hence we had eight years of a President who finally admitted to infidelities, lying, and perjury; we have civil rights leaders admitting to the very out-of-wedlock births that plague their communities. Some role models. And, there is little corresponding outrage or significant consequence. So, what's the average person to deduce? That it's all ultimately okay, and there exists no behavior that would make you a bad person, or wrong, or immoral (unless you count criticizing such behavior on religious grounds)—just temporarily embarrassed. I hope that the election of George W. Bush is signaling a significant spiritual, philosophical, and behavioral move away from that destructive way of thinking and acting.

Too many people find themselves on the receiving end of "single while married," and they don't like it:

" 'My right to stay out all night with the guys while you are pregnant is more important than your feelings or needs.' Boy, it was the last thing I needed back then, waiting up all night for the 'father' to come home. I learned great lessons from that: A man who loves you will stay with you and watch movies even if you only have the sniffles. That 'father' disappeared six months after our son was born . . . must have been important to maintain the nights out."

I have always contended that no woman should marry a man she doesn't believe would swim through shark-infested water to bring her a lemonade. Likewise, no man should marry a woman who doesn't have a patient sense of humor about guy stuff.

There are some clear-cut ways people determine to be single while married: money and spending, hobbies, addictions, internet "relationships," and outside activities.

"My husband is currently doing something stupid in our relationship. He spends money on big items, mostly motorcycles and parts, and recently purchased a newer Camaro without talking to me about it. He feels he deserves it and doesn't need to discuss *large purchases. We can't afford this. I feel he has betrayed me and after numerous times of buying, hiding the purchase, and me finding out, our marriage is doomed."*

I just love that excuse, "I deserve it." Where does that immature sense of entitlement come from? Spoiling from parents? A society which measures success in acquisitions? No matter how you look at it, it is egocentric. When we marry, as I remind listeners and callers, we give up the privilege of doing whatever we want whenever we want simply because we want. While to many that is a major catastrophic reality, most of us see this as a welcome tradeoff to have someone care about our well-being, to have something to live and work for outside ourselves, and the comfort of companionship. Happiness is not perfected until it is shared.

One female listener owned up to her selfishness about "friendships" outside of marriage.

"During my nearly eight-year relationship with a very wonderful man, there have been lots of stormy times that have at their root my determination to do what I want to do . . . have friends I choose to have . . . go where I want to go. This attitude that I have brought into our relationship out of fear that I would become my mother and allow him to steal my soul has done nothing but alienate him and cause him to be even more insecure and controlling.

"For example, at one point in our relationship, I had a coworker named David whom I was very fond of. I would come home and talk about things he said or things I liked about him, without giving any thought to how that made Russell (my fiancé) feel. My only thought was, 'He's not going to tell ME whom I can have for a friend.'

"I finally got the point that Russell said it was hurtful and caused him to be suspicious and jealous. I have since realized that to be good to him, and thereby good to us, I cannot have friends of the opposite sex that I gush over in our home. I cannot forget that the person I should be praising and adoring is the one I chose to be with and the one I love."

I'm often asked, generally quite angrily I should add, why married folk should not have close friends of the opposite sex to talk with, do things with, share, and so forth. I try to explain that we should not engage in behavior that brings unease or suspicion into our marriages. We should not use another person outside our marriage for intimacy and revealing of personal information about our partner (save for clergy or therapists in counseling). It is generally a lie to suggest that there is no aspect of man/woman stuff going on or that could potentially go on. At least one of the two likely has "designs," which is what motivates them to be so "understanding" in the first place. No married person should repeatedly put themselves in a situation with romantic potential. Religious people, for example, are never alone with a member of the opposite sex—they realize that how it looks and what it could become should be avoided out of respect for vows.

As another listener writes, some people will hold on to their addictions more tightly than they embrace their vows—denying, of course, that they are addicted—protesting instead that they "have a right!"

"My husband is determined to be his own man, and it is hurting our relationship almost as deeply as infidelity. My husband is an alcoholic. I consider it to be his best friend and mistress. He must be his own man. He gets angry so quickly instead of merely talking things out. Then, if I dared to defend myself from verbal attacks, I get the silent treatment for the next couple of very long days. I just love to pieces that man he is when he is not drinking, but when he is his own man, and does what he damn well pleases (drinks), I would rather be any other place on earth."

Another listener's husband has a hobby. Hobbies are good to relieve tension and experience creativity in a nonstructured way. However, some married people pursue a hobby as though they were single. One listener wrote me that her husband loves to hunt. She recalls that when they were first together, he would be away for many three- or four-day weekends. This was okay with her because, after all, they were dating and not married.

"We have now been married seventeen years and have three wonderful daughters and his hobby now takes him away from us a minimum of two to three weeks a year and on some weekends. The fact that he travels on the average of three days a week for business means he is away a significant amount of time during the year. He does not listen to my pleading for a cut in time spent hunting until the girls get out of high school He believes he has the RIGHT to do this, and calls any attempt on my part to communicate hurt feelings, as attempts to control him."

I hear from and about a lot of men who believe that their work or hobbies are some kind of inalienable right, against which responsibilities to family pale. That's why I was so glad when one of our editors quit working on my magazine, *The Dr. Laura Perspective*. It seems that he was working late every night at home on articles. One night his wife and children did not come home or call. He was frantic. When he finally reached them, his wife wondered why she should come home early in the evening when he wasn't really there. He quit the next day so he would have quality time with his family. I miss him desperately, but I so respect his correct decision.

Too many men and women get ferociously arrogant about their work and neglect their families while identifying themselves as some kind of heroes. One woman caller recently told me she was a great schoolteacher and thought that the numbers of children who benefited from her work far outweighed the sacrifice of her own children suffering through day care. I reminded her that the notion that being such a good teacher was more important than parenting should have come before pregnancy. However, now that she had a child, G-d blessed her with that responsibility that she must fulfill before she gets her professional ego massaged. I suggested she wait until the child was ready for kindergarten, and then start teaching while Junior was also at school.

Last, but not least, is the new phenomenon of cyber affairs. Frankly, this is pathetic. I have dealt with this subject on my TV and radio programs, as well as in *Perspective*, and I am struck with the complete lack of humanity and depth existing in folks who have cyber-relationships. There is no touch, no sight, no truth, no depth, no reality, no nothing of value. It is truly the epitome of getting an ego stroked. However, this passion for really being important to someone and finally getting needs met (no responsibilities or obligations are part of this fantasy, of course) has destroyed an alarming number of homes and marriages.

"My now ex-wife found it necessary to try to find her own self. Little did I know that our new computer was transforming my wife of fifteen years into a person I would never recognize as my wife. One day she asked for a divorce. I found out that she was actually having an online affair with this person that she was willing to give up everything for. Two months later I had convinced a judge to grant me custody of our sons (fifteen and twelve) and she left the state, and her sons, and moved to New Jersey with her new cyber-boyfriend. I was left with trying to explain to the kids why their mom had left."

I, for one, can't understand the degree of selfishness it takes to abandon, on a whim, all that has been built up and all who depend on you, for a flighty fantasy of sex and freedom. I can imagine imagining it! I just can't imagine actually doing it. It becomes easier and easier for people to behave this way since society has stopped condemning, judging, punishing, and shunning. I expect that the cyber-affair woman's family is probably hostile to anyone who says an unkind word about her—after all, family is family. Even when you abandon yours?

One man, a listener, sums up all this "single while married," mentality:

"I found that fighting for my rights or individuality is being selfish, shows lack of concern for others, and gives the wrong message to the kids. It is necessary for me to set the example. If you have self-esteem, you don't have to fight for your rights, you know who you are and there is nothing to prove. If I give up my rights or individuality to be there for others and receive the blessings from God in return, so be it!"

If There Is Only Me . . . Then You Can't Hurt Me

Some of what makes people self-centered in relationships has to do with immaturity, lack of experience, poor role models, personality styles, habit, self-protection, and some combination of the above.

For example, as one listener wrote:

"Being on my own for so long I got very used to taking care of myself and if I was hurt or in any type of bind, no one else had to know about it and it really just wasn't their business anyway. When I became engaged this affected our relationship greatly because it took me a while to realize that I can't become one with someone and still behave like the Lone Ranger. I had to share my thoughts, what I had, and very personal information. That wasn't easy, but I have to thank God for a patient and tolerant man who is now my husband. He taught me a lot and helped me realize he was there to help, not hurt me and I didn't have to do everything on my own."

As many people who have gone through decent therapy have learned, it is not unusual for people who have suffered to take it out on their spouses—a kind of "I suffered at the hand of another so now you owe me!" mentality.

This was (heavy on the *was*) the perspective of one listener:

"*I grew up in a sexually, emotionally, and physically abusive home—my father molested my sister, brothers, and me . . . as well as many of our friends and cousins. Because of our rough home life, my brother turned to drugs, my sister and I became promiscuous. I am astonished at how stupid and self-centered I used to be and how far I've come. At one point, I thought that because I was a wounded bird, that the world owed me something. When one approaches life as a free-for-all, there are no standards of behavior and nothing to live up to and for. I have built a decent, respectable life by having a foundation of values by which I live—with family.*"

While it is not unusual for people hurt as children to react in such a chaotic way, pushing away values and good people and good experiences out of unresolved historical anger, a fear of hurt or loss, or a discomfort with normalcy after so much chaos, the solution always is love, bonding, commitment, purpose. The solution always is getting back on the soul train someone threw you off.

That "pain" isn't always from childhood, although those experiences do have an impact on how you handle challenges along the way. Some people have had terrible experiences, which they generalize to all relationships.

"*I had come out of a very bad six-year marriage when I met my second wife. The first wife was very controlling and I did not like that. So, I decided I would not let that happen again. I never allowed my new wife and myself to grow as a couple. I decided that work was more satisfying to me than my marriage and family, in spite of the fact that marriage and family was always what I wanted. At the end of the marriage I was very lonely. My independence caused that. It's been a year since the divorce.*"

Self-protectiveness is alienating and lonely. Somehow, the person has chosen safety over risk, and without risk there is no gain, and without gain there is no intimacy, and without intimacy there is no peace and safety that comes from being known *and* loved.

I Hurt . . . Therefore, I'm in Charge!

When I talk to people on my radio program about their "life-long" problems and they go into their history to explain the origins of their issues, I remind them that there are two parts to ongoing behaviors: The first is the precipitating events (abuse, abandonment, etc.); the second is what are called "secondary gains." Secondary gains refer to the benefits of maintaining the problem. Here are two examples, one having to do with pain, the second with overeating.

"When I say something to her and when she does not complete a task I've asked her to do, she gets mad and starts yelling—then she starts crying and talking about how bad her childhood was and says no one loves her, no one cares about her. I do get mad at her when she won't do anything. The only reason I don't leave is I feel sorry for her, because she claims that she was abused, molested, neglected, and never taught morals in her childhood. I don't want to spend the rest of my life trying to fix something that will never fix."

I have talked to many women over the years who admit to holding historical pains up as a banner declaring themselves off-limits to demands, expectations, and responsibilities. It's a tough one to give up because all the sympathy and permissiveness makes life so easy at times; they feel righteous and in control. The perpetual suffering, pity, and aggravation are too big a price to pay.

Obviously, this is a "spite your face" type of behavior, because you end up not respected and not competent at anything that will be satisfying. One woman listener wrote about how her father made a big deal about her weight when she was a teen. He had put pressure on her to lose weight at that period of time when she was just going through puberty and it was a truly normal growth spurt. She was not overeating.

"To claim control of the situation, I began sneak eating. Fast for-

ward nineteen years later, I'm married to a decent guy, whom I always
promised I would get myself fit and healthy for. Twenty years, thou-
sands of broken promises, and unused exercise equipment later, I was
still eating . . . out of spite. That was how I claimed my 'right' to my
body. I am in therapy now, having realized that I need to claim
responsibility for my spiteful eating. My spitefulness has hurt my
marriage, but it has hurt me, too. I was determined to prove to my
father/husband that they could not control my body. I do realize
whom I have been hurting all along. Me."

Carrying over old problems into marriage and family is a
selfishness borne of unresolved anger and hurts; nonetheless,
it is a self-centeredness: me, my hurts . . . you won't get me!

Each individual must bring his or her healthiest, most
trusting, and least hostile self into a relationship. Using others today, simply to heal from or vindicate past pain, is self-
centered and destructive.

Bored Means Boring

It is amazing to hear from people who criticize their marriage or partner as boring. Actually, it means that all relationships can get boring. But it's often not the usual suspect (the
other person) that is the problem. The fact is that bored people are usually boring. They just blame it on others and circumstance.

That's why people get so shocked and annoyed when I tell
them that if they're bored they better become more interesting rather than demand that of their partner. It works, trust
me. Here's an example:

"I am married for nine years. About three years ago my mar-
riage was in serious trouble—mostly due to my being stubborn. If
my husband wouldn't give me what I needed, then I sure as heck
wasn't going to give him what he needed. We rarely talked, did

almost nothing together or as a family, we never hugged, touched, or kissed. I wanted him to love me first the way I needed, and then I would love him back, the way I felt he needed. He was a potato.

"I went to a minister for counseling. He told me to think of what I could do each day, special, just for my husband so HE would know he was loved. The entire session became about what I could do. It was about what I could give. My marriage is a complete turn-around. After just a few days of being 'my husband's wife,' he began to try to find ways to make me happy. I can't tell you how much the selfishness I had was the problem. Now I have the man of my dreams."

Another listener had the same revelation:

"I really thought my wife was no fun anymore. I saw a book about ten thousand ways to say 'I love you,' and realized I was really a selfish person. I started on the simple things like picking up after myself, fixing her dinner after a long day, leaving notes of appreciation. And wow! Things started happening. The gates of communication burst open and the sex and communication have never been better.

"GEEE, I never knew that giving lots gets so much back . . . I wish I would have known this many years ago . . . and how many years I wasted dreaming of leaving and finding the perfect lady when I had her all this time and I was too selfish to figure it out."

You Mean, There Is a You?

When babies are born, they are the center of their own universe; even their mother's breast is seen as an extension of themselves. It is a wonder and a shock for them to discover that there are other people, with opinions, desires, demands, expectations, power, and personality. When we grow into adults we supposedly have learned to navigate in the world of "others" and to get along with people, using skills we've developed along the way.

Sometimes we get stuck in the "me" mode and forget there is a universe of others out there. Sometimes all we need is a little nudge as a reminder. Sometimes we need a big smack upside our heads. Here are some expressions of that lesson learned:

➤　It's not that you're always wrong, it's that I'm always right: *"When I married my husband nearly eighteen years ago, our first three to five years were pretty rough. We both have our own faults, but it wasn't until I quit criticizing and trying to change him that our relationship really came alive."*

➤　We're not fighting, you are!: *"I have a very quick temper and seem to take it out on everyone around me at the time. We recently split up, because I was so tired of all the arguing. This all could have been avoided if I'd realized what I was doing then was being a self-centered, spoiled brat and needed to grow up. It takes two and I have to ask myself what I am doing to contribute to this arguing?!"*

➤　If we all do everything my way we'll all be very happy: *"I thought that if he could see that I was right, then we could do the right thing and all would be well in the marriage. I did not see that there were times when the right way or answer was not mine but rather what was right for us BOTH."*

➤　It's my life, isn't it?: *"I used to believe that it only mattered what I felt in this life since it is my life. Now I realize that this world does not revolve around me. The world is full of people who are in need that same way I am."*

It seems such a difficult task for so many to realize that happiness and love are not gotten by force of will, nor are they automatically granted simply because you show up. The greatest amount of getting is through giving. If you take care of the ones you love, even when you're hurting or not in the mood or they've done something to annoy you, it not only shows love, it primes them to be more giving.

Everything Except Each Other

The struggle against selfishness is difficult and never-ending. That is because we all want. We all need. We all have impulses. Self-control, as opposed to selfishness, requires effort and sacrifice. This includes making time for each other a priority. That means apportioning time for work, play, hobbies, children, extended family, religious activities, and community service. I sometimes weary at the complaints of those who are exhausted and stressed by their "obligations to students, worshippers, clients, patients . . ." I remind them that there is both choice and ego involved. The ego part is about the gratification they get for being so "wonderful" and "necessary." The choice involves the denial that they are acting on ego.

Perhaps a thousand cheering fans is more exhilarating to some that the grateful hug of a son or a husband (or wife)—but I'm not one of them. The legion may be sincere, but it still lacks the depth of the one-on-one at-home experience with spouse and children.

As "One" in the Eyes of G-d

One of the most profound truths is that G-d made us incomplete; and, it is not a Ph.D. that completes us. What completes us is a joining with our gender counterpart. One husband and listener wrote this:

"As far as being an individual, when you marry you are no longer an individual. That's why you are referred to as Mr. and Mrs. at the wedding ceremony. The people who have problems with losing their individuality were most likely insecure to start with. God said that the two should become as one. So, the answer is that you lose your individuality only to gain a new, and complete one."

Another listener completed this thought with the following observation:

"It's amazing how honest you tend to be with each other when you imagine God literally in your house as your 'boss.' We appreciate that we are each our own man and woman. But, when we come together as one we are unstoppable and inseparable."

That's it in a nutshell. When it's me or you, it's a fight. When it's you and me in the sight of G-d, it's a festival.

Selfishness not only cuts out your partner, it cuts out G-d, and without G-d, there is only "me." And "me" is ultimately alone.

3

Stupid Pettiness

> *"After all my years in combat, I've learned something I've carried with me throughout my civilian life. When I get angry about something, or at someone, before I act I ask myself, 'Is this the hill I want to die on?' "*
>
> —(RETIRED MARINE MASTER SERGEANT, A LISTENER)

I swear, on my radio show I think it would be much easier to talk someone out of outright murdering another person than it generally is to talk someone out of being *mad* or *hurt* (same thing, really) at some imperfection or perceived slight or personal style. And, forgive me, we women are worse than the men when it comes to being petty.

Last time I went through airport security we couldn't figure out why I kept setting off the alarm after I'd removed my belt, wallet, jewelry—everything but my fillings! The culprit was the wire in my bra! I mean, really, how high can you turn up the sensitivity on that machine before it gets silly. Same for women in general. Perhaps it is because we women are simply biologically fine-tuned (sensitive?) to interpersonal nuances, because we are the gender that gives birth, tends children, manages the neighborhood and family social interactions. How many times have you heard the story that when the matriarch dies, the family glue is lost? Often. How many times have you heard the story that when the patriarch dies, the family glue is lost? Never.

Whatever its evolutionary plan and benefits, the sensitivity to the actions of others is definitely set on max when it comes to women. Like airport security, moderate sensitivity is good for detecting problems to be handled, but maximum sensitivity actually causes problems.

This is not to say that men can't be hypersensitive or nit-picky—it's just not as general a rule for men as it is for women. If it were, so many women over so much time would not have had the age-old complaint of a tuned out, not-paying-attention, insensitive, clueless spouse or boyfriend.

Let me give you an example from a recent radio conversation with a woman caller. She complained that in November, at a neighborhood gathering, her friend-neighbor had invited her to a Christmas Night party at the neighbor's home. The woman also told her that she'd be away for the weeks before the party, having to travel to visit with family. Fine? No, of course not. Our caller was on the phone with me in January, complaining that the neighbor was rude. Her question for me was, "Should I confront her or just ignore her from now on?"

"Why," I asked, "why would you have to do either? What's the problem?"

"Well, when she came back from her trip she didn't call me to tell me exactly what time the party was. So, I didn't go. Then, I found out from another neighbor that she did have the party. She's a liar."

"Huh?" I answered dumbly. "What are you talking about?

You were invited. You knew she had numerous family obligations and then had to prepare for her party rather quickly. Why didn't you go? Why didn't you call and ask to help her? Why didn't you . . ."

"Well," she came back angrily, "she should have called me."

"Let me get this straight. If I invite one hundred people to a party telling them when and where, I am expected to call all one hundred just before the party again to assure them they're still invited?"

"Well . . . I was expecting a call."

"You know," I retorted, "if you were a guy you would have been over without ceremony and with a keg of beer on your shoulder. Guys don't get all bent out of shape about the details. They don't spend serious time mulling over the details of tone, innuendo, timing, intent, facial expressions, and the rest. They just get on with it. Why can't we?"

"I don't know. So, should I confront her or just ignore her?"

"I give up."

Generally, it isn't the large bombs of life that do the most damage, it's the gnawing away of serenity and good sense by pettiness that is the most destructive force of intimate relationships in general, and men-women relationships most specifically.

Save Me From a Sensitive Mate!

"Don't hang around with or get into relationships with sensitive People!!!!!," writes a listener who got out of a relationship with one of the few overly sensitive men on the planet. *"Thanks to being raised by a straightforward mother, I was not too sensitive. I was once involved with 'a sensitive man' and, as if that weren't enough, went into business with 'a sensitive woman.'*

Dr. Laura, I wasted too much time apologizing for things I did not say or mean. Thankfully now, both are out of my life, and I did learn that valuable lesson."

Frankly, her rule is a good one. I generally tell folks to avoid dealing often or in depth with the hypers—it's a you-don't-ever-win situation. It is impossible to get along with the overly sensitive for very long before you become completely paranoid, worrying and wondering if or what or when they're going to feel hurt or angry or something (and, of course, not deal with it openly at the moment—overly sensitive types suffer on for a while) and when they're going to blow up and accuse you of all sorts of things you don't even remember and didn't even mean.

When Petty *Is* Important

All that having been said, there are also too many times when people discount as petty issues or circumstances that deserve respect. Petty sometimes has a point; as my Rabbi, reminding me of a famous quote, said, "G-d is in the details."

One of my listeners makes this point:

"I am one of those people who can handle any kind of crisis but the everyday trivial little things set me off. Little things like not putting the cap back on the toothpaste, not cleaning up after oneself, not erasing the messages off of the answer machine, etc. I just feel if each person in my household did these little things instead of leaving them for me, then I could reserve my sanity for when they really need me. It's usually one person in every family who gets stuck with it all. How much do you think one person can take? Think about that the next time you're about to walk away from something that you usually leave for someone else to do. Give a helping hand."

In all fairness, that's a very good point. When I was in private practice counseling folks with similar complaints, I would ask them, "Yeah, it's usually one person in every family who volunteers to get stuck with it all. Why did you volunteer? Why not leave it there long enough for someone else to eventually volunteer?"

Letting small things pile up by not pitching in is setting up the more responsible or compulsive of you to pick up after you. That's instigating a problem. Though it is true that the responsible person has a choice in doing it for you or leaving it alone, does the family or relationship really need two sloppy, irresponsible, childish folks?

When you look at it that way, it seems unfair to regard a small issue as stupid when the other person considers it a big deal. One listener had an example that illustrates this:

"My husband does not like it when I leave my closet door open because it is in view of people who may visit. While I may feel this is not a big deal, I try to respect him, but I would never tell him that is stupid. After all, everyone makes a big deal over small stuff, whether you want to admit it or not. What's important to one person may be viewed as stupid or petty by another. However, we should not voice that opinion but respect the other's view."

It is true that a loving relationship is in the "small stuff." Keep that in mind, and bend a little bit to comfort and please your partner. As they say, "It's not much skin off your nose."

When Petty Is Really Very Important

I get calls from men and women who ask me if they're being petty—when they definitely are not! It's always interesting, and sad, to hear some level of serious incompatibility or insult, followed up by, "I know I'm just being petty. How do I get over this?"

"Sometimes I catch my husband looking at other women and it makes me feel like he needs more to look at than just me," one

listener writes. Well, gee, feeling a bit bent out of shape when our honey makes a quick gaze at a pretty body is just one of those realities of life. However, a quick look is one thing. What follows in the letter is another:

"I feel like this is such a petty pet peeve in the scheme of things. This just bothers me and when I have asked him not to do this, he says he likes to stay aware of his surroundings and challenges me that the girl is not going to jump him in the store, is she? I have tried to overcome this, but it irritates me!"

The truth is, this is not a petty peeve. It is the reasonable hurt of a wife whose husband throws his awareness that there are girls prettier than she in her face. This is abject insensitivity bordering on mental cruelty. My advice to her for the moment this happens? I have suggested that women (a) say aloud for all to hear, "You're right honey, she's gorgeous and sexy looking—I can see why you're hot for her!" or (b) move forward toward the woman/girl and offer to introduce them, again out loud. Trust me, the behavior stops. But we're still stuck with a spouse willing to hurt.

What a lot of people dating seem to forget is that those "small things" are just the things one is supposed to assess for potential long-term suffering or joy. It still amazes me that dating is seen more as a conclusion than an investigation. One listener complained that her new boyfriend, while nice when he's around, lies about smoking, and never shows up to dinner on time (work . . . maybe) and spends half the week traveling (work . . . maybe). She chides herself for being petty, especially after the hurt of a divorce.

I ask them, point-blank, "If you were not dating anyone, and I suggested a blind date with a guy who smokes and lies about it, isn't around half the week, and can't be counted on being anywhere when he says he would, would you want to go out with him?"

"No, of course not," they wisely say.

"Well, then don't," I respond.

"But, I'm not being petty? I mean, aside from that, he's terrific with my kids."

"And that's the problem—he solves only part of the problem. The rest of the problem is going to be left unsolved? Is that the life you want to volunteer for?"

This is a worrisome issue to me. It is disturbing when folks cannot or will not distinguish between genuinely bad behavior and whether or not they're being petty by being hurt or saying/doing something about the genuinely bad behavior.

Sometimes petty is just downright meanness.

"I'm a thirty-six-year-old male married for twelve years and have three children from two to eleven. We both have full-time jobs. My daily routine consists of getting the girls up, dressed, breakfast, lunches, seeing them out the door while my wife showers and gets ready herself. My wife always complains about something, especially if things aren't going her way, like getting to work on time. She will constantly blame everyone for her lateness. I usually get home early to clean the house, feed the kids, and interact with them, but it seems that the house is never clean enough."

On my radio program I recently reported on a study from England which concluded that the largest cause of the overwhelming divorce rate is the bad behavior of women! Feminism once stood for a belief that career aspirations and social roles should not be limited by gender. Today, feminists are applauding women engaging in stereotypical masculine misbehaviors: aggression, self-centeredness, abandonment of marriage, pornography, and promiscuity. More and more women decide they're entitled to their happiness no matter the cost to children, families, or society. The listener's wife's constant barrage of petty complaints is a symptom of a larger problem of this growing selfishness and insensitivity in general in our culture, and, more frighteningly, in women in specific. When the gender of nurturance, regeneration, and sensitivity becomes crass and coarse, the field of hope becomes barren.

"My husband is a good man in every way," my listener writes. Well, if that were true, we wouldn't have more to the paragraph, but we do. *"But he can also be brash, sarcastic, easily exasperated, and cutting. We were married for eighteen years and I felt constantly bruised, a condition that made it hard to love him and hard to feel love. We went to counseling, and our therapist made an off-handed remark that stuck with me. All those things about my husband that drove me crazy—she called them his 'style.' I knew then that they had very little to do with me, and everything to do with his style. Somehow, this perspective enabled me, finally, to take his comments in stride."*

Let me get this straight, if someone's bad behavior is something they do all the time, and they do it to everybody, not just you, then you're not to be upset because it's not about you personally? But that means you're supposed to take it and they're not obligated to change their style? This works?

Evidently not, because her physican put her on Prozac for an intense and worsening kind of hypochondria and depression. I guess we just needed to understand that it was "his style" to cope with being *petty* about his nasty personality.

"He thinks I wear my feelings on my sleeve," was the beginning of the letter from another *petty* listener. Turns out her new beau (she is fifty-three, he is fifty-six) gives her short shrift on the phone, he's moody without explanation, he spends almost all Sundays worshipping football instead of attending church, and lives with his ex-wife to save money.

"I know it sounds fishy . . . ," she writes, but she still worries that she's being too petty. Oh, puhlease.

To summarize the points so far: Hypersensitivity is annoying and destructive, people will call you petty when you're not, only to avoid taking responsibility for their own misbe-haviors. You shouldn't bury reasonable concerns by dismiss-ing yourself as petty. Good. Now, let's get on to types of, reasons for, and how to deal with pettiness.

Ya' Don't Even Know You Are!

I remember a story one of my psychotherapy mentors told in class which says it all about how habit, experience, and familiarity can make us petty and we don't even realize it.

He said that early on in his marriage he came down with a terrible cold. He lay in bed, suffering "terribly," wondering when his wife was going to bring a huge glass of orange juice, just like his mommy used to do when he was a kid.

The orange juice never came. He was getting annoyed at her lack of sensitivity. Trying to prime the pump, he hinted: "Ahh, could I have some OJ, please?" She complied, cheerfully.

He looked down at this shot-glass sized orange juice and became more upset. "What?" he yelled, "Can't we afford a real glassful of OJ?"

His wife was thunderstruck at the sudden rage and criti-cism that came with her doing exactly what she thought he'd asked for.

It looked as if he were being petty and overreacting, when he'd been playing out an old script: boy sick, momma bring lotsa orange juice, equals love.

He felt unloved when the OJ didn't come, and then slighted further when it came in a small container. Old script. New life. They don't match. That's where communica-tion comes in.

Old habits die hard—harder still when they're attached to sensitive emotions—but easier when the individuals have character.

One listener had such character:

"Before we were married, I had been on my own raising my two boys for twelve years. I figured I knew how to do pretty much everything there is to do better than most anyone (read: husband). All my life I have placed the utensils in the dish drainer with their business ends up—it keeps the part that touches your food out of any standing water, which makes much more sense to me than doing it the other way (read 'wrong' way, aka 'husband's' way). We argued over it and he finally saw it my way.

"We recently moved into a house with a dishwasher—my first. The other day I bent over to remove the clean dishes from the dishwasher and impaled my hand on a steak knife that was loaded—of course— business end up. I thought about hiding what had happened and clinging to my petty, but hard-fought victory. Instead, I chose to go to my husband and say to him, 'You know that argument we had when we first got married about whether the knives go up or down in the drainer? Well, you were absolutely right, and I will never question you about it again. Please forgive me.' He bandaged my hand with a smile, without comment, and with the utmost gentleness. And I love him all the more for not rubbing my face in it."

Coping with adult and childhood experiences teaches lessons. Sometimes these lessons result in behaviors that generalize from the one stimulus to almost all situations, relevant or not. That's when we get into trouble. For example, swinging at a ball when you're at bat is reasonable; swinging at almost anything that comes at you without distinguishing between a slap or a kiss, is not reasonable.

"My sensitivity to slights causes me to feel unloving toward my husband, which is not good. In my teens and early twenties I could be reduced to tears with just a look. Now I realize that most people are involved in their own problems and slights usually have nothing to do with me. I grew up in a home with a very grumpy, critical mother and a father that ignored or tried to ignore the unhappy climate in his home.

"In turn, I grew up very sensitive to any sort of verbal or nonverbal slight, real or not. There was a time when I blamed my mother for everything that went wrong in my life. Now I see she did the best she could in her own way, and I am responsible for changing the way I handle my perception of daily life. I choose to be happy."

The listener who sent this letter realized that her relationship with her mother, that of walking on spiky eggshells, was not what had to be with everyone. That is a remarkable, brave, and life-affirming revelation.

Familial patterns are tough to break. But they have to be broken, if destructive, or adjusted, in compromise, when you make a new family with a person from, of course, his or her own distinct familial pattern. One listener was brought up in a military family where accuracy and appearance were everything, and criticism was common.

"I did everything in my family to be perfect and avoid criticism. Then this guy came along that made teasing remarks and didn't get raving mad when I complained about his criticism, who even welcomed a healthy argument with me, someone I could argue with without being put down or iced out—I couldn't believe it! He knocked me off my 'miss prideful perfect pedestal.' He showed me there were other ways to look at something sometimes besides 'my way.' He gave me grace a lot sooner than I gave it to him. He is now my husband of sixteen years."

What a wonderful lesson, when we chose to learn one.

ASSumptions

Listen, I'm not sniffing my nose at sensitivity. Without it we all become concerned only with ourselves. It is sensitivity that tunes us in to others. When that sensitivity is turned on maximum, we sometimes become concerned only with ourselves. The surefire way to modulate that necessary sensitivity is through communication. I still am ferociously amazed at how willing so many folks are to react, condemn, and annihilate, and how many of those same folks are absolutely struck dumb when it is suggested they actually check to make sure their reactions are warranted. "Don't shoot 'til you see the whites of their eyes," could be translated into "Don't shoot 'til you hear it from their lips."

Here's a sensitive example of what I am talking about. This listener's father was diagnosed with cancer. She wrote cards to him and called him on the phone.

"I was unable to visit and I was told not to worry about it. A couple of months went by and I didn't hear from him. I tried calling again, no response. I stopped calling and sending cards of encouragement—I figured it was of no use to continue. My feelings were hurt that he didn't respond. I also thought that my father's wife just didn't want my father to hear from me. I had all these thoughts going through my head. In the meantime my father is going through chemo, surgery, etc., and his wife is with him all the time. The problem is I should have continued with the letters and cards regardless of my feelings. I wasn't the one in pain physically, and I wasn't the caregiver. My parents were going through so much. I should have done more and reached out instead of looking for someone to console me."

Bingo. One of the most significant dimensions of being an adult is to recognize that the world does not rotate around you or me or any one person as an axis. We are all on the spinning globe together. Everyone else has a life. Communication is the only means we have of bridging that natural gap. Without communication we only have assumptions. And you know what assumptions usually make of us? Check out the first three letters of the word *assumption* for the answer.

When I was talking about the communication vs assumption problem, a listener responded:

"How funny that you have this topic today. My fiancé and I had a very petty fight today—the fight seemed important to me but not to him. I had my feelings hurt because he spent my day off with his friend. He is a farmer, so I can ride around with him, but the mis-communication was that he didn't know I wanted to spend the day with him and, therefore, he assumed I wanted to do other things."

Sadly, the writer continues her complaint about his not seeing this, what she calls "miscommunication," as a problem. It wasn't a miscommunication—it was no direct communication at all. She wanted him to "just know," whereas he's treating her like an adult not an actress in a romantic fantasy. This isn't a petty fight. It's a serious problem when one person expects the other to mind-read and gets angry when he doesn't.

Communication is the most important key to just about every interpersonal problem. Perception, that is, how a person uniquely sees and interprets an event or comment, can make or break a relationship.

One listener wrote about the stupid issues he and his wife fight over. The prior evening, she had asked him to take his dishes into the kitchen after they had dinner in the living room. It wasn't, he admitted, that big a deal, except that he perceived her to be in a nitpicky mood, and he had wanted her to be loving toward him as he had had some amorous plans in store for the evening. He took the comment as her trying to treat him like a child and told her that he didn't need to be told to take his dishes into the kitchen. While it didn't actually start an argument, it put some emotional distance between them.

After thinking about it, he realized his perception of her parent-to-child request was an extension of his guilt for not having cleaned up as he usually did earlier in the evening. It was his own guilt, reflected through her innocent statement.

So why hadn't he cleaned perfectly? He'd put himself in

the little boy–mommy scenario. He had to struggle to put himself in the man–wife amorous scenario after that.

These sorts of inner struggles are normal, natural, and not unusual. If you are honest with yourself, as he was, you get by them. If you're honest with the other person, you get by them together.

Not all communication is done the "right way." And, not everything that comes out of your mouth, under the supposed banner of communication, ought to come out.

"Some of the best advice I can give friends now, after five years of marriage and dealing with many petty slights," writes a listener, *"is that old saying, 'know how to pick your battles.' I tell them that because life is entirely too short—don't waste it arguing with the person you love the most in the world. I tell them, 'If it's a petty issue or not, that's when you need to not argue and instead, communicate the most!'"*

Herein lies an important point: What are the limits of communication? The limit is when you get abusive, hurtful, nasty, sarcastic, cutting, threatening, and . . . well . . . you know from the experience of being on the receiving and giving end how that can go.

You need instead to communicate with information, praise, helpfulness, coming from a place of love, not from a place of selfishness or pettiness.

And while open, honest, and sensitive communication is a necessary antidote to building a mountain of resentments from a molehill of petty complaints, sometimes the river of frustration can't be permanently dammed up.

"My wife has these supersensitive antennas up 24/7. In some ways, this has been a positive for our relationship because it's taught me to be more aware of what comes out of my mouth. Also, any controversy tends to be dealt with immediately, thereby keeping things from 'festering.' However, I can tell you there is a tremendous downside, which does affect our relationship. It has to

do with that thing called 'perception.' When someone is this sensitive to everything around them, then they either perceive things to be more serious than they are, or they totally misperceive the message. This is complicated with a blended family of wonderful kids, but a constant monitoring of 'who said what' and 'what did it mean' is exhausting. I love my wife dearly and am devoted to her forever, but this is a real problem for me."

This is an opportune time in one's life to seek professional intervention. When our personality and behavior is destructive and repetitive, it is time for us to take some responsibility; not just because we're driving someone else crazy, but because who needs to live each day with that constant trickle of paranoia? In fact, we have an obligation to bring our best selves to our marriages—that may require a diet, spiritual guidance, more baths, and psychotherapeutic treatment.

What's My Problem?

Over the years, callers and listeners have communicated their stories and have shared the conclusions of their self-examinations to me. I am ever impressed with the courage it takes to face the demons within—in many ways that's much harder than the demons without.

There are a significant number of wellsprings for hypersensitivity and pettiness, some learned from history, some from the power that criticism or hurt feelings give us, some from attempts to survive.

Feelings of Inadequacy

Many people have been picked on above and beyond the average. All kids are singled out for things ranging from the superficial, like hair color and freckles, to the meaningful, like handicaps or heritage. Not dealt with well, these leave scars; and unlike scars on skin, which have diminished sensitivity, emotional scars leave the person extrasensitive and alert to slights not only on that subject, but in general.

Here are some more typical examples:

➤ *"I was always small for my size. Through grade school, because of my size, I was passed by for the sporting events and always picked last. As I grew to adulthood, I believe I carried some of that resentment with me to my personal and professional life. At home, when my wife 'infers' that I have done something wrong or not to her standards, I get the feeling that she does not value me. I will return the inflicted pain right back to her and we have a fight. And the thing is, she doesn't mean anything by it—I just 'feel' she's picking on me."*

➤ *"I am twenty years old and married for eight months. I have noticed how petty and supersensitive I really am. Nearly 99 percent of our disagreements are because I took something he said to me too seriously and consequently became offended. I can see this potentially causing a huge rift in our marriage as soon as he quits trying to talk to me. Why am I like this? I moved when I was nine years old from Denver to a small private school in Bothell, Washington. My entire grade consisted of sixty students. With such a small population there were really two groups of kids, the Popular and the Jocks. Well, I was neither one. I endured constant ridicule for five years. I began to think that everything everyone said to me was meant to hurt me. I really hate the way I am, but I'm not sure how to control it. It's an automatic reaction that was developed during the most impressionable years of my life."*

➤ *"Having grown up in foster homes, I had a huge chip on my shoulder. I was going to prove that all from foster homes were not trash. I was very defensive. I lost my friends and husband over how bad my behavior was. I would not let him criticize or parent our child because she was going to be the best and brightest of all children, because I came from foster homes. I took offense at everything because I took it as a statement that I was less because I was from foster homes."*

➤ *"I was raised in a competitive way and I was teased a lot because I was not as verbal as my sisters. Consequently I didn't see that teasing could be affectionate, I saw it only as making fun of me, a rejection. I really have to struggle all the time with the 'they don't like me' feeling creeping in."*

➤ *"When I feel the least bit slighted I tend to take out my insecurities on the people closest to me. I got this way from growing up with an emotionally unstable mother who drank and developed poor communication skills. I have become more aware that I do that and stop myself before I do, but I still have a hard time with it. When I am not doing things to tend to my spiritual needs (getting out of oneself) I find that I am more negative, ungrateful. I have come a long way from what I used to be like. I still have a ways to go but my communication is much better, my child is much happier."*

Therein lies the key. The solution, the saving grace for petty behavior in general—and especially the petty behavior that comes out of the scars of childhood emotional trauma—is "getting out of oneself"! The focal point of hypersensitivity is the notion, the incorrect notion, that everything is about you! As I tell people on my radio program, "Oftentimes when people don't acknowledge you or behave in a friendly, positive way, it's because they have intestinal gas pains, not because you are in the center of their thoughts in a negative way." This makes the point.

That's why I suggest that people solicit the other's well-being instead of assuming "bad intentions." For example, when you see someone not being as friendly as usual, before you get into fits of rageful hurt over being ignored or treated poorly, go over and say, "I notice you're not your usual self today, is something wrong? Can I help with something?" Get out of yourself. Try it.

Jealousy

When we offer our soul, spirit, body, and life to another, we are quite vulnerable. It is a definite time for hypersensitivity with respect to any threat or loss of that love. We can minimize such a threat by being psychologically healthy, picking someone psychologically healthy, communicating in a generous way, and behaving in a loving manner in general. Short of that perfection, as we all are, there is wiggle room for worry.

It is one thing to overreact anytime our partner talks about or to another person; it's another thing to react appropriately to real challenges to our intimacy (such as private meetings and communications) which need attention. It's yet another to react to the past.

I've had callers and listeners tell me about feeling threatened about their spouse or their intended going to a funeral of their ex. A funeral! Being jealous of the dead is too great a leap from reason for me. "If he loved me, he wouldn't go, because it upsets me," a caller would say.

Well, how 'bout this: If you loved him, you'd support his mourning and supporting the loved ones who are grieving.

How sad is it to be jealous of the dead.

Typically, though, it is jealousy over past relationships. When our partner is in constant contact with past relationships, the word *past* no longer applies—and there is a problem. Lately, on both my radio and television programs, I've been getting a lot of questions about a partner keeping old photos and letters in a "locked box, in a trunk, in the attic." Probably, there are more such questions because more folks are making, breaking, and moving on to multiple relationships, more so than ever before. And, with the evidence of past loves, one worries about becoming another inclusion in that memory bin—with good reason.

As one listener wrote:

"Although our relationship was going really well, I was overcome with curiosity one day when I was at his house alone. I am not sure why I did it (looked through a box filled with cards and letters from his past relationships), because I never wanted any details of his past relationships. He always made me feel special and loved. Then I started feeling insecure about our relationship, because I realized how strongly other women felt about him in the past. He told me that he was planning on throwing them away, anyhow, and if there is anything I want to know, just ask. I would never want him to leave his past behind. I want him to carry along all the lessons that he has learned thus far in his life. I want him to share those lessons with me."

Making someone you supposedly love erase any evidence of a past is a petty, annoying, and destructive behavior which alienates them from you—it doesn't solidify your importance in their lives. Only you do that.

On the other hand, I am reminded of an audience member on my television show who thought retaining pictures of an ex was healthy; so healthy, indeed, that he carried a sexy picture of his ex-girlfriend with him all the time—in spite of the fact that he had a new girlfriend. That's worth being petty over!

Manipulation

In "therapy school" we learned about "secondary gains." Those are the "perks" of having a problem. As the joke goes in my home, there are a few days a month when I get to whine, be grumpy, and eat Oreo cookies with impunity; hooray for menstrual cramps! That is a secondary gain; it's the "good news" part of the good news/bad news joke.

It's not unusual for people not to want to give up their problems totally because of secondary gains: sympathy, power, and a release from responsibility. The same goes with the annoying behaviors of petty hypersensitivity.

As one listener admitted:

"I used to display ultrasensitivity as a means by which to control and manipulate the men I would date. There were frequent occasions when I would sulk, pout, storm out of a room, or become offended at the slightest provocation for the intent of soliciting sympathy from the male-du-jour. It would work for a short period of time, but eventually my boyfriend would tire of it and beat a hasty retreat out of my life. It wasn't until a particularly painful breakup that I began to make a more honest examination of my actions and motivations."

On my radio program I generally describe this personality style as melodramatic—focusing on being the center of attention and controlling by displays of pain and hurt. Another listener wrote about her style of pouting or ignoring the person until she got the right reaction—which was for that person to *". . . plead with me about what was wrong, and apologize and finally ask forgiveness and show regret. I was good at this. It met my need to feel 'in control' and 'wanted.' I wanted everything to revolve around me as most petty and supersensitive people do. I made people feel nervous and uncomfortable and stifled—not knowing what would 'tick me off.' I lost a lot of friends and dates who gave up trying to meet my emotional needs. I finally know that I am just me, not the center of everyone's thoughts. It has been hard admitting this."*

I have often said that there is no love where there is fear. I might add here, there is no love where there is intimidation. Making someone feel constantly responsible for your emotions, having them frequently groveling for forgiveness for some perceived (and clearly unintentional) slight, and making them feel like a bad person for hurting you so often and easily, is intimidation.

Perfectionism

One of the most painful personality traits is perfectionism. The biggest problem with perfectionism is that perfect is not possible, therefore no goal is attainable. For so many people, such ultimate and perpetual disappointment breeds constant frustration and a lack of ability to enjoy the journey of life. The process of experience and learning is painful, not invigorating.

The ugly part of perfectionism is the beating others often take at the hands of a perfectionist. As one listener revealed:

"My husband, the poor guy, feels like he can't do anything right. I think it is because of my nitpicking. I have always been really picky—especially with myself. I am a huge perfectionist. I tend to have high expectations for myself and for my relationships. I think that sometimes my expectations are unrealistic, and that it's unfair to impose them upon others."

Perfectionists experience being human as a great insult, inadequacy, and failure. They are generally all too ready to look at harmless comments as proof of their worst fear. One listener who was going to school full-time while her husband supported them constantly felt as if she were not doing enough. She commented to her husband that she was proud of herself for going to class when she didn't feel well (heroism) and her husband responded with, *"Yeah, it's always good to go to class, especially since the reason you're not working is so you can do really well in school."* She took his comment as a criticism and demand that she be perfect in school, because it's all she has to do. Her husband was devastated by her hurt and wrath, because he thought he'd just been seconding her statement.

They cried over their problems together. She talked about feeling pressure to do well. He talked about feeling pressure to take care of them. And, she got it!

"Although I was still tempted to be a total brat and say that people didn't like to be reminded that someone was making a sacrifice for them, the thought suddenly struck me that all he really wanted or needed was a 'thank you'! If I had looked at the big picture from the beginning, none of this would ever have happened. I expressed my gratitude to my husband, and I know I need to remember this lesson if I want to continue to make my marriage work."

Imagine the following: You are looking through binoculars at a distant small entity. That is you seeing only your pain, perception, feelings. Now, pull back the focus and take in the rest of the surroundings. That's you looking at the bigger picture. If you take the time to do that before shooting from the hip, your relationships will work better too.

Self-Protection

One listener wrote about how her being petty was an attempt to protect herself from possible hurt. As I have said on air, putting steel windows up to keep out the dust also keeps out sunlight, the sounds of birds and children playing, and the fresh smell of the flowers. It's overkill. So is shooting first, and asking questions later. Yet, so many people, people who have suffered in the past, use pettiness as a steel window.

"I used to pick fights with the guy I am with now just because I was not used to a man not beating me or arguing with me. I lost him once but we are back together now. I realized that I didn't

have to argue or be beaten to be happy. Life is so much better for me now."

While this listener's letter sounds extreme, it actually is quite representative of a relating style that is prevalent: not admitting or showing too much affection, keeping the other person off balance, not letting the other person know how needed they are, or picking fights so that you don't have to be intimate and vulnerable. I find that many people stay in relationships with people who commit adultery, are violent, abuse drugs or alcohol, or are just immature and ratty—but decide to leave after the person "gets better." These are the folks who can't tolerate the risks of love.

Revenge

Being petty is a favorite way for some folks to get their anger out—anger with their partner or somebody or something else in life.

"I find that I become petty as a result of other 'more important' marital problems. For example, if my husband spends too much time playing games on the internet and not enough time taking care of household tasks, I become very petty and overly sensitive to everything real fast. After an argument, and once we both recognize the source of my pettiness, we are able to resolve the main issue and move on."

Of course, it would be better to communicate about the main issue up front and avoid all that ruckus.

The revenge is not just about venting, it is also about tit for tat. One listener wrote:

"I find it easy to be sensitive to just about anything when I am looking to bicker in the relationship. For example, I may feel that my boyfriend has been spending a lot of time without me, and I

become unhappy and even more insecure. Next time he's with me, I hunt for something to complain about, thus leading to a petty argument, still avoiding the original problem. It makes me feel like I'm back in control. Not being honest with myself and not trusting his love for me—leads me to see that I am simply protecting myself from being hurt."

The revenge motive doesn't necessarily have to be precipitated by your current relationships. It is sadly not unusual for people to take out on their spouse the hurtful rage from other, less safe places—like family, friends, neighbors, coworkers, and bosses. This is the experience of one listener who came to understand that destructive formula:

"The conclusion I came to (after a screaming match with my honey) is that I have put years of hurt and anger concerning wrongs done by family members years ago on him and created unrealistic expectations. I have resolved to do a few things . . . first, is to treat my honey like I would treat a good friend, with the same respect. Second, is to take care of myself in a more constructive and compassionate way—and start forgetting those ancient hurts."

This is a good news/bad news moment. The good news is that your dearly beloved is someone who will ideally love you warts and all—so you have the privilege of being open, vulnerable, truthful, and painfully real. The bad news is that sometimes we abuse that privilege to protect our image on the outside by not dealing with the people and the situations which put that burr in our shorts in the first place.

Getting Un-Petty

Many of the letters in this chapter have outlined the means by which people have gotten a grip on their pettiness. Here is a summary of their ideas and a few more of mine:

➤   Pray more often. Prayer is not only calming, it is humbling, and reminds you of your obligations to others. Since
much of pettiness is ultimately anchored in a self-centered
view of the world, spirituality helps you broaden your awareness and perspective. Pettiness as a self-focus which is the
opposite focus of religion. G-d's laws are about compassion,
understanding, obligations, consequences, patience, meaningfulness, and holiness. These concepts are bigger than any
one of us and require giving of oneself in humility. So many
people find this approach enlightening, exhilarating, and
transcendent. It helps you with the bigger picture.

➤   If it's that important to you—you do it! I have told
many people that instead of nitpicking others to death about
how something must be done, do it yourself. Take responsibility over those things that you cannot seem to be flexible
on. Perhaps if you then find yourself so overburdened, you'll
realize that doing it yourself, because it has to be your way, is
not the best or only way to go about things. Consider that it
isn't a choice between just "your way" or the "wrong way";
it's "your way" and somebody else's "your way," which is
just a different way; take the "wrong" part out.

➤   Teamwork is part of the blessing of a relationship. It is a
far, far better thing you do to find ways to solve problems
and grapple with issues as a team, rather than alone. It's this
teamwork that solidifies relationships; the mutual dependency will make you close. People too often forget that
mutual dependency breeds a familiarity of affection that
cannot easily be broken by gray hairs or an interloper.

➤   Risk not being perfect. When I was counseling people, I
often sent perfectionist types to a coffee shop and told them
to order Jell-O and just pick it up in their hands and squish

it. Why in public? Because perfectionists care about how they look. Why squish Jell-O? So they could have fun being silly. Frankly, I was amazed at how effective such a simple experience was in helping some folks loosen up.

➤   Communicate. Communication is the most important element in relationships. Communication avoids assumptions and misunderstandings. Ultimately, it is better to know the truth of where you stand and how others experience you (as painful as those truths sometimes are) because it gives you the power to grow and it gives them the knowledge they need to love you more.

➤   Stifle yourself. Sometimes it's wise just to shut up. This is probably one of the more difficult anti-pettiness techniques—I know it is for me. When your stress level is high and you have so much to do, it's tough not to lash out at anything that appears to add to your strain. Learn to use that moment to solicit support, not strike out in frustration.

Basically, the cure for pettiness is working harder to treat your loved one as though you loved him or her. This one is self-explanatory.

4

Stupid Power

"Sometimes it's not even that I need to be right,
but that I DO NOT want to be wrong."
—A LISTENER

As I've said many times on my radio program, "I love juxta-position!": when two faxes arrive from entirely different people from entirely different places and so naturally play off each other—for example, one makes a philosophical point for which the other is the living example. Juxtaposition confirms for me a sense of cosmic intention.

Juxtaposition happened two days ago. Right after I finished organizing my material for this chapter, having about an hour before dinner, I sat down to find a movie to watch for relaxation. What does the television turn on to? *Bus Stop*. What is the main point of this movie? Stupid Power. Whew.

The two lead characters are Cherie (Marilyn Monroe) and Bo (Don Murray). Bo is a very young, rich, spoiled, egocentric, overbearing, pushy, demanding, insensitive, but innocent and very cute guy who has come off the isolation of the huge ranch he was brought up on to find a wife. Cherie is a not quite as young, sexy, dim, definitely not innocent, honky-tonk stripper. Bo, having drinks in a good ole boy's joint, takes one look at Cherie through his drunken stupor and decides that she is the angel he's been looking for.

Cherie is used to guys coming on to her for "favors," but this guy wants her, on sight, to be his wife. He's boorish, loud, and very embarrassing. She resists. He demands. She resists. He kidnaps her against her flailing and screaming will onto a bus to go off to his ranch.

A snowstorm forces the bus to stay overnight at a bus stop. Here she plans to make her getaway. Bo roughhouses her into submission. The bus driver, stating he has the authority of the "captain of a ship," takes the young Muhammad Ali wannabe outside and gives him a beating.

At this point, Bo's old caretaker/sidekick really lays into him about how other people have their own feelings, desires, opinions, and wills, and that he has no right to treat the whole world as though it were an extension of himself. He tells Bo that this was a whipping he needed and that he owes everyone, especially Cherie, an apology.

At this point, the beaten, injured, and humiliated Bo can't imagine even showing his face.

The next morning, with his elder friend's urging, Bo does apologize to the bus stop keeper, the bus driver, and finally to Cherie, who, in fine codependent style just melts into his arms (after all, he's all changed, isn't he?) and off they go to the ranch to live happily ever after.

At least he did not get the girl until he was sensitive, gallant, and respectful . . . if only for twenty minutes. In real life, too many people don't even wait for that twenty minutes, or even a promise; they melt on the basis of their own hopes. Unfortunately, these kind of hopes are generally only postponed disappointment.

It Gets Bad

The following two examples of Stupid Power will give you a picture of the spectrum of this controlling and critical behavior, from the ridiculous to the unbelievable.

The first example came from one of my callers, a thirty-four-year-old man who had recently married. He called to ask me if it were okay for him to put a picture of his great aunt in his wedding album.

"Was she at the wedding?"

"Yes."

"Was she in the wedding pictures?"

"Yes."

"Is she someone important?"

"Yes, she virtually raised my mother and myself."

"Well then, what's the problem about having those pictures in the album?"

"My wife absolutely refuses to include any pictures of my great aunt."

"Why is that?"

"Because my great aunt did not RSVP in advance, but at the last minute showed up and my wife was angry that she had to arrange for another plate of food and setting at a table."

"You're kidding."

"No."

"Your wife knows how important this woman is to you, and she wants to punish this woman for being a last-minute yes-show by cutting her out of wedding photos?"

"Yes."

"I have two things to say to you, fella. One, make for yourself a second album with all the pictures. Two, good luck—having married a petty, vindictive, controlling person as you describe your new wife to be is going to be quite a challenge."

The second example is an episode I had with a young married couple when I was in private practice as a Marriage, Family, and Child Therapist. Her complaint was that he worked a long day, came home, and went directly up to his home-office and worked some more. They had two children. She was a stay-at-home mom. There was virtually no family time.

Well, it is easy to get into a knee-jerk dislike-him mode. After all, how selfish can one get? Wait, there's more.

When I queried him as to his schedule, it became clear that he had the work ethic in the extreme. It was not enough to do his best in the time he had. For him, there was an imperative to do it all and perfectly in whatever time it took. What he didn't finish at work he felt obligated to finish at home. He was his own prisoner.

It gets worse. She told me how critical he was of her, her child-rearing, her house-cleaning, and her appearance. It seems that he would walk into the house after a long day's work and run his hand over the top of the refrigerator to check for dirt. She was his prisoner.

Instead of getting mad at him for being such a controlling jerk, I thought about how terrible it must be to be him, much less be with him. He can never let himself off the hook, he can never let himself feel satisfied for a job well done, he can never let himself enjoy the love and comfort of his wife and children. For this man, there are never fruits of his labors . . . just labors.

In the first example, we have a woman who cannot adjust to change. Her discomfort turns to petty vindictiveness. In this second example, we have a man who cannot adjust to a full life. His discomfort turns to compulsive effort. Both of these people are to be pitied, because they are their own prisoners; both of these people cause tremendous pain to their spouses and children. Both of these people make lousy partners.

P.S. The young man did well in therapy. Eventually, he was able to agree to only an hour's work at home with his children at his feet. After one hour (sharp) his wife would give him a neck rub and some homemade cookies. She was happy to do that for him. He became better able to allow her to do this for him. His basic personality style was pretty resistant, but he could use manual overdrive and temper it a bit. Evidently, a bit was enough for her.

Oh yes, the rule was that any appliance he checked for dirt, *he* had to clean. Amazing how that behavior stopped dead!

Stupid Power Is Corrosive

"My impatience," writes one listener, *"coupled with a lack of sensitivity to our differences, has led me to this type of behavior. I've responded to what seem like 'dumb' questions (either the reply seems obvious to me or the question has been asked so many times I can't believe he doesn't remember) with a condescending attitude and tone of voice and, over time, this has eroded his confidence and our relationship. I think sometimes I'm just busy and frustrated with what seems like a 'bother and unnecessary' to me. I need to remember that he and I are different, and if he needs to ask things several times, that's okay."*

This letter makes a very important point. Differences in energy, style, personality, and experience are often met with exasperation. Think about it. What you grew up with seems so natural, so obvious, so clear. You have to resist showing annoyance and displeasure at what is new, different, and unfamiliar to someone else, because, unless you marry your own sibling, you're getting together with somebody with a whole different set of experiences and habits. Remember, they have to deal with you, too!

When I speak to callers, it seems so obvious to me that a core issue is the basic lack of communication between people. People are either afraid of laying things out and admitting certain desires or vulnerabilities, or they just reflexively believe that there is no need to communicate because they know all the parts without hearing them.

Stupid power is when you need to be on top, in control, in charge, one up, and so forth; you only need to hear enough from the other person—if you're willing to hear anything at all—so that you know where to go in your argument. That is, instead of listening to learn or connect, you're listening for strategy to attack.

This is exactly what another listener wrote to me about:

"My wanting to 'one up' or 'be right' in our eleven-year-old marriage creates a broken bridge in our relationship. There cannot be effective communication if I'm not listening to what he is truly saying, trying to be ready to counterattack with a one-up or a comeback. I know this is a defect in character of mine and we work at it by giving five minutes when he is allowed to 'talk' without my interrupting. I'm glad I have tools to work with now, so I can love better."

This last letter came from a woman who grew up in an alcoholic home. To protect herself from the irrational and self-centered ragings of alcoholics, she learned not to listen and to have a self-protective response. Unfortunately, this early unhealthy training ground led to self-protective behavior when it wasn't even necessary, simply because it had become habit. Her five-minute quiet and listen tool is a great way to break a habit.

On the other hand, when the perpetrator of Stupid Power is not so enlightened, it is hell for their spouse.

"My husband is one that practices one-upping on a daily basis. The result is his actions have made me a very different person. I no longer respond. A typical conversation consists of my saying something, him responding negatively, and then my shutting up.

The unfortunate thing is he doesn't realize how this behavior affects me. His needing to be the boss has me holding back and not saying exactly how I feel. Many times in the past, I have written him a note explaining how this affects me, and upon reading it, he took a red pen and started picking apart my thoughts. You're right, it's not a healthy marriage at all. Some day he may wake up, probably not, but it probably will be too late."

That's so sad. There is no winner here. He may be exerting his power to put her down so that he can feel up, but it's artificial. His being "up" is an illusion, and he knows it. He is just so terribly afraid of finding his flaws and potentially losing her love because of them. That's the irony. He's supposedly hiding his flaws, and still she doesn't love him anymore.

Sometimes people work it out. One listener admits her Stupid Power has stressed out her relationship—stressed out, but not destroyed it, because they have "an understanding."

"He knows that I do not like to admit that I was or am wrong. Because of this, he avoids certain subjects altogether. The way that I am dealing with this is to practice saying, 'I am sorry, I was wrong.' It is not the easiest thing to do, but I know that it is very important so that I do not drive my husband crazy. Thank God for people who are willing to work through these difficulties."

Not so bad. He knows her weakness and he doesn't go there. She knows her weakness, and she tries to control that instead of him. Not so bad.

Mine Enemy

I've often said on my radio program that the person you marry should be the one person in all the world with whom you can share your deepest, innermost, uncomfortable, shameful past and problems. Instead, many marry treating their partner as the enemy, not the ally.

"My husband and I both went into our marriage with very specific ideas about what our marriage was not going to be about. I grew up with an extremely domineering father who treated women like they were servants, not people. My husband, on the other hand, grew up with an extremely domineering mother who ran the house with an iron fist. So our ideas consisted of this: I refused to ever be run by a man again, and he swore no woman would ever control his life again.

"This is hindsight, of course, we had no idea this was the case when we said, 'I do.' We began to fight about everything. It basically boiled down to one underlying problem. He didn't trust me, and I didn't trust him. We both saw the other as the enemy.

"To make a long story short, I began to read my Bible and things concerning marriage began to pop out all over the place. I realized that being my husband's helpmate did not mean that I had to become a meek, trod-upon waif. Instead, I could stay the strong woman that I was and still prefer my husband over myself. Once I began to trust my husband not to run over me, and I understood that I wasn't going to become a doormat, he responded in kind. I started trusting him with my life instead of being in complete control. Amazingly, the same thing happened to him as he began to trust me with his life."

Where this revelation and metamorphosis does not take place, there is either all-out war, unilateral surrender, or an uncomfortable détente. The latter is a state in which nothing is shared because sharing is evidence of a loss of control.

"My children never witness their parents sharing hobbies, views, ideas, or common goals. We simply don't trust the other person not to try to take control. I believe it stems from a basic lack of trust in each other. I believe that it will someday be the straw that breaks this camel's back. I love my husband and I know that he loves me, but. . . . But, I also know that love cannot survive the two of us as we are now."

This behavior reminds me of a *Twilight Zone* episode where, after a global war, it appeared that two people were left alive: one man and one woman. Unfortunately, they were on opposite sides of this war. At first they simply tried to kill one another, as good, loyal soldiers would. Then, realizing the ultimate uselessness of this effort, he tried to make civil contact and have them cooperate for survival. It looked for a while as if they would connect; they were both young and attractive—the romantic possibilities were obvious (as was the parallel to Adam and Eve). Then, war posters would remind them of their identities, or some action or words would be misunderstood. In the end, there was no real, lasting trust. In the end, there was the end—of humanity.

And so go many relationships. Because of family wars, dating wars, and inner wars, the end is too often the tragedy of not being able to connect with comfort, with trust.

"In my life, I have been 'walked on' by many different people. As I grew into adulthood, I determined that I would not let anyone else 'walk on me' again. I took that determination into my marriage. I would always have to be right, because at all costs I would not be my husband's doormat. Then, one day, I listened. Instead of trying to be right, I shut my mouth and listened to my husband. Then, I listened to God. I began to realize that I needed to let God use me as the bridge between my heart and my husband's heart. A bridge MUST be walked on. So, now I have begun to make a commitment to be walked on, not stomped on. I desire a loving, godly marriage, and if it begins with me, then so be it."

I was so touched by this letter from a listener. It proves that change is possible, that the first change must be in ourselves, in our attitude, and perspective, and reactions, and that trust is a decision—one without a guarantee, and that's what makes change a brave thing to do. These acts of supreme risk give us the most potential return.

Power struggles may leave you "on top," but they also basically leave you alone. There is no real intimacy where power and control are exercised. While it is true that bad experiences with violent or untrustworthy or philandering partners can leave you armed for bear in making sure this doesn't happen to you again, it is also true that shooting before you see the whites of their eyes (or the black of their hearts) leaves your relationship dead.

Heterophobia: Men Are the Evil Empire!

In 1999, a longtime feminist, Daphne Patai, wrote a book, called *Heterophobia: Sexual Harassment and the Future of Feminism*, coining the term *heterophobia*. The premise of heterophobia is that the feminist mentality shifted from expanding choice for women to an outright visceral and frightening antagonism toward men, wherein heterosexuality itself is to be considered oppressive. I found this thesis true and the author brave to make it, as severe antagonism and retribution are generally directed to any women who break ranks to criticize anything female or to compliment anything male.

Over the years, many women have written to me feeling betrayed by the feminist movement, unsupported in their "choices" (like at-home mom), and synthetically manipulated to be angry at men—or the "patriarchy."

"Feminism has done little more than subdivide me into a fragmented image of a women," writes one listener. *"First, feminism divided me from men by making me afraid of them. A teen in the seventies, I was bombarded with messages of how I would be used by men and never treated with any respect. I was terrified and angry before the first poor guy ever looked crosswise at me. How do you even approach a marriage when you are convinced that what was once 'giving' is now 'being robbed'?*

"Then, feminism divided me from my sexuality. It told me that indiscriminate sex was my birthright (power)—that I should be able to sleep with whomever I chose whenever I chose and without feeling anything in particular. Funny, now I see that as endorsing the old male stereotype of sexuality and actually setting me up for the exploitation those same feminists had warned me against in the first place."

I have received thousands of letters repeating the same story about being warned about men as a fundamental part of the feminist mantra.

"I grew up in the midst of all this 'women's lib' nonsense, and actually bought the thought that fathers are not necessary. Though married, I did not stop and think what marriage was really about . . . working together. This is an art form I did not learn easily. I thought I was protecting myself and my boys by never depending upon my husband. If he did not see things my way, I did it my way anyway. When he became angry, I would threaten to leave with both boys because 'I have already been on my own and could easily do it again.' "

Fortunately, unlike so many others, this story has a happy ending. After she walked out on her husband, he was persistent in trying to talk with her. He got her to think. She realized that if he had treated her as she treated him it would have been ugly! After counseling, they are doing better.

P.S. Her son, then eight years old, came and asked her one day if he had a stepmother. My listener, confused, told him "no" and explained that a stepparent is the person who marries either the mom or dad after a divorce. It seems that most all his school chums had divorced parents, and referred often to stepparents. He just wanted to know if he had one. He was relieved to know he didn't if a divorce was what it meant. Perhaps more than anything else, that was the glue that cemented the notion of commitment, trust, and sharing for my listener. She didn't want to hurt her child. No better motivation in the world, I think.

But I Want a Controlling Guy/Gal!

It just doesn't seem possible after all these examples that anyone would choose somebody controlling with whom to partner up. But, every day on my radio program, I get calls from, largely, women, who complain, complain, complain about the very controlling behaviors they opted for when they picked the guy in the first place. In my first book, *Ten Stupid Things Women Do to Mess Up Their Lives*, I point out how some characteristics can seem exciting or tolerable while dating, because some people refuse to see the leaves, just the forest. In other words, they want to be married, protected, supported, or rescued, or they overestimate their ability to change a person's basic personality and consistent behaviors.

One listener wrote me describing how she fell under the spell of a controller:

"Prince Charming came into my life and promised me the world, and ripped mine out from under me. You see, the power of the controlling type, which he was, is the daily therapy that you receive from him. The words that he speaks to you are programming you, like a robot. Because of my fantasy, weaknesses, desperation, and insecurities, I became pathetic and he fed on that."

Another listener related how she married a controlling guy, just like dear old Dad, regardless of the fact that her mother ended up remarrying a wonderful man. Some kids will go to strange lengths finally to have that father-daughter relationship, even if it is with a bad father, and the relationship is painful. Perhaps she thought that with her, as opposed to her mother, it would be different. Well, her handsome, romantic Prince Charming went from the so-called compliment of jealousy to the punishment of violence.

When people have been victims of a cruelly controlling parent, they learn very early that to fight back they have to either beat 'em, join 'em, or be beaten by 'em. A child can't really beat a parent, except by indirectly causing them pain by illegal and immoral activities. Many are simply beaten down by that parent, and become depressed and passive. Some come to believe that there are only two modes of existence: to be the victim or to have the power. So, they take the power.

That's exactly what one listener wrote:

"I grew up in a home where my father has never lost an argument. He has always portrayed that his opinion is right and always reminds us of how we hurt him. I am finding sometimes in my relationship with my husband that I get on a Stupid Power trip. I think I know more than my husband in some areas. And I will get loud . . . like my dad . . . beating a dead horse to try to get him to see my point. I admit that I do that . . . and am able to control myself sometimes, and certainly recognize it and apologize to my husband for it. My father hasn't changed. At least I am really trying."

Other callers have told me that they needed a "daddy" to take care of them because they weren't doing too well at it themselves. For these women, having a cooperative relationship of equals would require them to hold up their end of the bargain—something they either can't or won't do. Hence, the opening for the controller. As one caller said, when I questioned her about agreeing to a relationship with a guy who seriously controlled finances, "I did at the time because I had a ten-year-old son, and felt secure. I was grateful for the relationship, yup."

Another caller, married for twenty-four years and with three teenage children, just got an inheritance. Her question? "How do I explain to my husband that I need control of my inheritance without throwing him into absolute cardiac arrest here?"

"Why don't you trust him to work with you on whatever new money is in the family?" I asked, innocently.

"Because he has taken control of that."

"I don't know what that means."

"Well, he always has had pretty much control of the money. I let him have control. I have heard you say before that anybody that has the responsibility has the power. I've let him do that. I've let him take care of the books and do the investing and that type of thing without my input. His attitude basically is that I've not carried my weight financially in the marriage and whoever makes the money should spend the money."

Because of this inheritance money, she wanted a change so that she could be in control. I reminded her that since she had agreed to a certain style of marriage, as with certain ground rules in a game, if you suddenly want to change the ground rules to have an advantage, the opposition doesn't react well. Her worry was well founded.

It is important to reexamine the match-up mentality in the first place. When people have deficits, some things they really ought to work on, they can either try to correct their weakness, or just get those characteristics *from* their mate.

"Exactly, I guess that is what I did. And he did the same thing."

"Yeah," I responded, "but your direction is chaos. His direction is control and accomplishment. What qualities of yours would he take on? He doesn't respect your characteristics."

"No, he doesn't, and he makes that clear."

"And that is precisely the point. Your characteristics are a contrast. You know what he got from you? A sense of superiority. Both of you have inferiority issues, you because of a lack of skills, he because of a sense of never being good enough. In marrying you, he is automatically good enough, even superior. You married him because he fulfills all the things that you don't need to do. Now, you have the money, and in your home, money is power."

I explained that money didn't make her competent, and the money being hers didn't make him inadequate. Nonetheless, they would both react that way, and possibly destroy the marriage. In situations like this, a very clever and competent therapist is necessary to help both these people move simultaneously toward self-esteem. She needs to exert the effort, to train herself, and to be confident. He needs to let himself be loved in spite of not being perfect. They need a therapist with the wisdom to see that she is not a victim and he is not the perpetrator. They've been an unhealthy team, ultimately each with the intent of protecting themselves and being loved. Unfortunately, Stupid Power games like these mutually eliminate love. There is generally only resentment and disgust and fear and loneliness.

Basically, the inappropriate exertion of power, Stupid Power, is an attempt to be something we're not, to protect ourselves from former or imagined enemies. It is proof that we still see ourselves as we did in infancy—as the center of the universe.

The King of Pain

When in private practice, I was impressed by how many couples fought over who suffered the most, therefore was entitled to the most. This competition was an Olympics for pain. One listener recently sent me a letter in which he named this strategy the King of Pain.

"When my wife and I argue, particularly about money, we often resort to what we call the King of Pain strategy. I'll talk about how I'm working two jobs, sixty to seventy hours a week, and she'll one-up by talking about how much more stressful her job is. Then I'll come back with how I'd love to have just one job, no matter how stressful—if I could have weekends off. We end up trying to show who is more

stressed . . . and lose sight of the money question that we started with. We found that by naming this phenomenon the King of Pain Syndrome, we are able to get back on track with the discussion that is important, rather than the one-upping. It allows us to laugh a bit at the silliness of our fighting, and lightens the mood enough that we can have a meaningful and useful discussion about the checkbook. Now, if only I had a crown. . . ."

The problem with jockeying for power in decision making is that competition is bad for intimacy. Competition always means somebody loses and feels demeaned or unvalued.

The irony is that when the King of Pain strategy is employed to get some kind of appreciation from the other person, it is only by trumping their pain that you win. When their pain is dismissed, they don't feel like being too nice to you at all! So, basically, it's a stupid strategy.

Here's some proof:

"Not long after we married, the contest began," writes one listener. *"I make more money and for some reason believe I am entitled to more praise, pats on the back, and other ego-boosting affirmations. After work, on a daily basis, the typical question of, 'Honey, how was your day?' turns into a battle of who worked harder, whose feet hurt or are the most swollen, who got the least amount of sleep, who worked the longest amount of hours, and who had the hardest day overall.*

"For just once, I would like to hear myself not buy into the game and just kiss him on the cheek and say, 'I had a great day. How about you, Hon?' But that is not my life. I make myself miserable. Tomorrow is a good day to start. Better yet, tonight is a good night to start."

What would she lose if she were comforting and interested in her husband? Status? Clearly, trying to be the one to get all the attention isn't working—it never does. There is terrific reward in being caring. If two people do that together, everyone is cared for without these Stupid Power manipulations.

At least this listener learned the lesson:

"I was constantly one-upping my husband to prove to him how valuable I was. The harder I tried, however, the less respect I had for him. Years after we divorced, I finally learned that it had nothing to do with him. I had never had any respect for myself, and therefore, I was trying to force it out of him. Sadly, I didn't learn this through therapy. I learned it the hard way. But, boy, did I learn it. Now, as a strong Christian, I have self-respect, self-worth, and a wonderful future."

"Being Right = Being Lovable"

One of the most remarkable revelations I ever had when I was counseling couples came from a session with a young couple with marital problems. It seemed that he had to be right . . . no matter what . . . every time . . . regardless of what he had to do to make his wife say that he was right. I'll admit, this guy was not easy to like. I really had to dig down into my therapist mode of thinking to be helpful. What I would tap into was the notion of "finding the pain." That is, I always assumed that the reason behind a person's awful behavior (unless they were evil, or sociopathic, or psychotic) was some pain. When I would register that flight plan, I could set aside the reasonable disgust that arises when confronting someone that annoying.

Sure enough, the pain was there. His father was an overly strict, martial-like disciplinarian and only showed affection toward this young man when he had done something right or gotten an answer to some challenge. Well, here's the formula for misery: the notion that if you can get your partner to see you're right, then he or she will be affectionate and love you. Problem was, he would figuratively beat her into submitting that he was right, and then couldn't understand why she wasn't affectionate and loving. You'd think something like this would be so obvious. With such early and severe training, he literally could not see what he was doing. When I tied the past and the present together for him, he was just stricken.

It was actually a nice moment; she reached over and comforted him. I pointed out that he was getting affection for being real, not right. It got quiet in that room for the rest of the session.

Differences Are Not All About Superiority/Inferiority

"After almost fifty years of marriage to an extremely sweet man," wrote a listener, *"now that we are retired and together daily, I find myself very annoyed with his misunderstanding of news reports and other topics. I find myself correcting him frequently and enjoying it. When in school together, I was always the better student of the two of us. I graduated high school at sixteen, he was nineteen. I love him, but feel guilty at what I'm doing to us."*

It is not just at retirement that we note the differences between us and our spouses—it is all the time! Differences should not be an opportunity for Stupid Power. Differences should be an opportunity for affection, humor, respect, patience, and even learning. Instead, I usually find that folks use differences as motivation for one-upping each other in moments of inappropriate gratification. Often the conflicts are over knowledge, opinion, ideas, perspectives, goals and dreams, reactions, and even something as mundane as putting dishes in a dishwasher or as sacred as playing with a child.

I get frustrated with the folks who really, seriously believe that because their partner does something differently from the way they are in the habit of doing it, that their partner is wrong. I often ask if the difference is dangerous, destructive, or illegal. The reaction I get back is one of puzzlement. I proceed to tell them that if it isn't a difference that is dangerous, destructive, illegal, or immoral, simply different from what they are used to—SHUT UP!

Wow! Does that ever get a surprised reaction! I continue by explaining that for the sake of a difference in how to make a sandwich, either somebody is hurt or everybody goes away hungry. I ask, "Is that your goal?" The answer is inevitably, "Well, no, of course not." To which I answer, "But that's what you are doing every day with the people you say you love the most!"

One listener confirms this when she writes:

"I used to constantly one-up my husband. It could have been anything. I one-upped him when he loaded the dishwasher by huffily reloading it the PROPER way after he had already done the job.

"I didn't want him in the kitchen at all because he was incapable of keeping it organized to MY STANDARDS.

"I didn't want him to cook dinner because what took me thirty minutes usually took him about an hour and a half.

"When he drove, I informed him of the superior way to get where we were going, and became frustrated knowing that if I were driving the trip would be much less stressful.

"Eventually, I found that I was CONSTANTLY IRRITATED with him. My irritation and constant nagging resulted in him not feeling needed, wanted, or even capable. I had broken him down. Many of the reasons I married him in the first place were the exact things I made disappear.

"While he was feeling less capable than ever, I was feeling more overburdened than ever. I had to do everything around the house to make sure it got done my way. I then complained that he didn't help enough.

"One day I was thinking about how things were going and I thought, 'Mary, all this seems to be stemming from you. You're

the one spending valuable time just trying to get things done. You're the one spending valuable time being frustrated over inconsequential things.' So on that day, I vowed not to one-up him anymore. It's truly been a challenge to keep my big mouth shut, but well worth it. The truth is, maybe the dishwasher isn't loaded very efficiently, but it's loaded and I didn't have to do it.

"Stopping one-upping allows you to feel love and respect for a person that you previously blocked by having negative feelings. Our relationship is now much more relaxed and rewarding."

Just keep in mind that you were not put on this earth for the express purpose of pointing out all your partner's mistakes. When you see a flaw, a difference in technique, or a characteristic which you don't prefer, sit back, breathe deeply, and thank G-d for having sent you somebody to love and to love you.

When It's Way Over the Line

There are certain circumstances which are either so destructive or outright dangerous that something serious must be done—be it psychiatric intervention, legal intervention, or a dissolution of the marriage.

Perhaps you remember the movie *Sleeping With the Enemy*. The rich, handsome, wonderful husband turns out to be a monster. Not only does everything have to be perfect (labels on cans all turned outward, cans categorized, towels folded just so, and so on), but he cannot tolerate any hint of negativity from her about anything, nor will he permit her to have any part of her life to herself. When she resists, he becomes violent. Scary, very scary. And not that unusual.

I get too many letters from women describing their boyfriend or husband's physical and verbal abuse. One woman wrote to describe her husband as very compulsive:

"He has done many strange things to get his point across or to teach a lesson. Because the girls were not in the mood for broccoli for dinner, he brought out about ten bags of scraps of food that he had hidden in the freezer under my frozen stored foods and sat those bags on the table to let them know how much we were throwing away. A lot of this was discarded food that he did not eat and was not put away. But some were scraps left over from meals. I store leftovers in the refrigerator. We do not waste that much food. To think that all this time he was hiding garbage in the freezer scares me. I think there is something wrong with someone who goes to that extent. It makes me wonder what else he will do. I am at the end of my rope. We tried counseling together, but that didn't work. I never know what is coming next, and that is scary."

Another listener wrote me that her husband of seventeen years lets nothing get by him, just in case he misses an opportunity to correct her. Before bedtime, he will check all jars to see if they are closed completely and properly. If one is not, she writes:

"He turns on me like an attack dog. He makes such a big deal out of it and it usually leads to a fight because he treats me like a child. He forgets about the whole thing in about two minutes, but I resent him the rest of the evening. Then when it's time to be intimate I push him away. I tell him why I'm pushing him away and he calls me petty. It starts all over again."

It seems that for some folks, domination and humiliation of their partner is a kind of aphrodisiac. That power makes them feel potent. Or, in some other cases, it isn't even "personal." It's just that being in control, alert, and on top of things (even if it means on top of loved ones) is satisfying enough to relieve life's anxieties and let them relax into sexual intimacies. No matter how you frame this, it is ugly and it is sick and it should not be tolerated.

In Conclusion

The power struggle cycles are exhausting. It is difficult to live a reasonable life with someone who is constantly or unpredictably angry, and it is difficult to live a reasonable life being angry about the small stuff. This approach to life is to relegate yourself to the slavery of impulse and the picayune.

One of the most interesting ideas I studied in my personal religious journey was the one of slave and master, and I believe it is relevant here. I try to be a serious Jew, and in doing so, have to take upon myself many "rules" (*Mitzvot*, in Hebrew, Divine Commandments). Some people have told me that having all these rules, like Kosher rules about food and Sabbath rules about not working on Saturday, make me a virtual slave.

They have it backward. Instead of being a virtual slave to my impulses and appetites, I make conscious choices. Because I wish to lead a more holy life, I choose to not eat bacon or cheeseburgers that are scripturally prohibited (with some Rabbinic input). I am not a slave to my appetite, I am a master of what goes into my body. What slave can say that?

The Sabbath is to be a holy day, wherein one is reminded that G-d created the universe and that G-d, unlike man who makes physical objects and land "holy" or sacred, has made "time" holy and sacred through this day. No man can control time—that is the one venue over which we have no power. As a religious Jew, I choose not to work on the Sabbath and to keep it holy. What slave can do that?

So that when you say, "I can't control myself—I can't help what I'm doing," you are basically saying that you are a slave, and not a master of your identity, actions, or possibilities. As I have said many times on my radio program, an irresistible impulse is simply an impulse that hasn't been resisted. You can choose to be the master. You can choose to say something nice instead of a criticism or complaint. You can choose to shut your mouth when you feel a nag or criticism coming up. You can choose to not rearrange what your partner has done, simply to "do it right." You can learn to sit with the discomfort of not having things your own way. The discomfort will pass once you get used to it—and then you will be the master.

Finally, in the words of a listener, you can learn to value the relationship as greater than yourself:

"Reflecting on a failed marriage caused me to question just how much it has ultimately benefited me to have put the emphasis on my needs, wants, ways, and schedules. It is clearer now that not a few of the struggles were power struggles. I am in a new marriage now, and I found a process to help me protect this relationship.

"Step 1: Deciding, once and for all, that this relationship is worth protecting from myself!

"Step 2: Becoming keenly aware of the feeling that starts consuming me and my thoughts when a power issue or situation is in the early stage and I am on the verge of saying, 'I'll show you!'

"Step 3: Pausing, saying nothing, and thinking for a moment, 'What would I tell my daughter, someone whom I love and value and want the best for, about the situation to protect her true needs and the relationship?'

"Step 4: Finding something much more beneficial and appropriate to do than I've generally done before.

"I had to work at it, but it works. It is my cure for out-of-control power-tripping."

There it is. It is simple. What makes it difficult to give up Stupid Power is the fear of what one is left with. If one picked a partner wisely, the answer is that it leaves you with peace and love.

5

Stupid Priorities

*"At that time, we realized that the most
important things in this world are our kids and each
other."*

—A LISTENER

Believe it or not, there are times on my radio program that I am, for microseconds, flabbergasted into silence. There are other times when I am so enraged that it's good I'm on radio so that folks can't see my eyes bulging with the incredible restraint it takes not to go through the microphone and throttle the caller. When are these times? Well, the flabbergasted moments are when a caller is so obviously the clear and present architect of his or her own pain; and the second, when I feel the impulse to throttle, is when the caller is so obviously the clear and present architect of a child's pain. Most of these circumstances have to do with Stupid Priorities.

One example of a flabbergasting moment was a call I got from a young man complaining that he and his wife were not close at all anymore. It seems that the time they do have together, short and rare, just isn't filled with that oomph that they had when they met. I queried him about their schedules. They both have full-time jobs and go to school full-time and have various friends and functions that they maintained from before they were married. He said this all with pride at how active, involved, growing, successful, and important they were.

"Ahh, I'm confused. You're complaining about the lack of intimacy, sexual and otherwise, yet you speak with enthusiasm about a schedule I would find anywhere from enslaving to punitive."

"Yeah, maybe, but that's what we like. We like being active. We're both smart and accomplished folks."

"That may be true, but it sounds to me as if you're not penciling each other into your schedules. What's important to the two of you is not anything that has to do with the two of you. I'm not surprised you don't have much of a relationship left. What I don't get is that two smart people just don't get it. A relationship and a spouse is not a bed you just crash onto at the end of the day. A relationship and a spouse needs to be a focal point of one's life."

"Well, I don't know about that. We each have goals and plans and are very supportive of each other's reaching them."

"Yes, I believe that. As you each support the other's selfishness, your own is supported automatically. Of course that works. But it doesn't give any warmth, texture, or meaning to your lives."

"That's not what I called about. I just want to know how, considering our goals and commitments, we can feel closer."

"Sir, damned if I know."

That's when I'm flabbergasted. Now, the throttling moment is merely an extension of the flabbergasting thinking. I remember this caller, again a young male, as though it were now. He called to find out if what he and his new wife were planning was "okay."

"How can I help you?"

"Well, my wife and I are married. We're finishing college and have plans for graduate school."

"Okay."

"Well, we also have a three-month-old child."

"Aahaa."

"And we work to support our bills and to pay for school."

"Mmmm."

"And we wondered if it were all right to have her parents raise our daughter for three or four years while we work and get our schooling done?"

"Are you kidding? Are you pulling my leg?"

"No, I'm serious. We thought, that way, the child would be well taken care of and we could get our education and careers under way. What do you think?"

"I think that this is one of the most morally vacant, self-centered, crass, cold, insensitive . . . (Now I'm mad!—I'm throttling!) . . . inhumane, unbelievably horrible suggestions ever made to me on or off this program."

"Why? If we get a good education and good careers, then we have a lot to offer our daughter. And, her parents did a good job with her—why not with our daughter?"

"I'm even more crazed now that you come back at me so 'innocently.' It is phenomenally sad to me to see even more profound evidence of the decay of reason and responsibility in our society—when a seemingly decent person like yourself can offer up a plan in which the bonding, nurturance, care-taking, loving, living, and being with your own child can get so easily put aside and rationalized as being in the ultimate interest of that child.

"Your suggestion is disgusting. If your in-laws raise that child, they will be the bonded mom and dad, and you folks will be the too busy aunt and uncle. You then think you will take that child away from her home and the only mother and father that matter as though she were a parakeet or an adopted hound? You think that those things in the future that you can offer her will be anything but meaningless indulgence—a payoff for your conscience? You think this will teach her the meaning of mother and father, family and commitment? You think this will make her think that she is important? You think this will help her move forward into life with confidence and hope for a loving family of her own in the future?

"Get off it, sir, and grow up. You guys got pregnant when you didn't want to, you got married 'cause you thought you should, but you're both living lives as single people with no obligations. I recommend you put that child up for adoption into a two-parent, mom-and-dad, covenantally married home, where they believe your daughter has intrinsic value. Thank you for your call—I hope I can get over it soon."

"Oh."

This call would not have been half as bad were it not a symptom of the prevailing societal values with respect to marriage (shack-ups and serial monogamy are now common), child-raising (nannies, day care, and baby-sitters the norm), and priorities (success is everything). And there is no shame for any of this.

As if in direct response, one listener recently wrote to me:

"My priorities were all backward, and so I lost the things that really meant the most to me . . . only I didn't know that at the time. (Well, really, I did know that, but I figured that once I was a 'success,' everything would be okay. So, I spent all of my efforts at being 'successful.' Well, I did not have much luck at being successful, and even worse luck at being happy, or making those around me happy.

"Today, I am an older person, with a disability (with which I am okay), but my former wife (who divorced me) has nothing to do with me; and my adult daughter doesn't have too much to do with me either, although she makes some effort.

" 'SUCCESS,' and the pursuit of it, have left me lost and lonely. If I may offer any suggestion to others, I would counsel them to consider what 'success' really means."

Show Me the Money!

I remember a fascinating moment in Synagogue during the 2000 High Holy Services. In seeming contrast to what this listener wrote, the Rabbi's sermon included a hope that all of us would become very rich. He wished us massive financial success as part of his blessing for the upcoming year. I could see that many in the audience reacted with discomfort—after all, a major part of anti-Semitism is the belief that Jews are avaricious. Understandably, there would be an initial negative reaction (albeit a silent hope that his blessing worked!) to a suggestion that money be a goal of "worship."

I know the Rabbi well, and understood what he was building to. He wished us all prosperity, not for our own benefit, but that we would have the power and the resources to help perfect the world. Money may be the root of all evil in the hands of many people without a spiritual basis. However, money is the possibility of great good for a great many. When money is a goal in itself, success is empty; when money is a means to a more noble end, success is a G-dsend.

The emptiness of success as "the" goal is highlighted in this letter from a listener who figured this all out, the hard way:

"My husband and I have been married ten years and have two children, six and eight. When we first married, we were living outside Seattle and both working in rewarding careers. We worked for the nice house, new car, designer clothing, exotic vacations, etc.

"When we had our second child, we realized that we couldn't continue the way we were going. There just wasn't enough of me to go around. Plus, all the money I was making was going to pay for

day care, parking in town, car payment, insurance, plus multiple meals to go, since we had money but not time.

"The wake-up call came when our three-year-old was molested in her day care by the owner's son. At that time, we realized that the most important 'things' in this world are our kids and each other. The material possessions don't mean squat in comparison.

"We quit our jobs and moved to a small farming town, budgeting down to one salary. Six years later, our marriage is now flourishing and so are our kids. I love being home and involved in our kids' school. We have home-cooked meals and eat dinner early, so we actually have an evening. The housework is done during the day, so when the kids go to bed I have time alone with my husband.

"We found that by rethinking our priorities and concentrating on what's really important, we were able to make life changes that strengthened both our marriage and our family."

I fear too many of our young adults today don't understand this family's decision. They'd probably just think of a lawsuit and a new day care. They are the product of rampant selfishness and devaluation of vows, obligations, and sacrifice for some greater good. They are the generation who watched their parents' infidelities, divorces, drug and alcohol abuse, selfish pursuits, materialism, and basic immaturity. For many, this kind of thinking is the norm, not the anomaly it should be.

As another listener reminds us:

"I just think that the 'ME' generation in our society needs to take another look at their priorities. That 'ME' generation are all going to end up in nursing homes because they are raising a generation of children that do not know an example of selflessness . . . only selfishness. Thank you for your time."

I loved the polite salutation about "time." Time is the one thing we humans can't buy, create, or control. Time is our gift from G-d. Time is our gift to each other—the most supreme gift—for it is only in the medium of time that we have the opportunity to connect, to love, to support, to bond, to nurture, to caretake, to heal.

Work Is #1

A mother from Dallas, Texas, called me on my radio program recently to complain about an event in her high-school son's "Career Orientation Class." According to the caller's son, the teacher, a feminist, disdainfully chided the girls in the class, reminding them that "they'd better pay attention to this class and decide on a career now, because if they didn't they would find themselves at-home moms wiping their snot-nosed kids."

I kid you not.

Thankfully, her son raised his hand and commented that he didn't see himself and his five siblings as "snot-nosed kids," that his mother stayed home with all of them and they were all good kids who appreciated having a mother and father who took care of them.

I told the mom to go to war with the school, calling on my Dallas radio affiliate to assist them to get parents organized to fight this corrosive and disgusting attack on motherhood, marriage, and family, and contributing to the growing confusion and ambivalence many men have for women in general, much less women who want to raise their own children.

I have been sickened by how many women call me, who have "seen the light" and want to stay home with their children, who have husbands, brought up by working and single mothers, who actually threaten them into working so that they can afford the goodies "they" always wanted. Men used to measure themselves by their ability to take care of their families—now they want their families to take care of them! Sad.

One woman listener pulled her act back together after a "near death" realization:

"My husband and I began our marriage as career-oriented people who understood the importance of personal advancement in our professions. He is a teacher/coach and I am a professional nurse.

"We both worked hard to earn a living and advance in our careers. After a few years, and with a young teen at home, I had the opportunity to advance to an upper-level management position. In order to meet the demands of the job, I had to work sixty to seventy hours per week.

"I prioritized a professional title, success, and money above spending time with my husband and son. As a result, my husband and son became very independent from me, and my husband became frustrated with spending evening after evening at home without me.

"The stress at home and at work resulted in health problems for me, including chest pain and hospitalization. Fortunately, I realized the damage that was being done, both psychologically and physically, to my family and me, and resigned from what I thought was the position of my dreams.

"I couldn't be happier. I don't have a prestigious title now, and I gave up income. But nothing is worth sacrificing my family over."

"But Honey, I Do It All for You"

When I was in private practice, as a Marriage, Family, and Child Therapist, it was amazing how many men, primarily, would justify their horrendous work schedules by saying, "But, honey, I do it all for you!" That, of course, would make the women grimace with annoyance and shrug with some embarrassment, as they weren't able to think of an apt come-back. For sure, they had nice things and would rather not give them up. Yet they were tired of feeling so not a part of their husband's lives.

Sadly, it now swings both ways; women as well as men creep up the ladder of their solo dreams, shouting down to their spouses, "But, honey, I do it all for you!"

"Bull," I would say to the protestor. "You'd do exactly the same if you were single. Yes, your spouse is benefiting with things, but they'd rather not make the sacrifice of relationship for things. You are the one determined to make that sacrifice, ironically in the name of sacrificing yourself for him/her. How manipulatively clever. How ultimately disastrous, unless, of course, you've got some honey in the wings who is all too ready, willing, and able to adore you and to let you sacrifice the relationship so he/she can enjoy the things."

One of my male listeners confirmed this mentality:

"I am twenty-eight years old and an avid listener to your radio program. I am the King of Stupid Priorities. The following are all the things I put before my wife and child: a two-to-ten shift job, my lawn-mowing service, the Navy reserves, and a full load in college with music and art projects.

"I love my wife and child, but I feel like I'm not a very good provider sometimes. I know what you would say, nothing should be put before your wife, but I do not feel like a man unless my family's needs are met. Also, I feel dead if I'm not doing something constructive. I'm not proud. I know I'm probably doing more harm than good, but I feel I'm in too deep and I can't give up on my dreams for fear I'll lose myself. I know this must make you sick, but, it's the way I feel."

He's right. It makes me sick. It also makes me terribly sad. Not only has he already lost himself, he'll likely lose his wife and child. When somebody feels dead without perpetual stimulation, they need psychological help. All people need challenges and stimulation—that's a normal part of being alive. When stimulation is the goal of one's life, and one is "dead" without it, one is already dead in the spaces that truly make us human—those are the places that derive joy and triumph from giving, sacrificing, loving, protecting, and simply "being with."

Work is not the only priority venue that can occupy folks to the extreme and hurt or destroy their relationships. Cleaning is another source of problems for some couples. Listen to these two comments:

"I used to think that a spotless house would make my husband 'feel' important, cared about, and proud. Come to find out that it is not as important as spending quality time with my husband. My husband and I work opposite shifts so that someone is always home with our fifteen-year-old, so now I clean when he is at work and my son is doing his homework or some other activity, and save my weekends with my husband and son without worrying about such a clean house."

And the second:

"My husband of one year is expressing that I prioritize all other obligations below his needs and the needs of the relationship. But, I must admit, I feel everything in my house MUST be in order for me to feel intimate. Confusion and chaos take the mood away. I need help in reconciling my thoughts and being attentive to his needs only."

The sad reality for people who need constant challenge and stimulation or everything in order before they can get to their relationships is that they really can't get to their relationships at all. The work and cleaning are merely screens, behind which they hide their fears of imagined, or in some part real, problems, weaknessness, inadequacies, secrets, anxieties, and so forth. The work and cleaning are how they make themselves feel intact, stable, and in control—all of which they fear will go away if they cease activity or become vulnerable and open in an intimate relationship. In other words, they feel safe and competent with a computer or a mop, not with the arms of their spouse or their children. This requires introspection and professional intervention and explains why they hang on to their determination not to give up what they're doing in spite of the obvious problems in their relationships.

"I'm Ready for My Close-Up!"

One of the tough realities a growing child has to face as he/she matures is that they are not the center of the universe. It's easy for a small child to feel that he or she is the center of the universe when every gurgle and scribble is oohed and ahhed about by parents and relatives. The first time that their kindergarten teacher tells them they can't take that crayon away from Mary, or that Johnny gets to go first, or that their drawing needs work, children recognize that life is a cooperative effort.

Some don't give up being the center of the universe easily, and getting attention and becoming the focus of others takes on many forms—some healthy, some not. It's all a matter of degree and balance. Some become entertaining, or even entertainers. Some become "needed," some become utterly dependent, some become perpetually ill, and so forth.

All in all, the "I must be in the spotlight" mentality generally brings darkness to the family.

"I have spent the last year and a half as a drama/debate coach at our local high school," writes one listener. *"I was able to go to the state level in almost every area in which we were competitive. I directed three plays (one being a full-length musical with a cast of one hundred). Both parents and administration thought I had done very well for their children. I thought that I had done very well until I realized that my son was about to be one. I lost his first year of life. My daughter was potty-trained by others.*

"I was so intent on being seen as the best that I became the worst mom and wife."

It is important to watch that ego! The ego-trap is an easy one for people to fall into. Being good at something makes one feel important—that too often leads to a sense of entitlement—that moves right into a sense of superiority—and that collapses relationships.

Work Is Not Everything—It Is the Only Thing

Too many folks get their primary sense of value and connectedness from their work instead of apportioning it between their work, their marriage, their children, their friends, their family, their community, and their inner spiritual life. If "all work and no play makes Jack a dull boy," then all work and no family and marital bonding makes Jack or Jill have a life without texture, beauty, meaning, and purposefulness.

This is exactly what one listener expressed:

"I worked fifteen years for a company and thought I would be there forever. It was a family-owned business. I put everything I had into my position. When I was pregnant with my first child, I worked right up to the delivery day. I went back in four weeks. It pained me to leave my baby, but the company 'needed me.' I was making good money but never able to go away for even a weekend, much less a vacation.

"Before I knew it my child was twelve. The owner of the company gave the store to his son and I was the first to go. In the beginning, I was devastated. But blessings really do come in disguise. I was hired in a totally different profession, make exactly the same money, work much fewer hours, and I'm off every weekend. My husband, daughter, and I are really enjoying all of the free time we have together making lasting memories.

"It doesn't make any difference how much money you make, or

how high you climb that corporate ladder, if you can't be around to enjoy the people you love and care about the most. The only regret I have is that I didn't lose that job ten years ago."

It is interesting to me how many of these letters about Stupid Priorities report a disaster as the way folks learn "the hard way" what balance and what priorities are essential for a quality, happy, and successful life. We can't be wishing disasters on folks in the hopes that they wake up and save their relationships with their spouses and children. This is the prime motivation behind this book—maybe you, or someone you love (but are starting not to like) could benefit from the stories of others.

Sometimes it's not simply that folks are totally selfish or insensitive of the needs of others; there are strong pulls, like the tide, which draw us along—much too far—before we start paying attention. What always surprises me is how easy it seems to be for us to "get with that flow." In addition to neglecting others, that we don't even feel a need for that intimacy ourselves. I often wonder why we don't miss it more, and how it really is possible to feel warmed only by success or power or money.

This listener got caught up in the flow, but eventually pulled himself out.

"I took a job as a gas station attendant in New Mexico. After a month or so, the current manager quit so I took the station over and became the manager/owner. I was determined to make it and began to work 105 hours per week—seven days a week—363 1/2 days per year for four years.

"I was offered several outs by God, or so I believe, but turned them all down. After all, I was the BIG owner—the BIG Kahuna (I was also the guy who cleaned the toilets).

"I only saw my kids and wife when they came down to watch me work—and I missed several years of my babies' lives.

"After all my EGO and posturing, the actual owner of the property put the land up for lease bids and I was outbid by three times.

In an instant I was ruined—absolutely nothing to show for the work.

"My firm philosophy now is 'WORK SUX.' Now it's family first. What matters is now I see my family and enjoy them."

Well, I guess G-d had to get very direct to wake this listener up!

"It's My Divine Obligation"

Speaking of G-d, in 2000 I was privileged to speak to a room full of Rebbitzen from all over the Bronx, Manhattan, and Brooklyn. Since these women, wives of Orthodox Rabbis, were from a traditional world, I was certain I would not be addressing the usual, more secular concerns about work and family.

I was wrong. It seems that along with the caretaking of generally a lot of children (the Orthodox value large families as blessings to and from G-d), they felt compelled by responsibility to the needs and demands of people and families in their Synagogues. Unfortunately, they found it difficult to balance doing for others, with having time for their children and their marriages. Rabbis have the same dilemmas.

I acknowledged that this was a real and serious problem, because they, in fact, did have responsibilities based on their commitment to being spiritual leaders. However, there are two points to keep in mind: one, being role models was a powerful way to serve their community, since making their families the fundamental priority was a way of teaching others how to structure their lives and deal with the pulls and pushes of others; and two, that they may be underestimating how much of sacrificing the family for "religious obligations" was really serving their egos—after all, it's always easier to be a hero on the outside than at home.

One listener amplifies these points:

"The biggest mistake in priorities I have ever made came a few years ago. I believed that God had put a ministry in my hands and that it was something that He wanted me to do. The ministry took on a life of its own . . . my family took second place, and often that second place was well down the line of things—because the ministry was so big and intrusive.

"My family and personal life became chaos. I THOUGHT that I was putting God first; in the end, I realized it was me that was first—that I was taking my own past, and trying to make a difference to absolve my own feelings and try to 'earn' God's favor. This goes back to my family and how they have made me feel over the years. I simply thought God was just like them.

"Now, I am out of this ministry, and since I home-school, I have really placed the priority on family. God has really blessed me."

Not that all caregivers in the name of G-d are egomaniacal, or attempting to repair ancient hurts and guilts, but those that are should heal themselves or get out. We each have to be careful to examine ourselves to see if our serving is self-serving. One way to tell the difference is to see who and what you sacrifice to do the serving and whether any of the serving targets include the folks you are the most obligated to, your marriage and family.

I believe the most successful ministers of spirituality hold family first. One perfect example is the Reverend Robert Schuller. He has an incredible ministry and an elaborate Church/School complex. I have the privilege of knowing his entire family, and not one of them has ever paid a price for his ministry, since they came first and became a part of the projects. His ministry is literally a family affair.

My local Rabbi, Moshe Bryski, is an amazing success with the development of Chabad Houses, adult education, children's Jewish Day Schools, and international networking for Jewish Outreach. He has some tough rules. He's always home for dinner and to help his many children with schoolwork, and don't bother to try to find him Sunday, that's family day.

These are men I respect because, as accomplished as they are, neither they nor their work has become a god, and their families come first.

"A year ago, I was never at home," admits another listener from the clergy, *"and my three kids were in day care from 6 A.M. until 7 P.M., only to be picked up and dropped off at a baby-sitter or family member's home until 11 P.M. There were days when my family did not even see me. The weekends were worse. I was gone all day Saturday and most of Sunday.*

"By now you are probably asking yourself just what in the world I was doing! My answer may shock you . . . I was serving the Lord!— or, at least I thought I was. I praise God that He woke me up to realize that I serve Him by serving my family first. This is a lesson that I am happy to say that I learned in time."

There are two issues here—one is clearly ego gratification, but the other is learning how to set boundaries and to say no, which again has some basis in ego. We all want to feel needed and important. When I was in "therapy school," we were warned against developing the "Messiah Complex." That was another way of reminding us not to get too big for our britches—not to develop an inflated notion of our own power and importance. It's easy to slip into that when people are looking up to you for help, answers, advice, and guidance. There's nothing more sobering and reality getting than the truths about ourselves we all get at home with our spouses and children! Boy, that's humbling—and humility is required to be a good helper.

One woman listener wrote to complain about how her "hero" husband used to be with just about anybody that called on him for help.

"Soon after I married, I noticed that he was everyone's favorite person to call for an emergency. Actually, looking back, I could see

it was happening while we dated—I'd just been blind to it. Even people who were casual acquaintances could call on a moment's notice and convince him to cut short a date with me, or our kids' birthday party, to deal with their needs.

"For several years I just lived in frustration, and without even realizing how dysfunctional I was becoming, began creating an occasional 'emergency' of my own just to keep his attention. When I saw our children learning to do the same thing, I realized something wasn't working right.

"We got counseling. Over time, my husband realized that his constant response to 'emergencies,' at the cost of family time, was just his way to feel better about himself. When he really listened to the kids and me talk about how neglected we felt, he realized that we should come first and things improved greatly and our family is much happier for it."

When our priority is our own ego, we can try to camouflage it as G-d's work, or what we have to do for the family, but the reality is always that we have Stupid Priorities, selfserving and ultimately destructive to our soul's and our family's life.

"I Don't Want to Grow Up!"

Sometimes people don't really want to grow up. Some of those people still get married—and some of those people have babies. All of those people hurt the ones they've vowed to protect.

The "I don't wanna grow up" types believe that being married and having children should in no way curtail their fun times. Sometimes it's their hobbies. (*"He has always been an avid hunter and spends great amounts of time, money, and energy on bow hunting. Often I felt as if I was low on his list of priorities after work, hunting, and fishing. When does it all end?"*) Or, it's hanging with the buddies. *(". . . Maybe golfing with the guys and returning drunk or four-wheeling with his pals. Our divorce was final and he hooked up with a twenty-year-old who moved in with him and got pregnant right away.")* Or it may mean just opting out of the picture altogether. *("He informed me that being with me and the twins would be like being in prison. I loved him with all my heart. I wanted the American dream. He wanted to go out with friends, and just not grow up. You know, it took him four days to go to give blood for our son, because he was too busy. I do believe that his priorities were a little messed up.")* These immature types choose their own immediate gratification over their obligations and well-being of their (supposed) loved ones.

It's very difficult to reach these folks. I remember that when I was counseling couples, the childlike member felt entitled to the fun . . . because: Their spouse was a drag and never wanted to do anything, the house was a mess, the children were a problem, they were entitled because they worked so hard, it's what they always did and he/she picked them knowing that, life is short, this is a free country, and on and on.

The bottom line is that these types do not live to give anything, hence they make bad spouses and parents—and they show their spots when you're dating. Some of you wish to be blind because "you're in love" or you're desperate, or you think it'll change, or it seemed cute at the time. Here's one letter from a listener who ought to jump ship—how obvious can it get?:

"My boyfriend is a full-time college student and also has a full-time job. He doesn't save his money because he wants to buy all of this 'new, fool stuff.' He has a car that runs pretty good and he has no ambition to move out and be independent of his parents. I, on the other hand, have been on my own for five years and I have a newer car, a decent job, and make the same amount of money he does, but he has a total lack of responsibility with his money. He wants a brand-new car that's about $20,000. And he can't

afford it. He doesn't want to move away from home either. His priorities as an adult are all backward and it drives me nuts!"

It drives me nuts that she even calls him a boyfriend. Clearly, there is no evidence that he will be a committed, responsible, trustworthy, or competent husband or father. He must be cute.

The Circus Juggler

Hopefully it's clear by now that a mature, responsible adult makes choices, and that those choices are made based on a value system that dictates priorities—and I do mean dictates!

Either just for the sake of curiosity or as a direct challenge, I'm often asked how I juggle a radio program, writing books, a charitable foundation, making jewelry for charity auctions, and being a wife and mother.

Actually, I tell them, it's really very easy. There are just so many hours in a day and just so many days in a week. From Friday sundown to Saturday sundown we observe the Sabbath—that means no work; which brings me down to six days a week.

Monday thru Friday, our son leaves for school at 6 A.M. I have to be at the radio station by about 11 A.M. to prepare for broadcast. That leaves me five hours to work on a book or column, or do the television show (which, by the way, was determined by me in contract to happen in the A.M. or not happen at all), or work on jewelry, or read a novel, or exercise, or whatever else occurs to me. Sundays I might work on a book until 12 noon, at which time the family takes little day trips for family time.

Every day I am home by 4 P.M. Our son gets home from high school (Orthodox Jewish) at 6 P.M. We have dinner together every night and then hang around to help with homework. After homework is completed, the "boys" (dad and son) watch a game.

I choose not to work at night—except in an emergency—because that's family time. I literally squeeze my career and interests into whatever is left over from family time. I travel very little, and when I do, the family comes with me, unless our son has to be in school; then, dad is with son at home for the one or two days I may have to be gone to testify for a bill in some state, or lecture about morals in advertising to an ad council.

Bottom line? I don't juggle. When you have to keep balls in the air, you make very little contact with any of the balls, and one always falls. Sadly, that one is usually family. It is easier to push aside family than it is to push aside a boss—a boss will fire you, while your family is expected just to tolerate what you do. Most of you find it infinitely easier to disappoint your loved ones than risk the same with work.

Many listeners have written to me about this juggling nonsense:

"I know firsthand how putting work, school, and hobbies as the top priority can hurt family relationships. About ten years ago, when I was a radio broadcast student, I was juggling my school, work, and family life poorly. I never turned down an opportunity to work extra airshifts or make personal appearances on behalf of the station. The result was no time for my wife or kids. I was trying to sleep evenings when my wife was working second shift to help support us while I pursued my dream of being a 'radio star.' The result was our children being on their own when I should have been there for them. Add to this an affair with a young lady who was also in radio and you can see how I let my ambitions and selfishness tear my life and my family apart.

"Fortunately, my ties to the church (albeit weak) kept me from finishing off the disaster. As I started to attend church more fre-

quently, I saw the error of my ways. I quit the jobs that didn't properly provide for my family. Life today is so much nicer for all of us because I finally figured out that family was a 'we' situation and not a 'me' thing. They have become my reason for living. They help me to be who I really am . . . dad and husband."

The family as "we" versus "me" is probably the most important concept under Stupid Priorities. Too many people marry and produce children not understanding or submitting to the notion of obligation and commitment. When you take on the care and raising of a spouse and children you, with grace, give up the privilege of doing whatever you want, whenever you want. Your family is not an inanimate object, like a bed, which you just come up and flop into after all the really important things in your life are taken care of. Yet, that is sadly how so many people treat family—and, it is an attitude supported by society.

Just yesterday, I received a call from a large city newspaper in a state from which the Governor was assigned an Ambassadorship, leaving the Lt. Governor to be promoted to the number one position. The Lt. Governor is a woman. No problem there. However, she is about eight months pregnant with twins and lives 150 miles from work. I was asked my opinion about the situation. Though it does appear that the dad may be the stay-at-home parent, these children are clearly going to have little to do with their mother for the next however many years she reigns as Governor.

My comment? It is a far, far better thing we do to parent our own children, and let those so unencumbered do the state politics. Choices have to be made. And here is yet another vivid example of how personal opportunity and ambitions are put before the needs of newborn, dependent, innocent children. And here is yet another testimonial to how family and children are less important than the "me."

And here is yet another opportunity for a strong, woman role-model to demonstrate how children don't really need mothers. Sickening.

And that is exactly what this listener remembers struggling with:

"I am the mother of three fine young men. When they were younger, however, I was influenced by the likes of Phil Donohue, etc., that told me I was not a whole person unless I worked outside the home. I went back to school and got a nursing degree, worked night shift so I could be home with my children in the day and wound up dependent on pills to slow me down because I could not sleep. I was always worn out. In hindsight, I did not help my family or my husband and did much to the detriment of my own health, because I thought I needed to be something. Since then, I have realized that only the peace of God, the love of my family, and the ability to do for others, not a career per se, is what is important.

"If I had to do it over, even with the loss of income, I would never have missed one day of enjoying all the joys that motherhood and the sweetness of a great marriage bring."

As Adela Rogers St. John is purported to have said, "You cannot wheel two pushcarts at once." This was in reference to her choosing a career over motherhood. In *Parenthood by Proxy* (in paperback called *Stupid Things Parents Do to Mess Up Their Kids*), I wrote about a female Army General who quit because she realized that her ambitions had robbed her children and herself of the mother-daughter bond.

It's not that woman can't or shouldn't work. I work. But, working should not be done at the expense of marriage, parenthood, or family. Priorities need to be set, decisions must be made and kept to. It gets easier and easier to say "No" to requests that would polish your image everywhere but at home.

As you've probably noticed, the folks who make the transitions from "me" to "we" seem to have a strong religious base. I don't think that's an accident. I believe when people "know" that they are part of something beyond themselves, and that there are divine values, they more naturally move from "me" to "we" because it is in the "we" that they truly satisfy the "me."

In conclusion, I received from one listener this warning to all the "women's libbers" out there who think they can have it all—while their all is mostly at work: *"I remember that one woman I worked for (house cleaning) made a speech to women's libbers about how she could keep her husband and her children happy. Well, while she was at work, her kids were at home taking dope and her husband was chasing me around her kitchen and her dogs were doing poo all over the house. Then, she came home and threw a frozen dinner in the oven. Where do these women get the idea that they can do it all?"*

The Stepford Parents

Every now and then, in between dealing with the hordes of parents who are too indulgent or neglectful of their children, I confront parents who are in overdrive with respect to their parenting—to the point of neglecting their own health and that of the marriage. Sometimes it's because they are more comfortable relating to a child than another adult, who has expectations and demands and the ability to be critical or rejecting, so they make the parent-child relationship their first—strike that—*only* priority. Obviously, this shuts out the spouse. That's the paradox—they're afraid of being vulnerable to their spouse, so they focus on the child, and in doing so push away the very person they're afraid of losing.

Other times, it's overzealous parenting. *"It took my husband and two kids and seven years of marriage to realize that we had gone overboard in our parenting. In our quest to become the perfect parents, we forgot that our love is what started this family in the first place!*

"I am a stay-at-home mom and have been for six years, so my days are kid-centered and so is my thinking. When he would say, 'Let's go out,' I would think that was not being a good mom and dad, and our relationship was starting to suffer. You are a better parent for letting your kids see that the love and respect you two share is what keeps the family going, and you should take care of it just as you take care of them—with all your heart."

This realization is even harder to make when the child has special needs. One dad who wrote to me has several children with a rare disease which will cause them all to die somewhere between the ages of sixteen and twenty.

"Well, Dr. Laura, we don't do it so well. Our lives are totally focused on the survival and quality of life of our children. I believe that when they die, the 'reward' for our years of self-sacrifice and dedication to our kids at the expense of virtually everything else, will be our separation and divorce. There is just nothing left between us outside managing our children's disease and our lives. I have tried on many occasions to get my wife to invest in our relationship and have been told point-blank in every instance that she is overburdened by life and that she has no intention or desire to add another load."

This is not an unusual scenario when there is an ill or handicapped child. It is remarkable how the normal responsibility to one's children can become exaggerated by guilt and a sense of martyrdom. I was caught in the crosshairs of this mentality because of a call I took with a woman whose son is seriously impaired behaviorally by autism. This boy, in spite of all efforts, is so terribly out of control that he becomes violent. Family members have asked them to come visit sometimes without their boy, so that there can be some peace during the visits as well as some peaceful time for the parents. I gently supported that option. Boy, from the letters, calls, and faxes from irate mothers of autistic children (who, by the way, had not heard the call, but were e-mailed angry comments from one listener), you'd have thought I said to euthanize them all! Telling someone she's entitled to some free time and that the marriage deserves attention was considered an evil act.

The truth is that when our children have problems of any kind, of their own doing or not, parents are often consumed with guilt for having "created" the problem. That inappropriate guilt has them lash out at any attempts to do other than "fix things," or at least sacrifice themselves on that altar. Additionally, some folks gain their value and identity from sacrificing themselves on that altar; the most extreme version is Munchausen's Syndrome, where parents, mostly mothers, actually make their kids sick for the resulting attention and to fulfill a need to be important.

A friend of mine is struggling with his three-year-old son's cancer. He realized that he and his wife were surely turning this sweet little boy into a monster by letting him get away with things, because of their compassion, and that they would self-destruct if they didn't ignore the inappropriate guilt feelings and spend time on themselves and each other. They made the necessary adjustments as best they could under the circumstances. Being basically centered, strong and in love with each other obviously helps a lot.

My Mother or My Spouse? Hmmmm

"I think that now that I am older and married, I realize how at the beginning of my relationship with my husband, I would drop everything at the tone of my mother's voice, or, if my dad would call. My husband would do the same with his parents. Now, the

two of us realize that the only way that our marriage is going to work is if we make each other our #1 priority.

"When people are married, the parents have to step back, and the couple needs to step forward, away from their parents into their own space."

Yes, indeed, but I can't tell you how many calls I get from guys whose wives won't move away from Mommy, won't stop calling Mommy several times a day, won't stop Mommy from just dropping in uninvited whenever she darn well pleases, and who won't stop checking in with Mommy for an opinion on everything the couple is deciding. Now, obviously, this kind of woman is a very dependent personality, and any guy who picks her is looking for a cushy pillow instead of a partner. The mistake these guys make is in thinking that she will automatically change from her Mommy's cushy pillow to his with a ceremony. Surprise!

This is no different when the guy is a "Momma's Boy." Women who pick these men actually want a guy who jumps through hoops at the mere mention, much less the sound, of a whistle. And they too think that the guy will take the whistle from Mommy and give it to Wifey. Wrong!

Some of these situations are blunt and explained in advance:

"My husband has always made it clear that his parents and brothers are more important in his life than I am. I have heard his parents say, 'Blood is thicker than water,' more times than I can count. I have also heard his Dad say, 'We are family, everyone else is an outsider.'"

Other situations come into view over time:

"I've been thinking a lot lately about how my life has not turned out the way I wanted it to, and not at all how I planned it. I just turned fifty this year, and I suppose you could blame my state of mind on a Midlife Crisis, or some such psychobabble. I think, though, that I just didn't set my priorities in the right place as far back as I can remember. I was always the 'good' little girl

who didn't want to disappoint her parents. At this late date, I can see that I just never grew up enough to set the priorities that were right for me. Guilt can be a terrible thing, especially when it is misplaced, and not at all appropriate. I went back to work for my workaholic parents twelve years ago—conforming to their desires and expectations, instead or mine or my family's.

"Your parents gave you life, but you shouldn't allow them to set your priorities after you've 'grown up.' "

People are often confused about their obligations to their parents compared with that to their spouse and children. When they call me, they ask about the Commandment to Honor Thy Father and Mother. For an extensive analysis of this Commandment, please read my book *The Ten Commandments; The Significance of God's Laws in Everyday Life* (Cliff Street Books/HarperCollins). Honoring your parents does not include dishonoring your vows or obligations in marriage. Honoring your parents does not mean that they get to, at their preference, make decisions in your life. It does mean that you must show respect and make sure they have the necessities of life—but it does not mean that you must sacrifice your family to do it.

Let me give you the basic concept of a proper parental relationship with an adult child through this story told to me by a wise Rabbi. There was a great flood, and the rains continued. The poppa bird was caught in the storm with his three baby birds. He wished to take them all to safety. Not knowing if there was time to take them all to safety, he picked up the first baby bird and carried him over the swollen, raging river. As they flew, the poppa bird asked, "Baby bird, will you always take care of me? Even when you have your own baby birds?" The baby bird, looking down at the swift current, answered excitedly, "Oh yes, Poppa, anything you need at any time, I'll be there to take care of you, don't worry about a thing, no matter what it takes."

The poppa bird dropped the baby bird into the river and flew back to get the second baby bird. The same dialogue occurred, and the second baby bird also was dropped to his death.

As the poppa bird flew over the flood waters with the last baby bird, he asked him the same question, "Baby bird, will you always take care of me? Even when you have your own baby birds?" This baby bird said, "Poppa, I can promise you that I will take care of my babies the way you have always taken care of us." This baby bird was carried to safety in its father's beak. Why? Because it is the order of things that when you leave your parents' nest, you take what you've learned from them, apply it to your own family, and that is the best way to honor your parents.

Catering to the whims of a weak or demanding parent is clearly a perpetual motion machine and causes the direct destruction of your psyche and your marriage; it is a display of disrespect for your vows, commitments, and obligations to your spouse. Where there are serious needs, as with a seriously ill or dying parent, those needs must be met with honor and compassion and compromise.

Neither spouse should put the other in charge of his or her own responsibilities to parents. Since each spouse is obligated to bring his or her healthiest self to a marriage, where there are clear problems with inappropriate attachment to the original family, mental health assistance should be used.

A Success Story Where You Least Expect It

I never cease to be amazed at which relationships do ultimately work out in spite of how horrible they seem. It impresses me how incredibly resilient and creative people can be when they are motivated.

One listener letter illustrates my point:

"I was twenty and he was twenty-six when we exchanged vows . . . and we were young and stupid. I wanted the fairy tale . . . he wanted his mother. Our sex life went downhill fast, and we blamed it on our priorities. He was spending all of his time on the computer, playing games and collecting photos of other women . . . while I was watching TV and blaming him for my unhappiness. I blamed his porn habits for my insecurities, and he blamed my poor housekeeping for his lack of interest in sex.

"I eventually packed my bags and moved home with my parents. After a month of internet correspondence with my husband, I went home. Things have never been better between us. We now talk each day . . . really talk. We make time for each other. We do things together and enjoy each other's company. My husband's porn habit is over . . . he trashed everything. I now clean the house and try harder to please him by doing simple things that don't really take much time, but mean the world to him (bake him cookies, rub his neck, cuddle with him on the couch).

"It was a matter of organizing our priorities and realizing which ones were important and which ones were selfish and stupid. I love him and want our marriage to work . . . and for once in three and a half years, the sun is shining on us."

It's the priorities, stupid!

6

Stupid Happiness

"My mother has been trying for years to find happiness.
First she tried to find it in my father.
Then it was in a bottle of beer.
And then she felt she could buy it at a department store.
She spent time in a mental hospital,
And she finally got her 'happy pill (meds).'
To this day, she doesn't get the message."
—A LISTENER

As I finished my breakfast this morning, on the very last page of the very last section of my Sunday newspaper, which I was reading before sitting down to work on this chapter, I found an ad for clothing. The model, middle-aged, with gray hair and glasses, is wearing a plain black, ankle-length shift, with a red, buttonless cardigan. She is smiling with great glee, and the only caption, outside of the designer's name, says "Practice happiness."

I immediately called my husband over to see this remarkable juxtaposition of "message" and the substance of this chapter, which I was about to write. It made me happy to experience such a coincidence largely because, as a religious Jew, I no longer believe in coincidences—they are events of meaning, assuming one is open to receiving the message. It made me happier to sit down and write—a process that makes me happy just by itself.

Why am I going on about this? Because it is for the lack of attention to and respect for such seemingly insignificant "happifying" experiences that too many of you jettison a perfectly good relationship, figuring that you'll find happiness in some other bed.

I know, because I hear these stories all the time on my radio program. It used to be that a man or a woman would leave a spouse because of violence, alcoholism, no support, serious character deficiencies, infidelities—serious issues. Now, I hear from both men and women alike, even with pregnancies, small children, or numerous children, how they just feel like it's time to leave, because they're not "happy."

What does that mean? And why should relationships end over a temporary and largely self-induced mind-set?

Is somebody under the impression that a quality, long-term marriage is supposed to make you perpetually giddy, or that happiness is a quality that must only be experienced emphatically, not subtly? You know, like Big Bangs versus a cool breeze?

The ad says it all: "*Practice* happiness." Happiness is a conscious decision, a determined attitude, an openness to nuance, requiring action and understanding on your part. Generally, and ironically, those people who say they are "unhappy" for reasons unknown, are generally behaving in ways which wouldn't bring any joys to anyone around them either, the same way that bored people are usually boring people.

I remember one particular day when I was in graduate school

in Manhattan. I was sullen and unhappy over stuff in general. As I was walking toward some subway stairs, an old black man, sitting in a chair holding out a cup, caught my attention when he said to me, "Hey, you're too pretty a young lady to have such a frown on your face. Smile. It's a beautiful day."

Yikes, was I ever embarrassed. Here was an old, crippled man, begging for coins, who looked happier than me, a young, healthy, woman, attending an Ivy League graduate school, on the way to a Ph.D. I've thought about that moment many times in the thirty years or so since it happened. Sure, there are things to be upset about, disappointed over, and frustrated by—but they don't ultimately have to determine happiness.

For the rest of that day, I *practiced* happiness—walking with a bounce, smiling at people, and making some positive plans for the day. Amazingly, I felt happy.

One of my listeners wrote to me about her realization that happiness is mostly a behavior, not a mysterious occurrence:

"I was married for the first time at the age of thirty-four, assuming that with my great career and self-confidence, I was ready to make mature and unself-centered decisions. After having two kids, I began to resent my husband. I did everything I could do to prove he didn't care and began treating him very badly. We fought over everything. I was sure this marriage wouldn't last and became very depressed and was irritable (unloving, resentful, and disrespectful) toward him all the time.

"He just wasn't making me happy anymore.

"This was about the time I started listening to the Dr. Laura program and learned that no one else is responsible for my happiness, and 'so what if I'm not happy,' I have a commitment and responsibility as a wife and mother.

"I started behaving differently toward my husband, and slowly but surely, I started feeling differently about my husband, marriage, and family. Now I am a 'committed' wife and mother, and

*a very lucky lady to have a husband who was willing to endure
the toughest first years of our marriage."*

Here's a woman who realized and accepted that, 1) the "feeling" of happiness must not be the priority our society appears to
put on it as "the" criterion for determining the value of our lives
and our relationships; 2) fulfilling our obligations, and behaving in ways which are loving and positive, make us happy in
and of themselves; 3) when we create pleasantness, in spite of
our mood, we create an atmosphere in which others flourish
and feed us back even more positively; and finally, 4) that feelings have no conscience or IQ—they are not to be revered over
obligation, morality, and common sense.

Women Talk, Men Shovel Snow

A woman caller was relating the terrible experiences of her
last two years: Several close relatives of hers and her husband's had died and their child had leukemia. She expressed
being exhausted, anxious, drained, and generally bummed
out with life. Her primary concern at the time of the call was
that her husband just didn't make her happy anymore. "He
doesn't comfort me," she lamented.

"What do you mean, he doesn't comfort you?"

"Well, he doesn't share his feelings or listen to mine. I'm
thinking of divorcing him, because I'm just not happy in
this marriage anymore. He's not giving me what I need."

"Well, what you need is a complete break from stress and
terror—but that's not coming soon, is it?"

"No, it isn't."

"And you're thinking that what you really need is to break
it off with him, because he doesn't understand, doesn't care,
and doesn't make you happy, right?"

"That's about it."

"Well, you're wrong—he shovels snow."

"What?"

"Your husband shovels snow to show you that he cares, understands, and wants to make you happy. Two things are going on here. First, is that bad stuff is happening, and it's difficult, if not guilt-provoking, to try to be happy in the midst of all this death and illness. Second, is that you are like a radio turned off; your husband is broadcasting 'caring' and you're not receiving the message."

"No, that's not so. He just isn't helping. And, what do you mean, shoveling snow?"

"When we women want to comfort somebody, we make them hot cocoa and talk for days. When men want to comfort their woman, they shovel the snow . . . symbolically, that is. Men *do* something to try to make things better—they don't ruminate—they do!

"I'll bet you can think of at least three things, under the category of shoveling snow, that your husband has done even in the last twenty-four hours to try to make things better for you— that's how he's trying to comfort you. Tonight, when he comes home, throw your arms around him, list off the three things, and thank him immensely for comforting you."

At this point I ended the call, having my screener take down the woman's phone number so that we could call her the next day after the "experiment." The caller was not all that receptive to my suggestion—in fact she was a bit hostile.

The next day she called back, glowing in gratitude and "happiness." She did exactly what I ordered: She threw her arms around him and thanked him for what he was doing to make things easier for her; he melted, she melted, and a great lesson was learned.

"Dr. Laura, you absolutely saved my marriage. I just wasn't willing to see happiness when it was there."

When life is causing us great misery, there is no one to

"get back at." That's why spouses often get the brunt of our rage, hurt, and sense of powerlessness. We imagine that they are a safe place upon which to vent frustrations, get even with life, and finally have some power. Sometimes we take it even further, imagining that if we get rid of them, we simultaneously get rid of all our troubles.

I remember once in "therapy school," at USC, reading an extensive research report suggesting that most folks who divorce regret it afterward realizing that it wasn't the panacea they thought it would be. The number of callers who did such, only to find themselves in similar predicaments with other people, realized a little too late that the main problem was that they took themselves with them wherever they went.

Happily Ever After

Keeping in mind that very few people live the concept of *practicing* happiness, it is naively assumed that a marriage *in and of itself* will be a wellspring of happiness. One of my recent website (www.drlaura.com) questions for my listeners asked, "Did you get married for all the wrong reasons?" One particular answer summarized many people's basic problem:

"I'm not sure what you mean by all the wrong reasons, but after ten years, I can see how naïve I was then. I thought (then) that marriage would be more 'happily ever after.' Sure, we both worked, but car troubles and minor accidents, financial strain, living far from our families, and a miscarriage in our newlywed period made me realize that marriage doesn't protect you from life like I thought it would.

"After all this time and two children (six and one), I'm glad we're best friends. We still struggle with finances, but because I stay home and we moved back to our hometown, we're doing better.

"We now look at life and marriage as a team sport, with each player trying to give 100 percent, not 50/50. This way, if one of you can't give your all, the other person more than makes up the difference. Overall, it's been nothing like I expected, but more than I could've hoped for."

How touching is that last comment? Hers is a philosophically brilliant insight: A quality, successful, happy married life can be gotten in spite of your expectations and demands and self-centeredness (which is a natural tendency that must be overcome). The key to enjoying the fruits of such an insight is encompassed in the Tenth Commandment, against coveting. The concept here is simple: If you determine to see value and feel gratitude for what you have, you will not be consumed by envy and disappointment. Instead, you will come to see your portion as different from that of others, but no less special, and no less significant, and no less worthy of respect and enjoyment.

Falling in Love

At a more innocent time in our culture, the notion of "falling in love" was the key in choosing a mate. Although falling in love is all about infatuation, projecting our fantasies on another person before we even know who they are and what they're about, it was assumed that this sexual and emotional high was sufficient motivation for marriage. This probably worked more often than not, even considering the predictable demoralization that occurs when you get that infatuation haze out from in front of your eyes (and good sense), because of the societal notion of commitment. Commitment is the bridge over all sorts of troubled waters; it gives people the substrate upon which to build a real relationship.

In our current less innocent times, infatuation is not necessary for sexual intimacy (just being around is sufficient motivation for some) nor as a reasonable condition for shacking-up and making babies out-of-wedlock. Of course, with the commitment part as denigrated as it now is, when the infatuation (synthetic happiness) goes, so do the people, right out of each other's lives.

Another listener wrote me about her experience with infatuation, and what she plans someday to teach her daughter:

"Our mass media is successful in portraying marriage as a 'mindless' institution, something to be entered into only if certain clichés are met (i.e., being weak in the knees, having butterflies in the stomach, and being obsessive about the other person).

"When I married my husband (now of six years) I felt none of those things. I was not nervous about our impending nuptials, felt no butterflies or any kind of obsession— Instead, I was thankful for the blessing of God and the opportunity to enter into a covenant with a man whom I knew would be my life partner.

"My feelings for my then fiancé were more than simple 'love' stuff. I knew he would be an active husband and father, that he would provide for his family and guarantee its security. I respected his mind, admired his achievements, and understood his motivations.

"When the day comes for my daughter to marry the man she believes she loves, I will simply tell her this: Marriage is the beginning of her love for her husband, not the result of it."

When I talk to men and women in sick and abusive situations, I ask them why they're there. Inevitably, I get back the answer, "Because I love him/her." I challenge that predictable excuse with, "No, you don't. Love is about awe, admiration, respect and appreciation. Do you have any of those for him/her?"

"No."

"Then, it isn't love. It's a sad kind of dependency and a

fear of life and autonomy. You are misusing the term *love* to describe unhealthy attachments and needs."

"Yeah," comes the next predictable response, "I know . . . but . . ."

If you're looking for true happiness with another person, you first need to be reasonably mature, psychologically sound, and able to deal with truth and reality. This understanding is the impetus for me to suggest to all clergy that no marriage should be officiated by them unless the couple undergoes premarital assessment and counseling. The fate of too many children, much less the growing instability of our society from the divorces, is at stake.

With premarital counseling, people must face their differences to determine their compatibility and ability to cope with differences; they will push through the infatuation stage and become more pragmatic about the qualities that truly are valuable in a prospective life partner and coparent of children. If I had the proverbial penny for everyone who has called me complaining about his or her spouse and who knew about some character and behavioral problem in advance, but who said, "Yeah, but I thought it would get better," I'd be a zillionaire. Practicing happiness also means taking responsibility for choices you know are not wise or healthy.

I'm Happy If You Like Me

Women, more than men, (probably because of inherent biopsychological differences), pin their happiness on being wanted by the opposite sex. In itself, that is not a problem— it is a healthy extension of the need for humans to bond and mate. What does become a problem is the indiscriminate way in which too many women play this out, and the superficial association too often made between sexual intercourse and true intimacy or love.

"I am a forty-eight-year-old divorced (six years) mother of one thirteen-year-old daughter," wrote one listener. *"The first thing I thought I had to do to find happiness after the divorce was to 'FIND ANOTHER MAN.' It's funny how women search for something so seemingly elusive as Happiness, most for a large portion of their lives, and it is usually right there under their noses. When my mother became terminally ill, she gave me new insight as to what my real purpose on this earth was; that in order to find happiness, I had to see how wonderful my life, my health, a happy, healthy child, being able to work, and so forth, really was. Suddenly, I realized that I was not going to be happy with any man, or anything, until I developed an appreciation for these wonderful opportunities and experiences of life."*

It's not that a husband or a wife can't make you happy—of course the addition of a kind, fun, loving, challenging, interesting, loyal partner, with whom you share values, ideals, and goals in common, is very happy-making. It's just that nothing, no one, no thing, will ultimately make you happy unless you learn the fine art of appreciation and gratitude for what you have, for what he or she has to offer, for the opportunities for giving, and for life itself.

This last concept, that of an "opportunity for giving," is an important one—maybe one of the most important concepts about happiness in life, much less in relationships. I have a charitable foundation—The Dr. Laura Schlessinger Foundation for Abused and Neglected Children. People from all over the country make blankets and clothing, donate toys, books, toiletries, jewelry, water bottles, and so forth, to fill "MY STUFF" bags which are delivered by the thousands to children rescued from their abusive homes, who have nothing but the shirts on their backs. Obviously, getting one of these bags means the world to a child with nothing, including hope.

I can't express to you how incredibly moving it is to get a letter from people who sacrifice much in time, money, and effort to contribute to this project, who THANK ME for the opportunity to give.

Giving makes us happy. Too bad we mostly think of getting things the way we want them as the primary key to happiness. Giving and behaving generously to a spouse under stress, for example, is a far better remedial concept than confrontation and demands.

I remember one man calling to tell me he was no longer happy in his marriage, because his wife always came home from work grumpy. He was thinking of a confrontation and/or a divorce. I suggested that he get a dimmer for the bathroom lights, fill the room with lovely candles, make sure there was a hot bath with bubbles and a glass of wine awaiting his wife at the door the very next evening. He thought I was nuts, but did it anyway. She was shocked, surprised, and a bit uncomfortable, but after the bath, very grateful. This small act of giving put his wife in a whole other mood and mind-set—and they were happy again. Giving. Try it.

Instead, too many, especially young people struggling with issues of identity and existential angst, get caught up in sexual and drug escapades, trying desperately to feel happy. One listener has been to that hell, and has lived to come back from it:

"I thought happiness depended on some guy loving me or thinking I was special . . . I didn't realize that happiness just happens when you follow God's plan for you. I am so fortunate and blessed to know, understand, and live happiness now. I am sorry I didn't listen to my parents as a teenager—I would have saved myself years of self-hatred, agony, and loneliness—not to mention the health risks.

"My pattern began as wanting and needing love and feeling special, and thinking that giving a guy my body would make him

love me—and then I'd be happy. I would plunge heart-first into new relationships, placing everything I had (heart, soul, mind, and body) into that guy. I would talk myself into caring for him so completely, when in reality, I didn't really care for him in particular. I was just so lonely and confused."

What is so sad is that in this hyper-liberal era, dripping with sexual exploitation in even prime-time television, the notions of modesty, covenants, sin, and shame have largely been obliterated, making meaningless sexual and romantic escapades all the more accessible as a false means to an end: happiness.

There is hardly a person alive who hasn't struggled with fears, weaknesses, spirituality, immature choices, stupid experimentation, and the like. Frankly, the more structure there is in our lives, imposed by family, religion, and society, the safer we ultimately are from our weaker selves during these difficult times.

Out of Weakness

Many of you have gotten into, and stayed in, relationships that you knew from day one were wrong. A feeling within you told you that this man or woman, though he or she had some good qualities, was someone you'd be better off without.

Why did you stay? Simple. You wanted to be happy. And this situation and person were available. You hoped it would work out, because if it did, you'd be happy. And, in between the ugly parts, you think you are happy.

I have found it astonishing how hard people will work with the wrong person in order to be happy—when they are so willing to throw out the right person when times are difficult. Why does the former individual struggle when he or she shouldn't, and the latter person not work at it when they should?

The answer, I think, is a paradox. In both cases, you say you want intimacy and happiness. But, in both cases you are avoiding real intimacy. In the first scenario, trying to make a round peg fit into a square opening ultimately doesn't work. Trying to make a bad choice work doesn't work. No happiness results, of course, but there is no real threat to one's ego either. In other words, the reason you're not "close" is the other person. You are now absolved and alleviated from the responsibility of personal responsibility and growth. Struggling to make things work with someone not psychologically available for intimacy is a noble struggle, giving you superiority and an external excuse for your problems.

In the second scenario, dumping the good spouse for "happiness," instead of working as hard as in the former situation, is yet another way of preserving ego: You are not happy because of your spouse. If you stayed and worked harder, you'd have to face the fact that you are contributing to your own unhappiness and problems, with either/or behavior/attitude. That's too uncomfortable, so, bye-bye.

In neither situation do you have to change (read: grow, mature, become healthier). That you are ultimately unhappy is your sacrifice to preserve your rickety sense of self.

"Out of loneliness," writes a listener, *"I settled for over a year, until my mother opened my eyes. She told me how it was not so bad to be without a boyfriend. So, I broke it off. And, as a good preacher once said, 'Don't try to look for the right one, BE the right one.' And that is what I'm doing now."*

That's right. I've told many a caller that the match they make for themselves is a reflection of themselves. In other words, the more you complain about your spouse, the more you telegraph your own weaknesses. For example, when you're not happy because the other is "controlling" (a favorite of women who want to be saved, and of men who don't have the strength to deal with their own dominating families), it's because you were willing to give up happiness (a healthy balance of teamwork in the marriage) to hide your weaknesses.

" 'Stupid happiness' is taking care of my boyfriend—I guess way beyond what you should have to do. I am a person who believes in taking care of a person. I put my all into my relationships, including my kids as well as the man in my life—because as long as he was happy, I was happy. Finally I realized I was not happy. I've learned my lesson: If he can't take care of himself, he won't take care of me," wrote a listener.

Instead of finding a nice, caretaking kinda guy, she believes for some reason that she cosmically doesn't qualify for such a good guy, and caretakes a selfish kinda guy, in the hopes that he'll get the message. But, takers are not givers or sharers. This listener obviously figured out that this seduction didn't work to change a person, or get her what we all need to be happy—someone who is loving, caring, and giving.

Some people tolerate the most horrendous behaviors, believing that happiness is ultimately out of their reach. "I was married to a man for seven years who had an obsession with pornography. I do not know how far it went, because he was a pathological liar. Even though the intimacy was gone, and in my heart I knew he was doing something deviant, I thought it must be my fault. Somehow, I was not attractive or thin or sexy enough . . . I let him have control of my self-esteem."

Other people settle for—as I described to one woman I was counseling about her bad relationship choice—the bits of cookies hidden in the pile of manure.

"He was possessive and overbearing. He'd make me feel sorry for him. As time went on, I discovered that he drank excessively, and at times he would threaten me and become violent. I kind of began to get a little frightened of him, but of course, he was always sorry afterward, blaming the alcohol. So I let it go. I know this is stupid, because I am really unhappy. Why do I stay?"

Some people have more clarity about what motivates them toward Stupid Happiness.

"I was divorced twice and feeling 'fat, old, and ugly.' So, I thought if I dated a lot of men, and then younger men, it would make me feel better about myself. I thought having so many men who 'wanted' me was an indication of my desirability. I even thought I was having a good time. I thought I was happy with my life. I thought I was getting over my failures.

"All I was really doing was degrading and disrespecting myself. I wasn't really happy. I thought I 'felt' good, but I was miserable because I was not 'being' good."

Abusing yourself, disrespecting yourself, allowing others to abuse and disrespect you, not living by deeper values, may make for some fun moments, even some satisfying moments, but you will not be happy in any more profound, long-lasting sense.

Living for the Moment

Looking for happiness in all the wrong beds and relationships is bad enough; trying to have a happy life by not thinking of your actions beyond the moment in which they happen is downright destructive.

Stupid Happiness is, in part, the talent for trying to create instant joy from the acts that normally do create lasting joy in most people's lives (love, sex, marriage, and children), but without the maturity and thoughtful consideration that needs to go into the who, when, why, where, and how these acts ought to occur.

What motivates such thoughtless precipitousness? Again, our weakness and fears. Our relationships have no hope when they're constructed of weaknesses. Believe it or not, our culture breeds a special kind of weakness that undermines our hopes for quality relationships. How? By its hope-lessness about serious, covenantal marriages. Here's one listener's experience:

"When I look back on my life, I see that I was living for the moment and not concerned about the future. I also believe that I was not able to value a marriage relationship, let alone a marriage bed. Our culture no longer teaches us to have that respect.

"Both of my parents are on their third marriages, and both lived with their current partner before marriage."

Fortunately, this listener, after following a few steps in her parents' footsteps, and with the complicit wink and nod of a society that has become proud of tolerance for the vulgar, realized that this was Stupid Happiness. She married a wonderful man, with whom she shares a religious life, and will be celebrating their twelfth anniversary.

"My Husband and I LEARNED to have respect for marriage," she concluded. Such lessons are hard-won in a society which celebrates hyperindividuality and promotes marriage as a kind of oppression.

That our society is so indulgent with respect to sexual behaviors in general has actually made it more difficult for people to rise above Stupid Happiness, because it virtually gives permission, and lots of opportunity, for the basest instincts and impulses to be exercised.

"I thought this lifestyle (stripping) was a good way for me to make a lot of money with a schedule that worked around school. I got paid to party and, at first, most of the drugs were free. I didn't use drugs that much in the beginning—but in time I developed a habit that went right along with my job and eventually it became a part of my daily life.

"I managed to sort of keep things straight for a couple of years, but gradually my life slipped into a downward spiral of drugs, drinking, promiscuous sex, and associating with all kinds of

degenerate, lost people. Once you are in it, it is almost impossible to get out, short of an act of God. The money is too good, and your habits are such that it becomes nearly impossible to fit back into the mainstream world. At first it seems fun, harmless, and almost glamorous."

This party scene may sound extreme, but I have been amazed how, to some extent or other, so many people fall into this ultimately vicious "fun cycle," marry, make babies, and then realize they are not with someone who is taking life seriously. This is because too many people mix up "fun" and "happiness" as though they were the same or that fun made one happy. That which makes us truly happy does not involve immorality or illegality, nor does it put us in places and with people for which we will eventually have shame. The activities contributing to happiness are those we'd want to pass on to our children, and point the way for our friends. Fun can, but doesn't always, fall into that definition.

Rushing to Fix Disappointments

Sometimes people eject out of perfectly good relationships because they want an instant fix to some serious pain. One of the saddest and most typical times for people to lose each other is when they've lost a child. One listener wrote me that they lost a child at birth due to complications, and found out that they were medically incompatible and would never have biological children.

"Instead of considering the alternatives they have out there like adoption, I decided to throw away our marriage. Then I met another man six months later and I have the most perfect little boy in the world, but I am still not happy because I want to share this joy with the man I love (my ex)."

Another listener started an affair when she felt her husband was ignoring her. She admitted not doing much to confront him.

"[I] lived in a huge world of denial, a corporate wife, big house, new cars, gifts of guilt, all the while living with this very mean and ugly man. I eventually started looking for someone to be nice to me. I had an affair for about one and a half years—and realized that I was no more a love for him than a good lay. My life was such a mess that I was just grasping for straws. I guess my point is that when you are hurting so terribly from one catastrophe, it is not wise to jump right on into another to make the first better. The happiness that you may get from that is only momentary."

Another listener, feeling unhappy in his marriage, in retrospect realizes he was stupid and selfish. He had an affair with a married woman, whose husband beat him up severely for it.

"A broken nose, cheekbone, and a concussion didn't wake me up. I still saw her until after her divorce. I still 'wasn't happy' and saw other women at the same time, drinking and partying and ignoring my kids.

"To make a long story short, the consequences of my search for happiness is: two STDs (one incurable but not deadly), my kids are in a single-parent family, my oldest son became a father at fifteen because of my influence, my oldest daughter had drug problems, and my youngest son had a run-in with the police.

"Because of your show, I started going to church and was born-again. I now have custody of my kids, and I have not been involved with anybody for three years, because I don't have time—my kids need me."

In his "giving" to his kids, he's now happy; trying to get happy through sex didn't work. Big surprise?

Sex = Pleasure
Love = Happiness

Why is it that I now get calls from men and women asking me if they're too weird because they're still virgins? They tell me that people make fun of them and dates tell them that they won't be interested in them for long, and nor will anyone else, if they don't have sex as part of the dating exercise. They worry and wonder if they're missing out on something, or making too big a deal over something that is so "natural."

One listener wrote that at nineteen, she gave up her virginity, because she thought it was time. It was a one-night stand—like the one her mother had that produced her. She wrote that it would have been nice to hold her husband on their wedding night some seven years ago, and know that he was the first.

"Sex is NOT love, no matter what the other person tells you. 'If you loved me,' you would . . . puhleeze! If YOU loved ME, you would . . . wait. It feels great to be loved, but it feels worse to be used and tossed aside like a used tissue . . ."

We too often put aside our morals and good sense, because we think that the sexy, fun-at-the-moment (pleasure) will equate to happiness. It might, but it's a risky way to go about it.

One young man wrote to me of his experience with sex as a teenager. He describes beginning a relationship with mutual interests. Then, slowly, it became less about caring, loving, and nurturing, and more about getting those few minutes alone to do sexual things.

"In time, I forgot why I had cared about her in the first place. I lost interest in protecting her, and only wanted what was pleasing to me.

"I was blinded by what I thought I wanted. There are two things I want to say about the situation of teen dating. First is that it is dangerous to pursue any physicality at all without the commitment of marriage. It feels good while you do it, but it can and often will hurt far more than the pleasure it gives. Second is that I hope teenagers would consider putting off dating until they

are older. When we date while we are in a position where we couldn't possibly marry that person, our relationship is shallow and meaningless. Plus, there will be the inevitable pain with the dissolving of the relationship."

I have included this letter, albeit about minors, because the mentality is sound for all ages. Sexualizing a relationship before its time (marriage) and being intimate without an ultimate point (marriage) does not bring happiness—although the temporary pleasure is seductive.

One man called me about whether he should give his "girlfriend" a second chance. It seems that recently, during one of their "problem periods," she had sexual relations with about five men. She's told him she's sorry. He tells me she's repentant.

"You can forgive her, then dump her."

"Why dump her? If she's repented, isn't that enough?"

"That's enough for saying, 'I forgive you,' for whatever that's worth. But when someone evidences behaviors that demonstrate such impulsiveness, superficiality, immorality, and poor judgment, she ought to be considered high-risk for failure as a wife and a mother. What she has told you in advance, in my opinion, is that when the going gets rough, she gets undressed in some other guy's bed. If you want to play, she's your woman. If you want a wife and mother for your children and a stable life, she's not your woman."

The caller couldn't easily get past the notion that he "loved her" (fantasies and unfulfilled hopes) and that their sex was wonderful (and that's an omen, isn't it?) It also made him "happy" to be so forgiving. The reality is, that when someone's sexuality is so tied into pleasure and self-medicating, they become a liability in the commitment department. Choosing not to read the handwriting on the wall, or failing to heed its message to keep the "dream" possible, is Stupid Happiness.

Happiness on the Sly

"Anything that's a secret—can't be good," were wise words from a very dumb movie I watched recently. That philosophy goes for happiness as well as illegalities. One of the most disgusting new advances in Stupid Happiness, brought to us by the miracle of the Internet, is cyber-affairs. It used to be that fantasies were about singers, movie stars, or some real people at work. Now you can destroy the lives of your whole family on a fantasy.

As one such listener wrote: *"I put the fantasy of a fairytale on-line 'perfect' relationship before the commitment of my marriage of over ten years to my husband and my beautiful family. I allowed myself to have an emotionally intimate relationship with someone through my modem, and it, of course, had a shattering effect on my feelings toward my husband. It was stupid of me to believe that sharing my innermost feelings with someone other than my husband wouldn't mess up what I have with him. Thankfully, I saw the huge mistake I was making and I willed to correct it. I adore my family and nothing is more important than the time and energy I direct toward them. I have found that the fairy-tale has been right here, in my reality all along."*

The Stupid Happiness part of this sort of behavior is obvious: Nothing and no one is perfect—and if he or she was, we each know better than to think we're a match! Thinking that happiness is only available and effective when everything is wonderful is to condemn oneself to unhappiness. How does one reconcile wanting our spouse to be a little different, for things to be a little better, for us simply to feel perkier and pleased more often? Frankly, for the best of us it's always a struggle.

And here is where practice comes in. You need to make strenuous efforts to attain joy. Celebrating what is merely mundane is to reframe life in a more positive way. Even putting nicer place settings on your table for a meal—if only for yourself—is uplifting. I listen to oldies, classic rock, on the way to work and sing along (albeit badly) with the lyrics from a more innocent time. I admit that nostalgia is a bit of a whitewash, but so what if it jump-starts our joyfulness at living. Living, with all its pains and challenges, *is* the ultimate in hope, because it brings opportunity.

If you don't use the opportunities of life wisely, you may very well find yourself using the secret shortcuts unwisely.

"I have been involved with a married man for seven years. I know he will never leave his wife. I am overweight and feel that no one other than this substantially older-than-me married man will have anything to do with me. I feel like a hypocrite at church when I say that I am happy to be single, when the reality is that I am having an affair. The affair makes me feel good in the moment, but when I am at church, I am riddled with guilt."

She's not any more fit, she's not any more healthy, she's not any more married. In fact, she's deeper in the hole than ever before. Once it was just that she was "fat" (which is a sorrowful enough excuse to damage or destroy some other woman's marriage and family), now she's still fat but she's also in an immoral relationship. That gives her a lot less to use to appeal to a nice guy; lotsa fat, little character.

Voyages on the starship Stupid Happiness generally lead nowhere, because they are ultimately self-centered; true joy comes from sharing.

Money Can't Buy Me Love

The thing that's attractive about money and what it can buy is that it's under your control, it's immediate, there's definite gratification, and you don't have to hassle with anybody over it. It's easy to feel good about yourself when you have buying power. Buying and possessing a thing is a lot easier than the effort that goes into making a good relationship work. There is a tremendous amount of positive feedback for having lots and lots of things. After all, there is a program showing you the lives of the Rich and Famous—is there a program showing you the lives of the Happily Married and Spiritual?

"When my husband and I first met, I used to do volunteer work in our community as many hours as I worked at my full-time, paying job. I started making more money and working more hours.

"I became consumed in my newfound HAPPINESS of material things. That was four years ago. Since that time, there has always been a piece of me missing, not completely happy. My problem was that when I gave my time and myself to helping others, I felt fulfilled. I realized that I was not here on earth solely to acquire things. By working to make each day better for others, I have learned my greatest lesson: True happiness is KNOWING the only thing I need is to give back to someone else."

This is also the main lesson of good marriages. These days, I hear more about what someone's husband or wife is not giving them, and nothing about what they aren't giving to their spouse. Oh, it's easy to say that you would be giving if only they would be/do such and such. The reality is, waiting around for happiness to be created for you in the fantasy of the perfect spouse (who, after all, has moods, stomachaches, worries, bad days, and so forth) is to stick a knife into the heart of your relationship.

Problems

All G-d's children have problems. Big problems or many problems certainly cut into our sense of feeling happy. Even then, sharing burdens with our spouse, rather than taking out our unhappiness on him or her, is, of itself, a kind of happiness. Perhaps the perspective we most need in times of strife is, as one listener wrote, to realize that even this seeming major catastrophe is *"a small bump on the road to eternity."*

In conclusion, neither you nor your relationship is or will be perfect. That should not stop you from doing the caring, thoughtful, brave, and compassionate things you need to, to bring pleasure into the lives of your family. And that should not stop you from enjoying the value of what you are privileged and blessed to have—if you would only see it that way.

If you're not happy, try behaving as though you were—see how that lightens life up for you and your family, and how that feeds back, lighting up the world.

7

Stupid Excuses

"I hear the word 'but' a hundred times a day!
An excuse always follows the word 'but.'
I think if we add an extra 't,' it would describe
most of us!"

—A LISTENER

"I asked my now nine-year-old son when he was two why he drew on the wall. His response was, 'I did it because I liked the color it made on the wall.' There you go—that simple!" writes a listener in response to my website (www.drlaura.com) query about Stupid Excuses.

It would seem that the truth ought to be that simple for people. After all, aren't we a country that brings its children up on the story of George Washington and the cherry tree? Don't our children learn about honor, integrity, honesty, and responsibility from stories of such heroes?

Actually, no, not any more. Now we bring our children up on politically correct revisionist history lessons (where there were no real historic heroes—just victims) and the nightly news from which they can know that a President is a proven liar, perjurer, philanderer, and was shamefully influenced by friends and family in granting Presidential pardons.

The so-called Village perpetuates the notion that there are darn good reasons for being dishonest, and that these excuses exonerate the wrongdoer. Scandals over what is considered a disability, requiring special treatment at work and remuneration from the government, reveal a degenerating system in which even laziness can be demonstrated not to be a personal responsibility. Even commercials on mainstream radio and television for a DUI attorney service chant, "Friends don't let friends plead guilty." (Remember when the chant used to be, "Friends don't let friends drive drunk"?)

It is no surprise that innumerable surveys demonstrate that young adults not only have become ferociously less honest, but have what they think are reasonable explanations for their lack of integrity and a lack of shame for their lack of integrity. These excuses cover the ideas most parents of our grandparents' generation would have given us a spanking for uttering: "Everyone is doing it," "You're at a disadvantage if you're honest because the cheaters get a leg up," "It really doesn't matter how you get to college because college is your ultimate ticket in life," "I have too much pressure," "I'm too busy to do the work," and so forth.

Of course, these attitudes seep into the personal arena. Again, recent polls indicate a growing acceptance of affairs, shack-ups, children out-of-wedlock, promiscuity, divorce, day care (modern child abandonment), and destroying relationships between the noncustodial parent and child because of a desire for a new sex partner or address.

These days, notions of honor, integrity, responsibility, and obligations are considered oppressive and retro. Excuses abound to alleviate each of us from our responsibilities to others. There have always been excuses. That so many of these excuses are being considered understandable and ultimately acceptable is new.

The reality is that without honor, integrity, responsibility, and obligations we are each so unrestricted that we're each ultimately alone, adrift, afraid, isolated, cynical, depressed, and grasping because there doesn't seem to be anyone or anything to trust. I know this is true, because I get the letters, calls, faxes, and e-mails telling me so from all over North America.

A lot of folks tell me that they learned the bad lessons of Stupid Excuses at their parent's knee.

It's Genetic?

No, of course it's not genetic. Being an apple off the wrong tree can be a problem, as one listener revealed:

"It would be easiest to state that as a child I was damaged by my mother's constant verbal abuse and derision . . . that I am unable to help my behavior. This is not true! What is true is that my mother did respond to all stresses by screaming, yelling, throwing things, and threats. This is what I grew up knowing."

And that became her excuse for blowing up—that it was just her nature.

"At the same time, I know that constant rage, angst, and anger are unproductive and self-detrimental. I have had to learn that I am capable of that behavior the hard way: There is nothing worse than seeing the tears in your children's eyes when your anger explodes and watching your husband stand bewildered that one minute I can be fine and the next in a fit.

"But, I had to accept that ultimately there is no excuse."

It is that last bit of honesty which paves the way for growth. Callers often ask me how they can possibly break such habits or behaviors, and break the habit of excusing away such bad behaviors. My answer is that it happens in the reverse order. First, you stop excusing it and begin apologizing for it. Taking responsibility should have as its core remorse for the hurt you've caused. Without that remorse, the "sorry" becomes its own repetitive excuse as the behavior continues. Actions then need to be taken to repair damage—where possible. Then comes the plan to make sure you don't repeat the bad behaviors.

One of the best techniques for this last phase is to anticipate situations and feelings somewhat in advance of the usual ignition point. For example, when you start feeling frustrated, pinned down, against a wall, angry, confused, or some other triggering emotion, either say out loud, "You know, I need to take a break for a minute—I'm starting to feel out of control/nuts . . ." or just excuse yourself and leave the room to calm down or refocus or reconsider. Or ask someone for help (counselor, minister, your mother!, Dr. Laura), or develop an "instead-of behavior" that you put in the place of the behavior you're trying to stop.

Whichever technique you employ, it admittedly isn't easy, as this listener's letter reports:

"There are so many times that I want to start yelling and yelling and yelling. However, I did enough damage the times that I succumbed to the feeling. I am trying hard to make sure that I control my temper. I try to use humor whenever possible . . . then I feel lighter because I know I am able to control myself . . . and ultimately not behave like my mother."

Making Excuses Is Very Human . . .

Human beings, like all mammals, are gregarious creatures and spend a tremendous percentage of their lives being dependent upon parental caretaking. This natural dependency upon family and community leads to "how to get along" behaviors. In other primates we see hierarchies set up and grooming behaviors and mock fighting, all geared to help the individuals in the group "get along" for the cohesiveness required to ensure daily functioning and survival.

Although human beings are not as instinctively programmed as lower animals, we do have typical behaviors that serve some of the same functions—a significant one is avoid doing anything to look bad and risk rejection and punishment. If you do bad, finding a way to hide or deflect that truth is the backup position to avoid disdain and consequences; whence come such behaviors as lying, blaming, deflecting, and attacking back (best defense is a good offense), strategies to preserve the image or power.

This behavior is very typical for kids who worry that their misdeeds will lead their parents not to love them anymore and who, understandably, want to avoid punishment. This habit of making up excuses gets severe in situations where parents have been hyperperfectionists or overly punitive.

Of course, the families who teach honor above all, and that integrity is essential to intimacy, attachment, and affection, help their children grow up into adults who will admit to shortcomings, mistakes, bad judgment, and bad deeds. Ultimately, those are the behaviors that lead us to admire and trust another.

. . . And "Owning Up" Is the Most Honorably Human

Maturity is partially defined by the willingness to be held accountable, without excuse, for your actions. Immaturity is partially defined by the unwillingness to do the same. As one listener admitted: *"I guess you could say I have tried for way too long to hold on to my teenage attitude—and I'm thirty. I was a really bad teenager and I always had an excuse for everything I had done. You wouldn't catch me taking blame for anything. Even it you watched me do it and I saw you watch me, I could still come up with a million reasons why I didn't do or why I did it because someone else made me.*

"I have taken this attitude to my marriage and it has caused major trust problems. I have been married for ten years and I want everyone to realize that it is hard when your mate looks at you wondering if you are telling the whole truth or making excuses."

The reasons for holding on to behaviors which so obviously are destructive are many; however, prime among them is the backward notion that if you're seen as wrong or bad then you won't be loved. The irony is that the excuses make others lose trust and respect, which in turn cuts into your being loved. In other words, you end up creating the very circumstance you're trying to avoid. However, it's hard to give up old patterns when you're under stress because you'd rather not take the risk. You'd better, if you don't want to mess up your relationships.

Some folks never learn and some folks don't care to learn because they wish more to protect their image with themselves and their power over others. So, the excuses never stop.

"The World Owes Me"

Anger and hurt often motivate self-protective maneuvers as well as vendettas. Sometimes these actions are aimed at those who hurt us, while more often such actions are aimed and fired with a shotgun approach. This listener admits to such an attitude:

"During my nine-year marriage, I became the queen of excuses. I'm the ongoing, reigning victim of the world. I had a difficult childhood, the result of a one-night stand, a mother married seven times, and

physical, sexual and emotional abuse by her as well as a number of her husbands.

"All that said, I decided in my mind that this world owed me something. I was always quick to announce my war wounds. But never, ever was I willing to address them. I received far more attention by whining about it. I was married to a wonderful man who did everything possible to assist me in addressing these issues and seeking professional help. But, I rejected all efforts. Instead, I used these things to excuse all my immature, selfish, and immoral behaviors, which I would blame on my past, my rough life, my pathetic childhood, and my absolute inability to trust anyone. Eventually, the poor man gave up.

"I continued my self-destructive and selfish behavior for ten more years. Had to hit bottom, and I did. It has been an amazing and scary and painful journey. But I have to learn who I am—and that is someone who has responsibility in life, and not a constant victim."

As this listener revealed, the main reason people don't easily change behaviors is that they are scared. They are scared of the truth, their weaknesses, other people's power over them, the unknown, change, vulnerability, and losing control. Sadly, these fears often override the good sense to move forward into responsibility; consequently, good relationships are damaged and lost.

And other people are just brats, narcissists, sociopaths, or downright evil. That's material for another book.

Oh, Puhlease!

It would be impossible for me to categorize all the types and styles and subjects and techniques of excuse-making which compromise the integrity of relationships. Under the title of "Oh, Puhlease," here are a cross-section of the most typical,

some laughable, all irritating, many obnoxious excuses people have given to my listeners and callers and, probably, to
you!

➤   In response to being queried by his wife, who has been
ten years sober, about why he's been slugging down vodka in
the closet for two years when they were both supposed to be
clean and sober, the husband said, "Because I didn't want to be
an influence for you to start drinking again." How noble! This
excuse explains the closet, but not the vodka—nice dodge.

➤   When his wife asked him why he sneaked a female
friend on a day trip for boating and camping with the children instead of bringing her along, he answered, "Because
there wasn't room in the truck for you and she was splitting
for gas money and entrance fees for the lake and was providing lunch." I see, affairs are now merely money and room-
saving efforts?

➤   "My husband's excuse when I asked him why he couldn't
just jump in the shower each morning instead of rinsing his
head in the sink and getting dressed is, 'I've just got a lot of
stuff going on right now!'" I guess soap and water are not
among the "stuff going on" right now or ever.

➤   When this woman's husband of twenty-three years
decided to have an affair and leave her for another woman,
his excuse to her was, "This happens all the time and it's all
your fault and it's because of the kids." I guess this woman
and her kids were also responsible for his infidelities with his
girlfriend too?

➤   To explain his not paying child support ($195 per
month) and not seeing his son (except for the rare times

when he does father-son things with his buddies—and a kid is required), this listener's ex-husband says that "I work twenty-four hours a day, seven days a week, and my boss won't give me any time off. And, I don't have enough money." Wow, I thought slave labor had been abolished!

➤ One woman listener has been shacking-up with a guy for fifteen years and has a twelve-year-old child with him. She keeps wondering when he'll marry her. He says, "When we have $5,000 in savings." Whew, I'll bet he budgets carefully—spending just enough to be under $5,000 in savings.

➤ One married woman is frustrated that her husband lies to get out of work—when he works at all—to get more money, to get out of doing something displeasing, and to get what he wants at the moment. They are seriously in debt, and when they almost got evicted from their home, she asked him why he bought the four-by-four pickup and toy RC cars and other unnecessary stuff. He countered with, "I deserve these things because I work hard for it." I guess he considers spending his life's work.

➤ One twenty-seven-year-old woman has been for one year dating and sexually intimate with a thirty-seven-year-old man, who has been divorced for six years, and who has two children, sixteen and eighteen. He tells her they will marry but he won't tell his children or anyone in his family that he's even dating much less planning to marry her. When asked why, he says that, "The divorce was such a shock, I just don't want to shock anybody more." Huh?

➤ Another woman wonders why after twenty-one years of marriage, her husband doesn't "get it." Evidently, what he doesn't get is that he shouldn't lie and hide important things from her, like giving loans to folks he hardly knows for business arrangements over which he has little control, and like going out of town for job training with a woman "colleague." His answer to why he doesn't tell her things in advance is, "You'll be mad." Duh, really?

➤   This woman's husband has been a truck driver for only four years. Evidently, he often acts like a jerk and when she calls him on it, his excuse for rude, obnoxious, or frustrating behavior is, "I'm a truck driver. We have an image to protect. We are supposed to be rude and obnoxious." Where is the Truckers Anti-Defamation League when you need them?

While these excuses may sound amusing, and some might sound awfully familiar, they are all too typical examples of the lengths people will go to ignore their responsibilities and obligations, to justify selfishness and insensitivity, to deny weaknesses and serious problems, to justify hurting the ones they're supposed to love, and to not grow, mature, and do what they need to do to preserve and protect their relationships.

Sadly, one of the most familiar uses of excuses is in the arena of one's own denial of fear, weakness, and laziness in taking steps to face the truths of a problem relationship— without doing so, no relationship can flourish or even survive.

I Know It Walks, Talks, Smells, Acts, and Looks Like a Duck—But, Maybe It's Not a Duck . . . ?

A prime example of this behavior was evidenced by a call I recently took from a forty-one-year-old woman, dating a thirty-seven-year-old man for less than a year. She'd been divorced for twenty years and has a twenty-one-year-old daughter. The conversation was long, and frankly entertaining, for although she was in serious denial about the realities of her situation, at least she had a sense of humor.

"Has he ever been married or engaged or does he have any out-of-wedlock kidlets?"

"No."

"Really? No? At thirty-seven?"

"No."

"You are engaged to him after dating him for how long?"

"Ten months."

"What's the problem?"

"Well, he's given me an ultimatum."

"Really . . . which is what?"

"Either complete the fourth step at Al-Anon or he cancels our engagement."

"Why are you in Al-Anon?"

"Because he is a recovering alcoholic."

"How long has he been clean and sober—assuming you know the truth? Users generally lie about such things."

"Ten months."

"What? You're engaged to marry a guy who's been a drunk for a long time, supposedly sober for the months you've known him? My understanding of AA is that they prescribe no serious relationships while they're struggling with sobriety and then the underlying issues. Not drinking, my dear, is only part of the picture. Why, after waiting two decades to pick a man, do you pick a drunk?"

"Well, doesn't everybody deserve a second chance?"

"For what? For friendship? For employment? For club membership? Why would you think of taking a relatively unproven second-chancer into your bed?"

"Well, I'm not perfect either."

"Since nobody is perfect that means that nobody is entitled to a healthy partner?"

"Well, no."

"All you're telling me is that you believe this is the one chance you imagine that you have at forty-one—he's younger? sexy? good in bed?"

"Oh, I'm not going to talk about that (giggles tell it all)."

"Well, my dear, if you really thought this was a good idea, you'd be doing Step 4 of Al-Anon, and you wouldn't be on the phone with me. Something told you this probably wasn't a smart idea. Tell you what, let's compromise. If, in five years, he is consistently clean and sober and has dealt diligently with his psychological problems underlying the drinking, his life, and his personality—I'll dance at your wedding."

The demise of many relationships is often in the denial that brings these people together in the first place. You imagine, hope, pray, ignore, believe that wanting someone will make him or her be more or different from what they are. Think about this though: Since you are not bothering to deal with reality, why should they be stronger or more motivated than you?

I was particularly moved by a listener's letter concerning her termination of denial (albeit twenty-six years into a long and ugly story). Her husband was in and out with lovers. Although the pain was excruciating, she believes that she learned her greatest lesson—from a child:

"I do not want to play the martyr anymore. One evening, after I dramatically told my husband to leave if he wanted his lover, the scene was dramatically played out, and the pain was so unbearable, so intense, that I went into a blank daze. My adolescent daughter walked over by me, crossed her arms, looked down at me, and asked, 'Mom, why do you think Dad keeps coming back?' I answered, 'Because he loves us and is confused.' 'No,' she said to me. Then again she asked, 'Mom, why do you think Dad keeps coming back?' 'Well, because he loves you kids, only right now he

is feeling ashamed.' 'No,' she said, louder. Once again she asked the question. This time I was quiet for a few moments as I stared into the fireplace with great thought and reflection. Finally, I felt like a bolt of lightning hit me, and I began to cry. I looked up at her and said, 'Because I let him.' She bent down and hugged me. I then realized that my husband was not to blame for my current state—it was me. I had lost all my self-belief and I was blaming him for tormenting me and our children. In my way of thought, I had no choice because I loved him. But just the same, I did have a choice.

"*Painful as it was, I filed for divorce. After four and one half years, I realize that I clung to a false hope, excusing anything to deny the truth. I was so afraid of losing him that I accepted being treated as no human being should ever have to be treated. My own fear was my great excuse. If I had perhaps not been so afraid to speak up earlier in my marriage, this situation might have turned out differently. No one likes to be verbally criticized or degraded, yet due to his threats of 'If you're going to cry and continue to nag, I'm not going to stay here . . . ,' I always shut my mouth. If I had, many years ago, stood up and replied, 'Then go, until you can calm down or speak to me with respect . . . ,' maybe, just maybe . . . he would have, or maybe not.*"

Her last comment points to the issue of excusing the behavior of your "loved ones" when that behavior ought to be dealt with. The excuses she made for tolerating bad behavior had her living in hell for almost three decades, concluding with her abandonment. At least her young daughter learned this important lesson: Stupid Excuses mess up your relationships because when you ignore ugly, unpleasant, unacceptable, harmful realities, those realities stay and grow bigger and uglier.

These Stupid Excuses for tolerating bad behaviors (and not mobilizing to improve the situation) include:

"*No one else was banging down my door for a date, so what was left?*"

"I felt indebtedness to him because he was older and had done wonderful things for me."

"I didn't want to make him angry because I wanted to be loved."

And, sadly, *"I am ashamed and unforgiving of myself for my past. Even when I try to believe more in the trust and forgiveness of God, I don't feel worthy of His grace."*

Yet, one listener wrote in that on the verge of marrying a man with whom she could not be open or comfortable, she found her courage and stopped the Stupid Excuses:

"So many times he said things, did things, and did not do things that I made excuses for. I was constantly worried that I would make him angry. Despite all of this, I planned a wedding that as the weeks passed was becoming a death shroud, not a joyful event. Finally one morning my soul woke up and started to scream. So I took a deep breath, sucked up all that fear, and called it off. I had felt betrayal, humiliation, fear, anger and despair. But it is NOT okay to live your life this way. Don't cower or turn a blind eye to faults that should never be accepted."

Excusing bad behaviors doesn't get you love, acceptance, safety, or a quality relationship—it gets you servitude under your own fears of losing what in fact you don't really have in the first place. Don't excuse bad behaviors when you're dating because you throw away what opportunity you have to improve that relationship or, if necessary, what opportunity you could have to find a better, healthier partner.

I Have a Darn Good Reason

The Past

When people call in to my radio program, it's usually to complain about what someone else is doing. If I suggest that they are somehow kidding themselves about the intelligence or ethics of their actions, or show how they are being provocative or petty, the dialogue generally gets tense. That's okay, because the hardest thing to do is to look into a mirror with 100X enlargement—nobody cares to see their pores that big! It takes a lot of courage to face that, and I applaud my callers, even when it's likely that they won't face up till sometime after the call.

One listener wrote to excuse her constant mistrust of her husband *because*—

"My first husband lied to me constantly for seven years. His lies caused great pain to me and others and even got him in serious trouble with the law. My current husband is very honest, and I know deep down I can trust him totally, but when he answers my questions my immediate thought deep down is I wonder if he is telling the truth. He has proved my fears wrong time and time again. How do you stop your immediate feelings?"

Obviously, this woman does not want a déjà vu experience—but she creates it in her mind with the excuse that she's been there and doesn't want to be there again. That's the irony—*she creates* her worst fear. So here she is, finally married to a good guy, messing up the relationship because she is stuck in reverse gear.

How do you stop your immediate feelings, she asks. You don't, is the answer. When you choose to not act on them by questioning him, checking up on him, being hostile toward him, or punishing him, all for nothing, then you automatically diminish the power of those feelings.

One of the prices of the new sexuality is that people are now dating, being sexual, shacking-up, getting hurt, leaving, and starting the cycle all over again. Unfortunately, instead of being a great liberating experience, mostly people are ending up hurt, negative, cynical, suspicious, and less trusting. This leads to more superficial intimacy (as you function to protect yourself from hurt) which leads to more hurt.

Money

While I often decry on my radio program the dearth of real men—men who sacrifice their dreams and desires to do what it takes to provide for their families—sometimes "providing for" is misused as an excuse to be neglectful of family for the sake of the money. One listener believes that his marriage is back on track and that he is truly his daughter's dad because of my radio program:

"The problem started back in August. I had just taken a new job as a manager for a restaurant. My wife stayed home after our daughter was born. At the time, money was tight, and we were living hand-to-mouth. My attitude deteriorated to the point that I was ignoring my family and working nonstop to make the extra buck and to get ahead. This went on until December when she finally told me she had had enough and put me out the door. Since that day, I have left that job and took a different one that lets me be a husband and father. Your advice saved my marriage, Dr. Laura. Thank you."

While financially supporting a family is essential, pursuing money can too easily become an end in itself, because you can buy lots of great stuff, feel powerful, gain status, and get a fat head, while starving your essential lifeline to a meaningful life: your family relationships.

Weight

Whether or not you like it or think it should be so, our appearance, including hygiene, posture, dress, weight, and fitness, matters in our relationships. It is all a sign of respect for ourselves and our obligation to the relationship.

Certainly, it is difficult to keep up with aging and gravity. Certainly, it is difficult to exercise and eat only the stuff you "oughtta." Certainly, it is difficult to carve time out of busy lives to do body maintenance. Certainly, one needs a mature outlook in balancing the physical with the spiritual and relational (so much for the cosmetic surgery junkies who take an important concept to the extreme). And certainly, one should never feel loved or not based on a bit of flab. A decent partner learns to graciously and lovingly accept the realities of aging in their spouse without comparing.

It is our individual responsibility not to take our relationship or partner for granted with lazy excuses:

"My husband recently announced that he is unable to participate in marital relations with me because of my weight. I am obviously overweight—I used to be 150 pounds and now I'm 200 . . . but I'm saying to my husband that size shouldn't matter and that dieting isn't easy; that if it were easy, weight loss wouldn't be the big business it is. He's just drawn the line and won't budge unless he sees some attempt on my part to lose weight."

I believe it is fair for him to say that he needs to see "some attempt . . . to lose weight," because it demonstrates on her part a respect for his point of view and the physical side of their relationship. It is flabber(pun intended)gasting how many people demand that their spouses be totally turned on to them and pleased no matter how much they abuse their bodies.

One other listener wrote: *"I guess that's my excuse. If he loves me, what difference does the weight make, especially since I am so totally wonderful otherwise."* It's not that the appreciation for all that you are is lost, it is that as you lose interest in pleasing your partner with your best self, so will your partner.

Feminist Propaganda

One woman caller recently spoke angrily about how her husband, who works out of town Monday through Friday, comes home on Friday night and expects her to be dressed in something sensual and to be "playful." She talked about how she is all week long with the house, the laundry, and the kids, and how dare he expect her to be his sex-kitten just because he's home. I reminded her that he's not been at a weeklong party either, and he misses his family and the loving warmth of his wife.

She was stuck in playing martyr and clearly hostile about his supposed freedom. I told her that in spite of her determination to make it be so, hers was not bigger than his—just different. I asked her two questions: One, what was wrong with his wanting her intimately when he got home? And two, what was wrong with her wanting him intimately when he came home?

My interpretation of her excuse for not being a loving, available partner was that she interpreted intimacy and sexuality as demands on her (instead of an opportunity for pleasure and bonding) and that she seemed to need to suffer in front of him as proof that she's worked hard too and that what she did was meaningful. I told her that these issues were standard feminist propaganda, that her husband was not tuned in to any of that, and that she'd better not mess up her relationship with them.

Booze

"I don't need an excuse to drink, because I don't have a problem. I enjoy drinking and I like the taste."

That comment from a caller about his problem with his wife's determination to get him to stop drinking is the most typical excuse for abusing alcohol—the outright denial that there is a problem in the first place. Of course, the pain in the eyes of spouse and children, the DUIs, the ill health, the money, time, and effort dumped into drinking, the sneaking or the grandiosity of "my right to do what I wish" are swept away with, "I don't have a problem."

Contrary to the moneymaking medical community's protestations of alcohol abuse as a disease (insurance payment for fees, lucrative programs), I still see this issue as one of character. Bad habits, even those that have a serious impact on the body and create states of compulsion, are still only influences over which you have a choice how to behave. There is not one ex-drinker I've spoken to in the span of twenty-five years of radio conversations who has said other than that a decision to stop drinking (usually with the connection to G-dliness) stopped the drinking—no other disease is cured that way—through will and grit and character.

I get very angry when spouses call feeling guilty for wanting to get out of bad relationships with folks with such seriously bad habits, the abuse of drugs and alcohol, pornography, and promiscuity, because the medical/psychological community calls them diseases (addictions) and not character failings (not nice to judge). This nonsense has trapped many a decent person in a situation of inappropriate obligation, imagining he or she is not being sensitive in making a judgment to leave. That's cruel, unfair, and wrong.

Pornography

"I didn't think this was a problem for you. We haven't had a lot of intimacy lately, so I'm just looking at pictures to remind me of what I am missing, that it is still there and someday I'll have it again. I am not contributing to the porn industry financially or the exploitation of these women, because I am not paying for the paid sites of magazines—it's all free. And, it's human nature for men to want to see naked women, it's socially acceptable. Besides,

why is it that you don't see it as just something to 'pass the time' or 'have as a hobby'?"

These were the remarks of one husband to excuse his preoccupation with pornography on the Internet.

My point of view is that, in all its incarnations, attention to the body or life of another person when you're in a committed relationship is abusive and threatening to the integrity of that commitment; it allows for attention and emotion to be directed away from family and loving obligations. No excuses change the truth.

You know, it's bad enough to not be willing to admit to skuzzy and hurtful behaviors. It's even worse to treat your spouse as dim, inadequate, stupid, not with it, or actually responsible for the bad behaviors.

YOU Made Me Do It

One of the most insidious excuses is to blame the victim of your behavior for your behavior. For example, "I'm not stubborn. You just don't understand."

One listener wrote: *"I keep my mouth shut when he is talking to me. Otherwise, I would cut him off or act defensive, because I'm so stubborn as to my point of view."*

Another blaming excuse is "I'm not vindictive, you've hurt me!" This latter excuse destroyed one listener's marriage:

"This behavior of vindictiveness was one of the things that caused the demise of my first marriage—I now have to struggle to keep it from taking root in my current marriage. If he doesn't do one of the things I think he should, like wash my car, I'll purposely not do one of the things for him, like cook breakfast on Sunday. All of this is in my mind and he has no idea that I'm even mad."

Obviously, these are issues of assertion of will, and an unwillingness to communicate or absorb the reality that you are now "two" and must take into account someone with a different history and point of view and will.

The most direct way of assigning blame to your partner for your behaviors is to do just that:

"Sometimes when my husband calls me names (f . . . g bitch) he tries to take the blame off of himself and attach it to me. He says that if I wouldn't such and such, then he wouldn't have to say it. He actually says it's my fault that he had to say it."

Folks who are physically abusive use the same excuse. I always remind both sides of that argument that anyone can provoke, intentionally or not—however, provocation does not dictate one automatic response. If there is an automatic, reflexive, typical response, it is a measure of that person, not the person who provoked. Ultimately, we are each responsible for our own choice of action, and don't let anyone convince you otherwise.

Tit for Tat

"The most stupid excuse I've heard (and used) is: 'I did this because you did that!' My husband and I wasted years playing the 'tit for tat' game when we could have better spent that time nurturing and loving each other. Fortunately, we figured it out and began 'acting' to each other as opposed to 'reacting,' and as a result, the last couple of years of our twenty-year marriage have by far been the best."

The tit for tat game is obviously childish and clearly destructive. Why then do we adults do that? Because of hurt feelings. When our beloved does/doesn't do something that contributes to our sense that they love us, we hurt them for hurting us—imagining that that will make them love us better? I don't think so.

Sleight of Hand

Magicians are really experts at distraction. They subtly move your attention away from the action that creates the illusion that magic has happened. Little children do that when they point to something in the distance as they desperately try to conceal the cookie-before-dinner crumbs on their chins. When we grow up, we're supposed to face our wrongdoings and our agonies in a more courageous manner—especially with that person we're supposed to trust more than anyone: our husband or wife.

One listener wrote about her horror in finding out as an adult that her father was a child molester.

"This has destroyed me in many ways. I have been directing my anger at my husband, because he is an easy target and it keeps me from having to face the anger I feel for my father. I called a therapist and I am now in the process of fixing me. I believe that our spouses take a lot of the blame for the problems that have to do with other people as well as ourselves."

She's right. The irony is that because we feel the most safe with our spouses, we excuse our mistreatment of them as we blow off steam and rage meant for less safe persons or places. When she faces her dad, she will have to give up much of her past—taking it out on her husband avoided that.

Oftentimes it's not an issue of deflecting from a third party, it's the inability to assume responsibility for your own misdeeds.

"One behavior that I am not happy about and even dislike is when I get angry at my husband, and during the argument we are having, I begin to shout and yell. It is usually when I am right that my husband in an effort to win the fight begins to push my angry buttons. My husband is provoking, to say the least, and my excuse is that he pushed my angry buttons and got anger. He thus doesn't have to acknowledge any wrong or any correction that

*may be needed, because he's been able to prove that I have some-
thing to work on also."*

Although that sleight of hand is clever, she has the tools to
take it away from him: Disarm her angry button; then, he's
stuck with himself.

It's Never Over

*"I'm sorry that I allowed my unresolved anger to nearly destroy
my marriage, however, I am glad we were able to rise to the occa-
sion and move forward."*

That was the happy ending to a story that doesn't generally end that way for many people. The scenario was that her
husband had done something hurtful, had repented, and
wanted to improve the marriage. However, *"I was really angry
thinking about what he put me through and that he 'owed me' big
time for the hurt."*

I always remind couples and individuals that having hurt
that lingers after an assault on the marriage and the partner is
normal and expected. Once you make the recommitment to
accept that person back, and determine to work on the relationship, issues of punishment have to be put aside or the end
result, an improved relationship, won't be forthcoming. Using
the "I've been hurt excuse," though valid, is destructive to relationship reconstruction plans. At some point, you've got to give
up the rage and the behaviors it stimulates.

It's Not an Excuse—It's My Values

*"I am a Vietnam vet. I have been married twice. At one time I was
very promiscuous—not during marriage. I am seeing a lady that I
am very fond of. I listen to your show faithfully and agree on most*

subjects. I am in my fifties and feel that your warning about sex outside of marriage applies to everyone, not just teenagers. My lady friend disagrees. She pointed out that we are adults. . . . My reason for following your advice is because of my own personal convictions. She expects an answer soon. She thinks morality is a stupid excuse."

Note: It's not a good plan to have someone in your life who dismisses your core values as "excuses." Values are never an excuse, they are valid reasons. The man's lady friend is disrespectful, controlling, and selfish (Proceed directly to Chapter 9: Stupid Mismatch!).

8

Stupid Liaisons

"Recently at a company party I got heavily intoxicated and had a near-sexual liaison with my boss's nineteen-year-old daughter.

I am fifty-four, very happily married, with a son, who is, incidentally, the young lady's boyfriend.

I don't consider it too serious as all that happened was she performed oral sex on me a couple of times, while all I did was gently fondle her.

What bothers me about the whole liaison is, I think, that it could have become a very big mistake.

I almost cheated on my wife, nearly betrayed my son and boss, and came close to making a drunken idiot of myself with a young woman, whom I consider a very dear friend of the family."

—A LISTENER

Let's see, he got drunk, had sexual relations with his boss's daughter, who is also his son's girlfriend, betrayed his vows with his wife, and he *thinks* he only got *close* to doing something wrong? How Clintonesque! How grotesque. Sadly, these days, how *not* unusual.

In today's moral climate, where the air is thinning by the day, not by the altitude, many folks describe what used to be seen as outright affronts to their vows as "mere" or "almost" or "innocent" or "misunderstood" or even "reasonable" or "necessary" or their "right." Also, as this warped thinking goes, they rationalize not having really done anything wrong by splitting a definition into submolecular particles; if it wasn't intercourse to orgasm, so this argument goes, it wasn't sex. Oh, puhlease!

The point needs to be made that even putting yourself in a compromising situation *is* a breach of your vows which brings hurt, confusion, and mistrust to what should be a safe place: your marital relationship.

Instead, I get calls about women going drinking and dancing in bars at night without their spouses, husbands and fiancés who go to stripper-joints and participate in lap-dancing at bachelor parties, lone spouses traveling and socializing evenings with members of the opposite sex under the banner of "business," spouses car-pooling with either unmarried or unhappily married members of the opposite sex, married men/women spending family time (and secretive time) "helping" unmarried women/men with their home or feelings, perpetuating friendships with "ex" lovers, developing hobbies and activities with others outside of the marriage, having on-line "friendships," spouses flirting and gawking in plain sight of their husband or wife, taking vacations with buddies to a singles resort, and a host of other behaviors that, in spite of denial with the intensity of a pit bull bite, are clearly disruptive and destructive to intimacy, trust, and ultimately, love.

Beyond that, these behaviors are downright cruel. Even to attempt to rationalize away behaviors that cause your spouse pain, is to virtually spit on him or her. I just love it when some guy or gal calls about their impossible spouse, who is just hypersensitive about their innocent friendship. When I challenge what is basically the choice of a person who supposedly doesn't really matter over the person he or she is supposed to love, cherish, and protect, their response is generally a frustrated silence or a protestation of rights (to play) over oppression (of marital vows and obligations and downright thoughtful decency).

This is the point at which the offending spouse gets even more ugly. Adding sulfuric acid to injury is the typical behavior when confronted by their hurt and confused spouse. When callers tell me of their spouse's misbehaviors, it's usually in the form of: "I just want to know if I'm being fair or unreasonable. Is it okay for him/her to . . . ?" referring to one of the above behaviors.

Generally my answer is, "No, that behavior is grossly inappropriate for a married/engaged person. That should be obvious to you. Why do you feel you even have to ask me or any other third party about it? Why are you not trusting your own point of view?"

"Well, because (he/she) says . . ."

"Wait! Let me guess. (He/she) says, 'You're wrong,' or 'It means nothing,' or 'You're hypersensitive,' or 'You're insecure,' or 'You're controlling,' or 'You're immature,' or 'You're not happy with yourself, and you're trying to drag me down,' or something like that. Right?"

"How did you know? You sound like you're hiding somewhere in my house."

"Because, my dear, that's exactly how all people intentionally hurting their spouses talk. It's their way of alleviating themselves of any shred of guilt, to make you back off, shut up, and let them do what they selfishly want to do—which they've somehow convinced themselves they have a right to do."

Of course, it's not unusual for these do-badders eventually to collapse in a heap of begging for forgiveness for "losing their heads" and "getting off track," or, my favorite under-statement and misnomer, "making a mistake."And then I get the sad calls: "Am I obligated to take (him/her) back?" or "I took (him/her) back but I can't trust, can't warm up, can't let go, can't feel love. So, what do I do?"

Here are the choices: Stay and suffer, stay and go crazy, stay and pray, stay and demand things to change, stay and take the risks, or leave.

Love Shouldn't Hurt

How can you say you love and care for someone when you bring that person pain, uncertainty, embarrassment, anxiety, and insult? Wait—I know the answer to that one—you don't love them! Justifying actions that clearly hurt and demoral-ize your spouse is self-serving, not loving, and is psychologi-cally abusive. Here's a tip: If your actions hurt the one you love, they are the wrong actions. Period.

Love is an action based on the conviction of commitment, not on the ebb and flow of emotion. The emotion of feeling overwhelmingly drawn to someone, sexually turned on to them, or fuzzy all over when they walk into a room or the thought of them comes to mind, is intermittent, fragile, and too easily pushed aside by such other competing emotions as boredom, depression, health issues, financial circumstances, familiarity, annoyances, and so forth. It is the sense of oblig-ation due to the seriousness of the commitment that pro-vides the impetus for appropriate behavior in spite of momentary glitches in "that loving feeling."

And, most importantly, it is the *behaviors* of loving that help stimulate and perpetuate those "loving feelings." That's right! Your behaviors largely determine your feelings. If you require proof of that, remember all those times when you felt down, but spiffed up your dress, stiffened up your lip, and marched into the fray—the very act of behaving undepressed and confident put you in the position to reinforce those healthier feelings. The same works for intimacy; behaving in a loving way taps into those stored-away positive feelings for your spouse and generates positive reactions from his or her feedback and makes you feel even better and closer.

Yeah, but I Want Those Feelings Quick and Dirty

"I was a new mother and in a marriage that I felt was killing me. I set my sights on a person that I knew would bring me the excitement I wasn't getting in my marriage.

"It took me three long years to realize that the grass was not only greener, but much more bitter. I'm thankful that my daughter has a father who was insightful enough to see that her mother would come around."

This listener's letter is very typical for both men and women who find that being married and having children is not the fantasy experience they imagined. With maturity, commitment, and communication, people learn to make the best of life's challenges, difficulties, and disappointments. Without maturity, commitment, and communication, people look for ways simply to feel better rather than make things better.

For some, drugs and drinking work. For others, it's walking away from the scene—thereby creating the crime. For still others, it's the clandestine affair which makes them feel those fantasy feelings again. Not all in this last category acknowledge what they want. More often, the perpetrator convinces him- or herself that this is just an innocent flirtation or friendship through which they can relax in a way they can't at home with colicky babies, a tired spouse, or a busted washer-dryer.

No matter how you spin it, it's self-serving, wrong (check out Commandment Seven), doesn't solve the true problem(s), and risks everyone losing everything.

I recently took a phone call on my radio program from a guy who admitted that he hadn't been acting mature in the marriage. For several months, his wife and child were at his in-laws' house. He said that their separation absolutely had the intent of a time-out and that they would get the marriage back together. Evidently, they'd been talking on the phone daily about their problems. It seems they were both (immature and superficial) party types before they married, and then before their child. She grew up to face the challenge, and he'd been annoyed that she wasn't "fun" anymore. He continued to have "fun" going to bars and being with his buddies. She left. He wants her back.

He called, because he'd been lonely for female companionship so he connected with a woman and has had her to their house (!) for dinner (she cooks) and sex. When I challenged him on the fact that he indeed hadn't changed a whit during this time-out period, in that he still demanded immediate gratification, he then told me that he wanted to end it, but the girl wouldn't get the message. Here it comes: The girl had arrived at his house minutes before he decided to call me. He let her in.

I told him that I was stunned that he had engaged in these activities in the family home and that even now he let this woman into the house. He seemed "helpless" to know what to do now because "a relationship" had begun with this woman. I suggested he lead her to the door, tell her not to contact him anymore or he would file a report with the police for harassment. I don't know if he did that last part or not. I told him also that he had no choice but to tell his wife about what he'd done—especially because this woman was not going to let go.

This sounded like the plot to *Fatal Attraction.*

If it isn't a lover who won't let go, then it's a pregnancy, attempted suicide, extortion, sexually transmitted disease, public humiliation for your spouse and children, disruption of generations of family ties, legal and financial battles, demoralization of your children and the loss of their foundation of safety, trust, and respect for you and for marriage. It's dirty, face it.

In Your Dreams

From my experience on-air, it is definitely a more female tendency to dream and fantasize about an old lover when the realities of life and adult responsibilities hit minutes or years after the honeymoon. One caller said, "Um, I have a question. I've been married six years and I am still, um, every once in a while, seldom, like probably once every other month, having dreams about an old boyfriend I had."

"Okay. Now, when did it start and what else was happening in your life and/or marriage?"

"Oh, um, probably, I don't know—ah, six months after I got married for probably five years now."

"Six months into your marriage you learned something about life, about marriage, about love that you didn't like. What was it?"

"Well, freedom. The freedom was gone and, and um, just that, you know, the excitement is over after six months. Or, the newness of it all. And I think that I just wanted that newness again. Or that flirting. I was wondering if I should write in my journal more to try to figure out my feelings?"

"That's your question? If you should write in your journal? This is a typical female behavior, and I'm a woman so I can tell you that daydreaming, writing in journals, talking to your friends—all make you believe that you're doing something, but truly these behaviors are to avoid dealing with the core problem."

"So what is dealing with it?"

"Good question and the real point. Dealing with it is to realize that in the beginning of your marriage you were doing all this fun stuff and now real life has hit and you have to go out and buy each other Kaopectate and you have to do bills and you have to do all this stuff which is not as much fun. By the way, it obviously can never be the same unless you get divorced every six months from everybody you've married. You've gotten lazy in this relationship and have been waiting for feelings to carry you away or for him to create a mood. What have you done to make this marriage warm, loving, and meaningful—other than write about how unhappy you are and fantasize about Prince Charming?"

"Right. I didn't look at it that way."

It is normal for relationships to have to struggle with reality. What is becoming normal, albeit unconscionably wrong, is to ignore commitments and vows in order to "feel good." I have suggested walking around on a Prozac drip to many people who think the epitome of a good life is always to feel perky. Truth is, real happiness is a more moving experience than feeling perky—but it's only earned over time and with depth. Don't be one of the too many these days who looks for the omnipresent nipple of your infanthood. Much of the value, meaning, and purpose in life comes from giving . . . not feeling.

Back to Yesterday

A listener writes:

"My husband has and sees no problem being friends with ex-girlfriends and ex-wives . . . from twenty years or more. Should I not

get upset and let him go to dinner with these female friends? Also, for your information—this is my third marriage and his fourth."

Do you realize that these two people have seven marriages between them? Do you realize that these people will likely increase that number in the next few years? Here's why: She's afraid of the vulnerability of intimacy so she married men who can't be intimate—then she doesn't have to look inside when she's got something so real and obvious to complain about; he's afraid of the vulnerability of intimacy so he maintains innumerable superficial female friendships which lead him to be able to say that he doesn't have a problem at all. As for his ex-lovers' club, some people are human flames—they crave the constant presence of hovering moths around them. What they don't experience in depth, they make up for in numbers. The women who participate just love the flattery.

A match made in purgatory.

Not all "going backward" is about superficiality of intimacy. Sometimes it's about restoring our egos, which often goes hand-in-hand with a special kind of revenge.

"When I was in college, I fell in love for the first time. Our relationship got out of hand, and it turned sexual. He graduated and left me with the impression that he'd come back for me. Years passed as I waited for him and didn't date anyone else. After several years, he told me he was involved with one of my friends and that we had no future together. But, stupid me, still holding onto a fantasy of romance. After graduating I met a very nice young man—handsome, kind, honest, intelligent. Then, it happened. My old boyfriend called me. He wanted to be friends again.

"I said sure, but had other plans in mind. I wanted to get him to love me again, and then I'd break his heart and leave him like he left me. My new love hated my having a relationship with him and told me he loved me and that he wanted to marry me but that I was compromising the security of our relationship by continuing to have contact with my ex.

"The game was over. I sent my ex one last e-mail and told him not to write or call. Now that I have a stable, healthy relationship, he thinks that I'll just drop it all for him—no way! That was that."

Actually, this listener came awfully close to losing the healthy part of her life in order to "heal" her damaged ego. I've seen so many people fall into this trap. They sacrifice their current moral growth and maturity for the option of erasing a rejection from their past: If they can make that person love them after all, well then, they'll be all right, perfect, wonderful, or whatever. Truth is, the involvement, or lack thereof, by some one person is not an indicator of anyone's worth. And self-esteem is harder won than that— and that's why people choose easier ways. Mind you, the easier ways are always substandard, and exact a terrible price.

Be Careful—and Stop Being So Stupid

I just love it when folks try to soft-sell me that their extra-marital intentions are truly honorable—and that this honor is worth the destruction of their marriage? "Well, no . . . but . . . ," is the soppy answer.

Here's an example that is all too typical. Fortunately, it has a happier ending than most.

"I started noticing how much stuff my husband was doing for my friend's family, and NOT doing for his own. I started noticing what kind of parent she really was and how she dressed and acted around my husband. She was no friend of mine! She was the kind of person my mother always warned me about. That person who likes what you have so they try and take it from you. I told my husband what I was going through and that we needed to dump her like a sack of rotten potatoes.

"Well, of course, he said I was losing my mind. A few weeks after I tell him all this, she has decided to move closer to her ex-husband for the children. Yeah, right. Anyway, my husband says he'll help her move. Fine—the faster the better. Okay, here's the BEST part. He comes home mad as heck. She had put the moves on him. He was disgusted and very sorry for not believing me. At last, she is booted from our lives without a tear being shed."

I seriously doubt that he didn't see what she saw. I believe that he enjoyed the hero status he got from the "friend" for helping out, while at home helping out was simply what he was supposed to do. I believe the flirting made him feel masculine and desirable, whereas at home the mood hardly struck. I believe he was moving toward the "I never really meant for anything to happen . . . ," excuse, but in the end, his conscience got the better of him.

The moral of this story is that you should never put yourself in a situation that could remotely lead to compromise. This specifically includes being alone with a member of the opposite sex for friendship, business, just talking, just eating, just sharing, just driving, just anything. It is simply a fact that proximity is dangerous in and of itself because it allows opportunity for inappropriate feelings to evolve. To show respect for your marriage and your vows, you should never let that happen.

This might be at great sacrifice—but what price your honor and your marriage? In 2000 there was a widely publicized event that dealt with just this issue. A military officer, experienced and decorated, refused to be confined to close quarters with a woman also in the military. He cited his religious beliefs (Catholic), and his vows to his marriage as reason to ask for reassignment or to serve in this assignment with another male. Political correctness being as powerful as it is, he has been severely punished and his record tarnished. This was an outrageous conclusion to a situation that could have been handled with respect. Then again, in today's culture, the only allowable intolerance is toward religious belief.

His character, conscience, and marriage stayed intact. Incidentally, if this were standard military procedure, fewer women would have to be excused from service due to pregnancy.

I Need to Be Needed—I Need to Be the Good Boy/Girl

Sexual or romantic fantasies are not the only motivating force behind Stupid Liaisons, the immoral or unhealthy outside relationships that damage marital intimacy. The unilateral need to feel important in a generic sense propels many people into situations that substantially detract and distract from marital commitment and activities.

As one listener explains:

"When I was married, we decided that I should stay at home to raise our children. I gave up my career and my life to do so. During this time, I lost contact with those I used to work with for years. Our life was different now. One of my friends, another at-home mom, was an alcoholic. So, needless to say, I thought I would fix that one. I would take care of her daughter. I would lie, cheat, and steal from my husband and children. I would say I was home when I had been over at her house trying to help her stop. I would give her gas money or pay for groceries when we hardly had any. I would cheat time with him to give her. Worst of all, I would blame him for not supporting me in doing this wonderful thing.

"My female friend and neighbor across the street made her way into my husband's bed. The worst thing is that I knew it was going to happen. I thought I was worthless, because I could not get my friend to stop drinking. My nonstop drinking friend had taken the life out of mine and the friend across the street was just using me to get closer to my husband.

"The end of all of this is that I left, thinking he was the a—h—e of this whole thing. It has taken me three years, talking to my ex-husband about good and bad times, and growing up, to realize I can't save the world and to use better judgment about what is a friend."

Making an identity, building an ego, feeling important through rescuing makes those rescued your means to an end other than their welfare. You need them to improve because that is how you are measuring your own worth. Some people become workaholics to serve that inner god, others find broken friends and try to fix them.

Some just turn over their lives to whoever wants a piece, because they interpret that behavior as that which will bring love and avoid all negative judgment or confrontation.

"I have been with my husband for twenty years. He has a bad habit of letting people walk all over him—not only his family members, but also people who work for us. I attempted to talk to him about this, but he never would listen to my point of view. There was always a reason why we should forgive and forget. Then, once we did, they would sh— all over us again.

"But this along with other behaviors has started to make me feel worthless."

At first, it would seem that this listener has a very weak husband. How sad. However, that is rarely the true story. This type of behavior is more self-serving than self-sacrificing. This type of behavior is generally about building a reputation through the flimsiest of means.

This is a point I've tried to drill home many times on the air: Your attempts to feel wonderful and important by having no boundaries or standards for how others outside the marriage affect you and your family is self-serving and damaging. By the way, not holding people accountable for their actions doesn't really help them. Repetitively saving their undeserving butt doesn't mature them—but it does make you feel superior. And even reflex forgiveness at its worst does not suggest reissuing a "use me" proclamation—so don't go touting forgiveness as your excuse. Please do note that along this route of self-congratulation, you willingly sacrifice the well-being and affection of those who really ought to count on you for support and protection. You are all too willing to sacrifice them for the "audience"—in your mind, the folks at enough of a distance see you as a hero. Those at home know better.

Shut Your Mouth!

I have often said on my radio program that without gossip, much of human conversation would cease and that quiet would rule the land. What some people don't get is what gossip entails. E! and A&E biographies are largely gossip. The tabloids major in gossip. Much of what passes for news is gossip. The Internet is filled with gossip (or porn). And a lot of what people talk about to each other under the umbrella of conversation is gossip.

People even gossip to themselves. A recent caller was complaining about her boyfriend. It seems that he read her journal, in which she had commentary about him and an ex-boyfriend. Evidently, he was upset by the content of what he'd read. She clearly was calling to complain about this breach of privacy and wondered if she were morally obligated to explain about the things he read. I suggested that no matter how he got this information, gossip from her friends or her journal, if she wished to continue a relationship with him she'd better clarify the upsetting points.

I frankly don't understand why people write disturbing, unflattering, scandalous things down on paper if they don't intend someone to read them. So often, in hearing about this journal-keeping, it sounds more like a place to air things that ought to be disciplined, or an opportunity to vent the ugliest, weakest, most unfortunate parts of ourselves, our thoughts and feelings. Perhaps that's the venue of spiritual or psychological counseling—where at least the venting is toward growth or depth of understanding of oneself.

I have harped endlessly on how spouses should not share their problems and complaints concerning each other with mutual friends or family. They are likely simply to side with you—so much for an unbiased sounding board. Meanwhile, you've breached the sanctity of the marriage, embarrassed your partner forever, having painted a one-sided portrait of him or her.

There are countless calls from folks who regretted telling friends and family their gripes and problems in the marriage, specifically because after the relationship normalized again, friends and family were still polarized, rejecting, critical, even hostile to the partner and the renewed relationship.

As one listener put it:

"I would like to thank you for a very practical and broad-reaching recommendation I've heard you make to callers lately. That is to refrain from discussing personal matters with uninvolved parties. We women are certainly prone to spilling our guts out to each other for little to no reason. I've always regarded it as a form of dishonesty to tell half-truths of any kind.

"I am now reduced to sharing only the most benign and anemic bits of information about my life. I admit, the more I told them the more needy I appeared. No explanation could convince them of my sanity once their sage advice had been given. I failed to take into account the destructive potential of an idle tongue."

Therein lies yet another problem in "sharing" personal information: When the advice isn't taken, then you have trouble.

On-Line Is Not Just a Chat

"When I was pregnant with our second child, my husband started several on-line friendships. He started pulling away from me, chatting at all hours of the night, sometimes about things that were none of her business. He even made long-distance phone calls. He told me one week after our second son was born, two weeks before Christmas, that he wanted a divorce. But I told him he promised me forever, he promised our children forever."

The Internet has made escaping from responsibilities and reality possible from your very own living room chair! That these cyber-affairs have become a part of our culture is evident in the new growth industry: the therapy of cyber-addiction, yet another behavior that has nothing to do with character and everything to do with outside influences and brain chemicals. I repeat, the only irresistible impulse is the one not yet resisted. This is not a disease, it is a lapse of character based upon weakness and selfishness.

At least this listener is honest enough to admit that chat-room relationships are to salve the ego, as a pretense at solving the problem:

"My husband and I were having problems that most couples have once they have been married for a time. We never seemed to have enough money, he never seemed to want to talk to me, and we did not agree on how to raise our children.

"It wasn't too long before I had my own computer and was chatting with people, spending more time with them than with my young boys. Before too long, I had met a 'wonderful' guy that hung on my every word. Of course, all my 'friends' in the chat-room encouraged me to divorce my husband and get involved with this guy in real life.

"I separated from my husband, breaking his heart, and took my kids to live in a different town. One morning, I woke up. My husband had come to pick up the kids, and I looked at his sad face. I

realized I couldn't let this man go. After all I had done to him, he still loved me. My husband and I listen and respect one another again. I can't believe how much I almost lost."

The main problem with all kinds of affairs is that they pretend that the sole source of the problems is outside you and that another "him" or "her" will solve the problems. You know better than that . . . eventually.

Yo Momma!

I used to say on the air that in the span of the quarter of a century or so that I've been on the air, I haven't gotten any father-in-law complaints. That's not true anymore. I think I've gotten five in the past three years. That still leaves thousands and thousands of complaints about mothers-in-law. They run both ways, that is, the woman's and the man's mother. There does seem to be something special about that mother-son relationship which leads to a lot of competition between daughter-in-law and mother-in-law.

Many mothers of sons have a hard time understanding that they need to turn the baton over to another woman. Instead, they may play a sickening game of tug-of-war over the loyalties of their sons. In doing so, they put their sons in the middle, as if they must choose between their mother or their wives. This can get very cruel, even evil—demanding that their sons come to visit, bring the children, but not "that woman." The sons who do that are the boys, not the men.

Many times the handwriting is on the wall, as one listener doesn't seem to see:

"I feel my fiancé chooses his family over me. He takes their side and defends them when I need him to support me. Now he is talking about when we get married and he finishes his term with the

Air Force, he wants to move onto his parents' land and rent from them. I really don't want to do this, because I feel it could destroy our relationship. He doesn't understand why I feel this way. I don't think he's gotten the point that he's on his own, and mommy and daddy aren't going to be there every day to hold his hand."

Actually, my dear, no he's not, and yes they will. You have to decide if you're going to be there to watch it.

The stories can get a whole lot worse when she does stay there to watch it:

"I knew my husband had a close relationship with his mother. His first commitment was still to his mother after we married. The day I told my husband we were expecting our first baby was the day I realized he hadn't detached himself from his mom. His response was, 'You're not going to have it, are you?' This was one of those moments in life where it starts going in slow motion, and you feel like you're having a nightmare. I was in shock and disbelief. He said he absolutely could not have this baby because his mother didn't want him to—I guess to keep him as the baby and to keep him with her and away from me or any other woman. He said that it was ultimately my decision, but if I had the baby he couldn't guarantee he'd be there next year. He gave me an ultimatum—the baby or him. And it was all so his mom wouldn't be hurt."

Well, she aborted the baby. Later, when they did have a child his mother had nothing to do with it, continuing an exclusive relationship with her son. The listener ended her painful letter:

"I wish I would have left him when he gave me the ultimatum just weeks into our marriage. Why would a husband, an intelligent, educated physician, keep as his first priority his relationship with his mother before his wife and child. I will never understand it."

I will never understand catering to it.

One male listener wrote to me admitting that he almost lost his wife and son by letting his mother intimidate him.

"Mom had always been a strong presence in our house, but I never realized the magnitude until my wife and I had our first child. Mom's domination became unbearable, but she would not lend her support or cooperate with us. When we tried to delicately confront her, she physically attacked my wife and had my older brother beat me up. After four years of her nonrepentance, and my calling Dr. Laura for advice, I gave her an ultimatum to own up and make amends, and we haven't heard from her since. Although I miss her, peace has been restored to our home."

Of course, I'm always happier when ex-communication is not the necessary option. One woman caller told me about how her father would just show up unannounced to spend the day at her home. She wanted her privacy with her husband and child, but was afraid to hurt her father's feelings—especially since she was living on land he gave them.

There's the hook: Be careful about taking such "gifts," when you understand your parents well enough to know that they feel their gift gives them appropriate entitlements, privileges, and power.

I told her to go to the door when he knocked, not let him in, and tell him: "It's a bad time now for a visit. Please give me a quick call when you're available so that we can pull this together better next time." And then, with an "I love you, Dad," give him a hug and close the door. Of course, he'll be hurt, even outraged, and I hope not vengeful. You might even have to give him back the land and actually take care of yourselves and build a future together from the bottom up. Greed is obviously a big part of this picture—those controlling parent-types count on your greedy dependency, wanting it all and now.

One listener has had it and has decided to call the meeting to order:

"I am a stay-at-home mom of two beautiful little girls. For me, the most stress comes from my in-laws. They have been coming to our home every weekend for the last two months. They stay in our home from Friday until Sunday afternoon.

"While in my home, they constantly tell me how to raise my children, and they do not follow my rules for my children. If I put them in time-out, they take them out. If I remind them to say, 'Yes, ma'am,' or 'Yes, sir,' they tell them they do not have to say that to them.

"My husband and I have discussed this, and he is nervous about saying anything to them about coming down all the time and about following the rules of the house set for the children.

"Well, I've simply told my husband that if he doesn't figure out a way to tell his parents—then the children and I will start staying at the most expensive hotel in Nebraska on the weekends while he spends quality time with his parents."

Well done. Sad that it had to be done this way. Better if each spouse would take responsibility for building a mature, adult relationship with parents and not constantly behave as though fearing being sent to his or her room without dinner!

It's Us Against Them

Many times callers struggle over the proper place for their loyalties: with their spouse or with their bio-family. "But, it's my mother/father/sister/brother . . . ," is often the lamentation which reveals a sense of "blood thicker than marital vows" confusion. Although I work very hard to have people fulfill their obligations of respect and honor to their families, I remind them that they have established a new family, over which they have primary responsibility for welfare, nurturance, well-being, and survival.

I remind listeners and callers that being supportive of their bio-families does not include sacrificing the welfare of their home, spouse, and children. For example, one caller was feeling guilty, because his parents had been pushing him to take in his wayward adult brother, out on parole again for drug arrests. My caller had several small children and a wife, who was not enthusiastic about having that big a problem to take care of or worry about or defend against (as he had bad friends and a bad temper). My caller, a decent man, didn't want to disappoint his parents, let down his "blood," nor upset his home. He didn't know what to do.

I told him that support and help came in many forms. That is, helping his brother find a place to live and helping him drive to a special appointment for a job interview was helping his brother. Calling his brother on the phone or meeting him during a lunch break to offer moral support was also helping. I told him that I believe he had no moral obligation whatsoever to put his family in jeopardy in the hopes of rehabilitating his brother. Additionally, this clearly did not put the burden where it would do the most good: on his brother.

"But what about my parents?" he asked.

"What do you mean?"

"They're going to be angry with me—disappointed in me. What do I do about that, and what do I tell them?"

"Tell them that you respect how much they care about their son and how much they want him to be and do better. Tell them you understand their desperation in wanting to protect and fix him. Tell them you have all those same feelings about your own family—and that your family comes first. They'll have to think about that one for a while, because it provides a catch-22."

It is not unusual for in-laws to put unreasonable demands and stresses on the marriage of one or more of their kin.

Why is that so? Same schoolyard clumping of mini-groups with an "us agin' them" mentality, an inability to let go, a selfish determination to control, a hostile reaction to change or difference, inherent emotional and psychological problems, and maybe even too much time on their hands.

During the week in which I worked on this very chapter, I had innumerable such calls. One was from a woman annoyed that her mother-in-law had for the past five years (married ten) yearly sibling-only reunions with her—that means no spouses (like my caller) and none of their children. At first, I responded with dismay that my caller would be upset about one night out of three hundred and sixty-five; except, it was for five nights, Thursday through Sunday. Another caller wondered whether it was okay for her husband and two adolescent children to spend six weeks vacationing with his parents without her, because she had to work (he was a public school teacher with the summer off). Yet another caller said her husband had received only two plane tickets as a gift from his out-of-state mother, enough for himself and their son. "Does that sound right or nice to you?" she asked.

"No."

"When we were dating, one of the things that was a bond between my wife and me was having to survive difficult families, in which we didn't seem to fit or have much in common. We seemed to be in sync about keeping our distance, protecting privacy and adult individuality."

This listener had difficult in-laws in stereo. Which, of course, made it a lot easier for him and his wife to band together in mutual support—or so the writer thought.

"After we married, even as the pattern of destructive/everyday evils continued on the part of my in-laws (who turned out to be really disgusting, compared to my merely frightened, confused, annoying family), my wife insisted on having much more involvement with them than I thought healthy, and she would never

stand up to their rudeness, destructive comments, and manipula-
tions. It turned out that doing it 'her' way meant doing nothing
except eating dirt, and having a wedge grow larger and larger
between us, and seeing my wife continue being emotionally/psy-
chologically crippled in general."

It is in these situations that I always prescribe serious psychotherapy. Without the growth of personal dignity and a
respect for the integrity of oneself and the new marriage and
family, such Stupid Liaisons will be destructive to the potential happiness and success of any marriage.

And sometimes, when a healthy balance cannot be
reached, withdrawal is necessary:

"It was a very painful decision for my husband not to have any-
thing to do with his family. I am grieved that my husband had to
make that decision." This listener's marriage did survive the
attempt of his family to break them up because, due to her
heritage, she was "not one of them."

"Now, Honey, You Are Not Allowed to Play . . . With Grandma/pa!"

Another point of confusion about honoring your parents as
an adult with a family to protect is the issue of serious bad
parental behaviors: drug use, shacking-up, consorting with
drug dealers and child molesters (here's the "but I love him,"
and "he's different now" excuse to ignore), blatant affairs, a
series of lovers, vulgar language, violent behaviors, and so
forth—I've heard it all. So much for the wisdom and sobriety
that's supposed to come with age!

Not only do more and more older parents engage in such
seamy behavior, they often try to entangle their children in the
fray by asking for lodging with the lover (while still married to
the other parent), demanding that they have access to the

grandchildren (who would be at some risk), offering their adult child an entry into their immoral or illegal activities, and generally asserting that they should be accepted without judgment for whatever they do simply because they are the parent.

No way. Your first loyalty is to the family you created in love and commitment.

Your Adult Children

Now that I've made it clear that your obligation is to your marriage and family, what about when your children become adults? This is especially complicated when you are in a second (third, fourth . . .) marriage with all the sense of guilt for messing up your children's lives with a broken home, and not being there to do what a father/mother is supposed to do on a daily basis. This scenario generally includes a grossly inappropriate overindulgence of bad behaviors by your adult children, an attempt to rescue them no matter what their own responsibility and need for accountability, and a general continued messing up of their lives and your marriage.

Here's a commentary on this issue by a listener:

"My husband has two grown kids who have their own partners and kids and he continually bails out his daughter with any problem she may phone him with—which is fairly constant.

"I have kept out of things until I had to mention something to him about boundaries and why he still feels he needs to give her money. I got the reply that it's none of my business and I wouldn't understand because I've never had my own kids and that I should keep right out of it.

"This excuse I've heard more than once as an excuse for bad boundaries and from parents who enable their kids throughout their adult lives; the result inevitably is that the adult child never

learns consequences for their own choices. In fact, he is making up for his own guilt for his parenting style and it infuriates me."

The guilt-ridden mishandling of children from a prior marriage is probably the major contributor to the statistic that second marriages collapse at greater rates than first. It is natural for in-laws to favor their own; and for "parents" to do the same; it is natural for there to be issues with ex-spouses because of history, extended family, and children; it is natural that there be unresolved personal, emotional problems due to the loss of the prior marriage; and it is natural that you realize navigating this isn't as easy as you thought it would be—the new love partner isn't a panacea.

It Often Does Come Down to a Choice

So many times I've heard the phrase, "I don't think I should have to choose," when a caller is complaining about someone their spouse doesn't get along with, isn't treated well by, or outright disdains. My answer: "Yes, my dear, sometimes you just have to make a choice."

"My sister and my husband do not get along at all. Although I care about my sister deeply, I only see her when my husband is not around. If there is a family function, such as a reunion or holiday, they are both adult enough to put their differences aside for the good of the family. I do not believe, as much as their personalities conflict, that either of them should be put in a situation where they have to bicker and argue.

"When it comes down to it, my sister and my husband do not make me choose a side to go on. They hate each other, but they don't expect me to hate either one. I would take my marriage in a second over my sister."

This listener letter demonstrates that there can be honor among enemies, and that she realizes that her ultimate loyalty is with her husband. That means, no, not for the sake of mommy's feelings make sure that everyone is always happy and getting along. Sometimes, that just can't work. Some personalities clash. At least they are being civil and not demanding that she go to war for either's sake.

If, for example, her sister were doing some of the horrible things I hear about, like making false reports of rape or child molestation against him, then it is clear, she must be completely eliminated from their lives.

Another listener, whose best friend was blatantly rude and mean to her fiancé, was asked by him not to invite the woman to their wedding.

"This upset me, because I considered her my friend. However, I agreed. Well, this terribly hurt her feelings, but I have to say it was the BEST thing I ever did. My husband means more to me than anything, and I am proud to say that 'I stood by my man!'"

If the criticisms and warnings of friends and family about your spouse are well-founded (physically violent, abusive of alcohol/drugs, blatant infidelities, destructive personality) you must contend with these truths—a head in the sand is a tush in the air. In general, the petty attitudes, and turf wars of your friends and families, their warped personality styles and ugly attitudes, must not be allowed to mess up your marriage.

You have to choose. You have to stand by your man/woman!

9

Stupid Mismatch

". . . Some advice my mother gave me:
'Don't date anyone you know you wouldn't want
to marry.
You never know whom you will fall in love
with.' "

—A (MALE) LISTENER

"One thing I have learned is that if you are determined to be stupid, no one can stop you!" writes a listener.

Why would anyone be determined to be stupid? First of all, the recognition of being "stupid" is largely hindsight. While in the midst of having some relationship or making a questionable relationship work, so many naïve and well-meaning to unhealthy and self-destructive motivations rule the day. Let's face it, once you make a decision, it's hard to let go of dreams, admit error, defeat, or failure, or accept that something you believed so great isn't. This is where all the armor of denial comes into play, as you use excuse after excuse to avoid recognizing the truth that needs to be faced for a healthy and happy life.

Two factors rule in not giving up a Stupid Mismatch. The

first is the fear that you are actually the problem: If you were different or better in some way he/she would be different. These self-doubts are powerful immobilizers. The second is the fact that breaking up is hard to do. All loss hurts and dumps us into an unknown. For too many of you, the ugly known is more appealing that the unknown. When I have helped people face the unknown, it is clear that most see it as a deep, black hole. I ask them to recognize that deep, black pits are exactly the foundation for planting a tree. It's all in the perspective.

Insta-Intimacy

"I have a son who was born out-of-wedlock. In fact, I only knew his father for eight weeks and got pregnant by error and then found out that his father has been arrested over twenty-five times for DUI's, driving on a suspended license, amphetamines, robbery, battery, and spousal abuse. He was even responsible for a DUI death of a girl he was dating while he was married. Surprise? He lied about everything.

"When I learned this man had been driving my new vehicle while on parole, I flipped, and broke it off at four weeks of pregnancy."

Even though she had the good sense to break off with him, it's far from over, and it probably will never be. Even from State Prison, he is filing suit to maintain rights to their son. In between his prison sentences, he harasses her at home and work. She is scared as well as physically and psychologically stressed out.

Is this an unusual situation? Actually, no. Because of the relaxed societal views about unmarried sex, too many men and women are getting insta-intimate, engaging their hearts, souls, psyches, and genitals in a situation that has not yet engaged their brains. The result is a constant flow of mismatched liaisons that lead to broken hearts, babies out-of-wedlock, sexually transmitted diseases, disappointments leading to hurt and a lack of trust in relationships in general, fearsome situations with threats of violence or worries about suicide, and embarrassment leading to more stupid decisions like marrying anyway and isolation to hide shameful situations.

It is true that one stupid decision tends to lead to another especially when you are desperate to deny reality ("This can't possibly be true") or try to transform an ugly reality into your dream ("With my love he/she will become what I should have picked/waited for in the first place").

One listener wrote to me about his experience of "not waiting":

"I broke one of your cardinal rules of dating and asked a woman to marry me after only six months of dating. I'm a forty-seven-year-old college-educated male and have been divorced over ten years. I've never shacked-up or remarried.

"My kids are grown, and I thought the time was right for remarriage. I met 'Ms. Right' six months ago. She was forty-four, intelligent, educated, affectionate, caring, of the same religion as me, and physically attractive. She said and did all the right things. We 'fell in love' within a month. Within four months we agreed to marry. She chose the engagement ring, and we picked a date. Sounds great, doesn't it?

"The day I was to give her the ring (three days before Christmas) she called and broke it off, saying she didn't want to get married or see me again. She refused all my requests for an explanation.

"It seems that I had overlooked the warning signs. I excused the facts that she had been married twice, had an abortion with her second husband whom she married six months after her first husband. She had been sexually involved with four men in the six years since her last divorce. It seems that she had broken up with all of them after six months of dating!

"I knew ALL THIS, and thought I was different and could change her life by being such a good guy. 'I'm not like the rest, Sweetie, I'm different and I'll save you emotionally!'

"Well now, after being dumped, I feel like an idiot for not seeing the signs. Dr. Laura, you were right. You NEED TIME to really get to know another person and watch for the warning signs."

Yeah, but he saw the warning signs. Unfortunately, that didn't stop him. Ill-placed hope is simply postponed disappointment.

Don't Have Sex Before You See the Whites of Their Eyes

Having sexual relations before any true relationship (read: marital commitment) is established is stupid behavior. When I talk to people about morality and G-d's Commandments, it is in the context of providing a view of rules as guardians, not oppressors. Religious proscriptions have the ultimate goal of preventing you from hurting yourself and/or others and to give you the purpose and motivation for a meaningful, joyous life.

The current ferocious cultural movement to disassemble the power and importance of religious motivation in behavior and decisions is frightening. If I weren't afraid of sounding too weird, I'd probably call it satanic. When, in 2001, young adult college students at SUNY at Albany can join a University-supported S&M Club, and their counterparts at Penn State can attend a Sex Faire complete with "pin the clitoris on the vagina" games, clearly the boundary between civility and perversion has been corrupted. In this milieu, it is understandable that young as well as mature people begin doubting their values and seeing their spiritual lives as perhaps downright silly.

Nonetheless, we must persevere. And sexual intimacy outside the realm of a marital husband-and-wife commitment leads generally to tragedy.

"I am thirty-two and just ended my second marriage. It had lasted two years and involved five children: his, mine, and ours. I was pregnant before we got married, poor judgment on both our parts. We fought a lot about the children. He abused my boys mentally and physically. Counseling went nowhere because he was not much of a talker. I found out, though, that he had a lot of stressors in his life. His mom came out of the closet, and he had numerous affairs on his first wife. He'd already had one on me.

"We married because I was pregnant, and we thought it was the honorable thing to do. Wrong. It has cost not only money, but irreversible pain and hurt in many innocent lives."

I remember a wonderful public service advertisement from a Christian organization that had a young male adult asking his grandfather about "Safe Sex." The grandfather's answer was to hold up his left hand and point to his wedding ring. "Safe" here doesn't only mean protection against herpes, AIDS, venereal warts, and so on, it means safe from misunderstandings, emotional hurts from rejection and loss, unplanned pregnancies (miscarriages, out-of-wedlock births, abortions), and the obvious confusion that comes from imagining that sexual intercourse, or even pregnancy, is a promise of true intimacy, love, or commitment.

When people, especially women, have sexual intercourse with a number of partners, their self-esteem suffers, which usually leads to even stupider choices in a match as they feel "less valuable." I know. I've gotten too many of those calls.

Promiscuity is, in and of itself, Stupid Mismatching since it brings together bodies and hopes without rational, meaningful foundation.

Newton's First Law of Physics

An object in motion tends to stay in motion unless another force impedes its progress. Unfortunately, when dealing with human endeavors, the opposing force isn't always good sense.

"I was involved in a mismatched relationship for five years. We were complete opposites, and I knew it from day one. I kept telling myself and even my partner that we needed to cut our losses and move on, but he was always so sorry and wanted to work on our issues together. I told him that he wasn't a bad person, just not the type of person I wanted to be with, but he kept insisting.

"It became a habit.

"I kept trying to break up with him, and then he would say he was sorry. By this time, I was so bitter and angry with myself for settling and with him for mistreating me. Well, I kept hoping he would change, but of course he didn't, things just got worse.

"Till one day, when he went to a boat show on a Saturday and never came home again. So, in the end I was hurt—but it is probably for the best, because now I can find the right match for me."

Habit. Momentum. This listener also wrote that she had completely lost respect for herself and for him, she felt unloved, she realized she was being mistreated, she was miserable, they'd have angry fights, and still, it went on until he left her! Now, on top of all that frustration and disappointment, was the hurt of rejection in spite of the fact that she ostensibly didn't want him.

It is that patterning which leads me to believe that it isn't going to be easy for her to find the "right match," since she sees her painful problems only from the perspective of the victim, and not the coperpetrator of her own misery.

Until you understand more deeply your own motivations for choosing and staying in a "bad" or "mismatched" relationship, the chances of your moving on to a healthier one are small. "Wherever you go, there you are," is one of those clichés that actually makes sense. Where you are and what you do when you're there is a measure of yourself, not of the circumstances. For many of you anxious to put the blame for your problems outside yourself, that's a bitter pill.

"How Would I Know What's a Good Match?"

It is true that familial and societal influences have an important impact on personal expectations. As one listener wrote:

"On a 'to do' list, my then future husband wrote the number one item was pot, then the bills he needed to pay from that week's paycheck. Two children later I divorced him. He still smokes marijuana to this day, and I have fatherless kids.

"I talk to them often about making better choices than I did and about the importance of two solid, loving parents. I partially attribute this to the fact that I came from a broken home with a mother who worked and whose interests lay more with boyfriends than with her children.

"I had and have little to no clue as to how a good male-female relationship should be. I'm still trying to gain some footing for the bad choice I made twenty-two years ago."

At least she's willing to admit that these were her choices, that they weren't good, and she takes responsibility for the problems they've wrought and what she owes her children now. With this openness, there is more hope that she'll find a better "match."

You Only Think It's a Mismatch

One of the most difficult and uncomfortable concepts for people to assimilate is that of "water seeking its own level." I get call after call from people complaining about their relative's, or friend's, rotten partner—without whom their relative or friend would be or do better. When I try to explain that their relative or friend picked and wishes to maintain that partner, they struggle against the notion. Instead, they go on about manipulations, situations, and machinations.

Why? Because without that perspective, there is little hope for their relationship with their relative or friend. If their loved one is charting his or her own course, they realize that there is no place for them on that journey, and that they can't really save that person. It's over.

One caller epitomized this truth:

"I am thirty-four, and I've been with my thirty-seven-year-old boyfriend for sixteen months. He's never been married, I've been divorced once. We have no kids."

"What can I help you with?"

"I told him the other night that I have decided I want to go into counseling. I have some issues with some insecurities and mistrust, and it's affecting my relationships."

"How?"

"Distrust in how he feels about me. Questioning if there is somebody else. Just insecurities."

"Is he behaving in a way which would lead any reasonable person to have mistrust?"

"Not really."

"Not really means yes, but not big. So tell me what the yes is."

"The yes is he gives me some mixed messages at times that are real conflicting."

"What does that mean in English?"

"Well, sometimes he will talk in regards to our future together and be real clear that he wants a future with me, and then the following week he tells me things like, well, maybe we're not meant to be together. Maybe we are fooling ourselves."

"Okay, let me ask you something before you start paying $200 for forty-five minutes of therapy. What you have described is flip-flopping. Why do *you* need to go to therapy for your insecurities when *he* flip-flops? Normal people react with insecurity when somebody keeps flip-flopping on them. That is a normal response. Now, what does your average, reasonable, normal person do when they are in a relationship with somebody who flip-flops constantly?"

"I would suppose get out of the relationship, but I don't really want to get out of the relationship. Let me be clear. I've done flip-flopping as well."

"And now you've found someone to do it with."

As the conversation progressed, the caller showed a deeper awareness of "wherever I go, there I am." She said that she didn't want to go into another relationship and do the same thing. She also revealed that he didn't want her to go into counseling. I explained that his reaction made total sense in that he was too afraid to face his own problems and weaknesses and realized that if she got healthy, she would no longer want to be in an unhealthy relationship. Unhealthy people match up with unhealthy people. Healthy people match up with healthy people. One of the unhealthy parties will always try to undermine the other's attempt to get healthy, because they don't want to be alone.

"So," I continued, "at the age of thirty-four, you have to look at your life and ask, 'Do I want to stay unhealthy to have him in my life—never get better, never have better, and to be tortured like this forever?' "

"No, absolutely not. It's unfortunate, but it makes sense. Because, in other areas he's got a lot to offer."

"That's nice. But, when people aren't stable, what they have to offer becomes useless. It's like a beautiful mahogany table where all the legs are different lengths. What value is that? So it's nice that he has good qualities. You do, too. But with respect to bonding, you are not healthy, right?"

"Right."

"Then you are going to have to let go of the security of him."

"That is absolutely true."

"And this point is the point at which most people fail. They don't let go. They don't get healthy."

Picture two people crouched down, side by side. One decides to stand up. The other can either stand up with the partner or pull the partner back down. Those are the only two ways they can function together. Beware the person who tries to pull you back down.

In spite of all unfortunate family influences and subsequent problems and inner turmoil, you are still the only one responsible and capable of deciding your course. As one listener reminds us:

"My husband and I were married for two years. During that time is when I realized what kind of character I wanted in a man—characteristics my husband didn't possess: ambition, strong spiritual leadership, self-motivation, enthusiasm for life, and love of children.

"I strongly suggest waiting to get married UNTIL YOU KNOW WHO YOU ARE. If you don't know who you are, how can you know what you will need in a husband and a father to your children?"

Too many of you are not thinking of life beyond the present moment. So much necessary growth, self-awareness, and maturity must take place before such an important decision as a life's mate can be made. It takes being on your own, making a place in the world for yourself, finding your own identity, and growing spiritually. That takes time and patience.

Without taking that time and having that patience, you may be trying to find yourself in someone else's problems.

The Fear Factor

"I married him because I was so terribly afraid. I was so scared of raising two children (one from a prior failed marriage and the other our son) all by myself. Fear is a powerful force, because it disrupts our perceptions and our rationale. I kept hoping that he would become what I wanted him to be. I was wrong about that, too," wrote a listener.

The man in question was an alcoholic, chronic liar, and had actually left her to run off for a time with another woman when she was five months pregnant with his child. Right after the wedding, though, he was back with not only that "honey," but others, too.

Her postscript was reassuring:

"It was not until after I left him that I found out I was fully capable of raising my children all by myself all along. I hadn't needed to drag myself and my children through all the heartache after all."

Though it is reassuring that she's finally copped to her own responsibility, it is sad that her children, like those of so many other folks ill-equipped to take on responsibility for even themselves, will still have to pay the price.

Her story is not unusual. If there is one predominant theme for people expressing the reasons for their "Stupid Mismatches," it is fear:

"My husband is a wonderful man, but I married him more out of my fear of not being able to take care of myself rather than my love for him and a life we can build together. I got married for what I thought was security. I have the home, the cars, and various other toys, but I don't have my own self-respect."

Other Stories:

➤   *"I hung on to that relationship because I didn't think I was good enough for anyone else. At times I feel angry and bitter for the bad experiences that I had and the way I was treated. One day I came to the realization that I was guilty, too. I held on to that relationship until I felt strong enough to get on with my life. When I finally realized that I was good enough and that someone else would love me, I could let go. My life is completely turned around."*

➤   *"I have had a boyfriend since I was fifteen years old. One right after the other, I just couldn't be alone. I started dating an older man. Within three months, I learned that he was emotionally unstable, verbally abusive, and an alcoholic. I was terrified of him. Why did I date him? I didn't want to be alone. I didn't think I'd ever meet anyone. These were reasons that ran through my head so I settled for what was available.*

"The one good thing that came out of that relationship was that I actually stopped trying to find a man and started trying to find myself. I slowly became comfortable being alone. My Stupid Mismatch came from a fear of being alone or unwanted. I found myself."

It is disheartening to read so many pained letters from men and women who grabbed at relationships as a drowning man might grab for a straw. It is sad to hear from so many people who equate being wanted by someone, regardless of their qualities, with their own self-esteem.

As one listener wrote:

"It is true that self-esteem comes from accomplishing goals. To this day I keep adding things and goals to my life that validate who I am. I no longer need someone else to do that for me."

Good! Because, that's the only way self-esteem can be gained—through the "self." Or else it would be called other-esteem.

Love Is NOT Enough

It drives me absolutely crazy when callers, describing the disgusting, horrendous, destructive, immoral, cruel, stupid, and downright evil behavior of a husband/wife or boyfriend/girlfriend, ultimately pacify themselves with those four fateful words: "But I love him/her." Yikes! One of my listeners wrote to me to describe her four-year boyfriend as not giving her a ring, but hinting about a future, as not bonding with her children, as mean to her kids, as flirtatious with younger women and as one who double-dates with his twenty-four-year-old daughter's married friends, with his daughter as his "date." She then wrote:

"If this sounds like my problem, I really want to know. I had a very bad marriage and can be needy, despite my independence. Like my son, I am also very emotional and easily hurt. As I am not getting any younger, I am thinking that it may be time to move on. But when I think of losing him, I get very sad.

"I thought we were the loves of each others' lives. Now I'm not so sure if that's enough."

If I had her on the radio program, I'd ask her what in heaven's name he was actually *doing* that gave her the impression that she was the love of his life? And, I would want to know what in heaven's name she thought love was? Love is not about infatuation and lust. While emotional and physical passion are a part of love, infatuation and lust are not about the object, they reveal more about the subject. With infatuation and lust as the basis of your attraction to someone, when you get to know the real person, you become more disillusioned than with a love that grows slowly. The love that grows when lust and infatuation are controlled, is the love that grows of respect, awe, admiration, and trust, and is the love the lasts through all four seasons.

There is no "love at first sight," there is only sexual attraction and the romantic projections of our fantasies. There is no love where there is fear. There is no love where there is no emotional health or ability to communicate about emotional and practical issues. There is only desperate attachment. I work very hard to get folks to recognize that their desperate attachments are cementing them into destructive relationships, and to get them to stop using "love" as their rationalization for tolerating what they shouldn't, and to change what they should.

Recently, I had a talk with a Hassidic Jew about the formalities of dating in their community. He spoke with a glowing appreciation of the specialness of women, of love, of marriage, and of family. He related that Hassidim do not date until they are ready for marriage. Hassidim do not have any physical contact until after the wedding—and that includes holding hands. Hassidim spend hours upon weeks upon months, talking about all the realities of life, their feelings, joys, perspectives, plans, and goals, they meet each other's families and become close, and then they decide if it's a match.

I went to such a wedding. I have never been more moved by the meaningfulness and beauty of a wedding. These two really knew one another, they were totally supported by extended families and their community, and they believed that their union was a blessing to G-d.

Neither of them had past sexual relationships, abortions, or hurt feelings from failed marriages that so often lead to a cynicism or crassness in relationships. Since their relationship was not sexual, they were not distracted by mistaken notions that sex and love were the same thing. Their attraction to each other was strong, but determined to be made even more joyous and meaningful through marriage.

My point is that sexual passion and desperate attachments lead people to believe that they are in love, and that love can conquer all. These are two dangerously wrong beliefs.

"The first time, yes, we were young, and I was obsessed with, not in love with, him. The second time, ten years later, we realized we were in love, but there were other considerations—were we of the same religion, morals, beliefs, money thoughts, child-rearing thoughts, and a lot more? We spent about two years after he asked me to marry him figuring these things out and THEN I got a ring and we set a date and were married within six months in the most spiritual ceremony I could have imagined.

"Also, since we are of the same thoughts in so many ways, and we are both moral people, divorce is NOT an option, so we work out all of our problems. We don't fight or get nasty. We disagree and then we come to an agreement or understanding. No one wins or loses."

Clearly this listener was willing to grow into love, not assume its existence through passion, and was wise enough to realize that commonality in attitudes, goals, and morals is the Safe Marriage prophylactic that would truly make a difference in the quality of their lives and relationship.

I particularly enjoyed a letter I got from a twenty-seven-year-old divorced man who said that he and his first wife thought that *"Love would pay the bills and wash the dishes for us.*

"We had some pretty serious problems. I recognized that, but was too weak and wimpy to do anything drastic enough to do any good. A week before the wedding, we had a huge blow-up type fight about some basic differences in our philosophies of living. At one point, I suggested that we postpone the wedding. To which she replied that A) we would never get married, B) everybody has come to town already, C) we can't get the money back from the reception hall.

"We went into counseling. I knew that I either had to conform

to her notions and play dead, or be myself and live up to my potential, and that meant leaving. I was out of there.

"One of my main thoughts was from a question I read in your book Ten Stupid Things Men Do to Mess Up Their Lives, which was, 'Do I want this woman to be the mother of my eighty-nine children?' I know, Dr. Laura, that I should have asked that question and many others just like it before I ever asked her to marry me. I now look at dating in a whole different light."

In conclusion are the tips about the "questions to ask while you're dating" submitted by a listener who learned the hard way from her first Stupid Mismatched marriage:

➤   "If you do want to marry (again), learn to share control.

➤   You have to like, respect, even love yourself (not in a prideful way) before you can share with someone else. Get over all your hurts before going into another relationship.

➤   Do not marry someone whose family hates you or whom your family hates. You marry the family, too—and it's hell.

➤   If you have to justify why you're with that person, especially when there are red flags flying everywhere, he/she is not the one! You don't love 'em. You love having someone around.

➤   Don't sleep with the person before you marry. You CAN wait and it's more rewarding.

➤   Wait until you are in your late twenties or early thirties to get married. Travel, work, do things in groups, and have fun. Then there is never the excuse, 'I never experienced life,' or the blame, 'You kept me back from the things I wanted to do.' Also, you learn more about yourself and about life if you take the time to grow up.

➤   *Be able to support yourself and live by yourself for a while before you commit yourself for life to someone else. Then you know you're not desperate.*

➤   *If you are divorced and have children, wait to get remarried after the children are grown up. Concentrate on the children. They want and need at least one of the parents committed to them."*

Surviving the Stupid Mismatch

It is possible to get through life with someone with whom you are a Stupid Mismatch. Sometimes you might both grow and change in healthy ways that bring you closer together. Sometimes you will simply learn to accept the differences, cooperate in ways that limit conflict (like division of labor), and learn to enjoy the companionship, shared history, and good moments.

Other times, the ultimate loneliness that comes from the disconnect, which is a natural part of a Mismatch, brings challenges.

"They say that opposites attract. We sure did. We love each other, but that's about it. My husband is a devoted sports enthusiast. He coaches, trains, educates, and socializes in the world of sports. I feel out of place in his world. After occupying my first twenty-five years raising our kids, I'm finding we don't have much in common and I don't know how to meet him at his level. He isn't interested in the couples that I enjoy socializing with. Now that we're both about ready to retire, I'm wondering what the heck we'll do with each other!"

In these circumstances, where the Mismatch is not about unhealthy or destructive behaviors per se, I generally suggest that the more malleable of the two simply involve him- or herself in the activities of the other, period. That means this woman should go to the games her husband coaches, and hang out with his friends, and even learn to play some sport with him—like golf. Sometimes, after they get over the feeling of "giving in," people discover that they just haven't tried to expand their own horizons enough, and that they really do enjoy some aspects of the activities. Even more, they enjoy the closeness to their spouse. And, as often happens, the other less malleable spouse often feels more motivated to do the same.

Admit It, You Saw Those Ugly Red Flags

There have been times when a caller has tried to convince me that they didn't see the red flags. Once I pound on them, generally they retreat to, "Well, it wasn't so bad," or "They said they'd change," or "I thought I would be the 'perfect match' for him/her, and all would be well."

Callers admit to making excuses for drinking, violence, and various other ugly behaviors for many reasons. They don't want to be embarrassed by a(nother) marital failure; feel responsible for the problems ("You make me hit you/have an affair/drink"); believe that they're fat, ugly, and/or stupid and can't get anyone else or better; believe their love will change him/her and then they will earn his/her undying gratitude by loving him/her the way they wanted to be loved; their hormones have the better of them, besides which he/she is so good-looking and charming and so forth.

As one listener wrote:

"I was the idiot who came up with excuses to justify it all. I wasted my time sitting up half the night trying to think of ways to change him. I was the one who betrayed my faith. I was the one who almost turned my back on my own dreams."

You can't help being incredibly impressed by the folks who steel themselves and move on—some before marriage and children, others, sadly, only afterward. Where there is a profound Mismatch in fundamental values, attitudes, expectations, goals, morals, and spirituality, a healthy marriage and family will not grow. All differences are not compatible, in spite of the fact that some degree of opposites attract from a need to complete an incomplete self, yearning for its other side—as when an introvert is drawn to someone outgoing.

As one listener wisely wrote:

"A fish and a bird can fall in love, but where will they live?" We live in the details, not in the "what might be." We must have the courage and wisdom to face those details if we are to have a good life and provide one for our spouse and our children.

"My boyfriend of a year and a half, I love sooo much. I could marry him, but we believe in two totally different religions. I tried to ignore that fact for a while, but I finally realized that it would never work unless one of us converted to the other religion. I most definitely was not going to. This hurt so much, but it was the only way."

She was right. One of the most joyous bonding elements of a marriage, and for a family, is a mutually embraced spiritual life as a family worships together. People often underestimate the impact of an unshared religious life until they have children. Then, the Holy Wars begin.

I always tell people on my radio program, that there is the good news and the bad news about giving up someone who is a Stupid Mismatch. The good news is that you're freed up to do something healthy. The bad news is that it hurts for a while. It would seem that the bad news outweighs the good news most of the time. It is sad how many people can't sustain themselves through the painful, hurtful, difficult period of transition. Rather than set the focus on what will be possible, they set their focus on the now, the loss, the pain, and the disappointment. This leads straight to finding a way out of the pain. This leads straight to self-doubts ("If it's *me*, then I shouldn't leave him/her"), and excuses ("If it weren't for the drinking/job/sprained ankle, he/she wouldn't be doing this and that"), and finally what I call "noble-ization" as the best rationalization of them all ("I shouldn't think only of my happiness, I am hurting his/her feelings by judging/leaving him or her").

Don't go there. Surround yourself with wise loved ones, both friend and family, pray, talk to a secular counselor, see your clergyman, call my show! Or else this listener will be speaking for you:

"But ignoring those red flags got me only bruises and humiliation. It took away my personality and individuality. I had no opinions. The square peg (me) did not fit in the round hole, so I tried to change the shape to make it fit."

It is ironic that she used the round and square imagery to denote a mismatch, because another listener suggests that marriage and family life is only for "round" people, because:

"It's a circle of love. People who drink, lie, and cheat, who aren't emotionally healthy, kind, and compassionate, are the 'square pegs.' Thus, you can't make them your spouse without it being a very painful mismatch."

The moral of this section is to be "round" and find other such "round" folks to be your friends, and definitely your spouse.

Too Young, Too Foolish, Too Needy

Whenever callers tell me they're getting married, my first question is, "How old are you?" My second question is, "How old is he/she?" If those two numbers are too disparate or their sum is less than "fifty" I groan, grunt, and generally make rude noises of disapproval.

When callers tell me, after years of torture, disappointment, and anguish in really bad marriages, that they know they married too young, and wish they would have spoken to me all those years ago, I usually answer, "Yeah, but would you have listened to me when I said you were marrying too young?" "No," is the honest and typical response.

In a controlled environment where everyone knows everybody and everybody married early after parents researched, selected, and advised about a partner, where fidelity, commitment, and "till death do us part" is the norm, where expectations are modest and responsibilities taken seriously, there may hardly be a "too young" to marry.

Most of the world is not such a controlled environment. Most neighborhoods are amazingly fluid, the divorce-move-away-remarry-divorce rate is very high, shack-ups (temporary nesting) are the norm, children are born into nonexistent families, and the general expectation drilled into each person is maximum personal gratification. In this environment, there is definitely a "too young" to marry.

Why? Because there are so few shared strong values. Because there is so much anonymity. Because there is so much social stress. Because there is so little family and community for a proper, healthy education and so few role models of mature, responsible, stable relationships.

With social sexual norms at an all-time low, the easy investment of emotion and physicality misleads young people into believing they are experiencing something valuable, when they are not, and that they are experiencing something valuable with others who are valuable, when they are not.

"What did I do to mess up my relationship? I made commitments that I was too young to make. I failed to see the flaws that haunt our relationship today. I failed to heed advice that I received when I could still act on it. I failed to assess my personal strengths and weaknesses when I made decisions. Hindsight is 20/20, but I

should have asked for glasses when I was young—and not the rose-colored variety," writes a much sobered listener.

The mentality of a young person is generally largely unformed, too simplistic, coated with insecurities and ignorance, and steeped in fantasies and nonobjective thinking:

"Like most young men, when choosing a prospective wife, I only cared if she was attractive, and said she was attracted to me. Subsequently, I married at nineteen to a pretty girl with a great figure who was twenty-one, 'cause she liked me. I did not look at her past tendencies, such as she slept around and already had a kid out-of-wedlock that she gave up for adoption, or that none of her relationships lasted because she was vain and only cared about getting her needs met. Just 'cause someone is attracted to you and says they love you is NOT enough qualities to marry someone. I learned it all the hard way at my kids' expense."

Young people, seventeen to almost twenty-five, are at a stage in their lives when they are just beginning to be adults and are just starting to develop a unique, autonomous self. It is a difficult time, emotionally challenging, and somewhat frightening. It is not unusual to find both young men and women hurrying into relationships to find instant adulthood, maturity, security, and stability:

"Basically, I was too young and too immature to be patient to find the right man for me."

"I knew this man I was to marry was not a match for me. I was warned by parents, family, and friends. I carried on with the wedding out of Stupid Rebellion."

"When a person marries young, they have no way of judging their partner's attributes as compared to others. There just isn't enough experience for that. Youths take people at face value, and think only about the present. At age eighteen, that's what I did."

So many of the regretful testimonials I receive from people admit that the main problem of their Stupid Mismatch was the natural immaturity of youth.

It is natural to want to be loved, to want to have someone dear, to want to feel grown up and established, and to want to feel secure. When young people are virtually saturated with a media and social culture that glorifies attachments, no matter how superficial or fleeting, it is not surprising that they, in their innocence, want a piece of that action.

I have been sadly surprised by how many young men (and older, for that matter) have no sense of what it is to be a "man" anymore. I can't tell you how much disdain I have heaped on young men who call me, who marry before they have jobs, while they have debt, and with expectations of their wives working (dumping kids in day care) so that they can have the luxuries with which they were brought up or believe they should have "now." They tell me they'll be living in their parents' basement or supported by their in-laws.

I tell them that there was a time that defined manhood, and that it isn't now, by a man's ability and willingness to take on responsibility and prepare himself for his obligations. Now, all he's got to do is "find him a woman"!

Yes, there is a "too-young," and it generally leads to a Stupid Mismatch specifically because it is a carnival game of shooting at the first target that comes across, or the one that titillates for all the wrong reasons:

"First off, I married too young, which is the first mistake. Ask any seventeen-year-old and they will say they know it all, especially in the matters of love. But love was really lust. Things I was aware of, I chose to ignore as irrelevant. But the problems in my marriage today are a direct result of looking away from the problems in the beginning."

I am always impressed when people are open to admitting their weaknesses, because it is only in that assessment that you can begin to know where you have to work on yourself to build strength:

"Neither of us were ready emotionally—I didn't know how to

respect myself and share my perspective on what was right in a relationship; he didn't treat our friendship like it was anything important. Most important mismatch: I was a wanna-be-strong Christian, and he could've cared less. I didn't respect myself enough to end things, because I liked the 'security' of having a 'boyfriend.' "

In a prior era, where such realizations were countered with the realization that vows are commitments, people would strive to persevere and work through problems. In our disposable tissue culture, the same is not true. Serially broken hearts, marriages, and children's homes are now the more typical result.

As one listener, now much wiser, advises:

"I would advise young women to date men very close to their age, refuse to have a sexual relationship until after they are married, meet friends of the men they date, get to know the family, and establish trust before investing too many emotions into a relationship. Otherwise, what you allow yourself to fall into is a false sense of security."

Wise words.

Too Old and Too Foolish

At the other end of the spectrum is the older man or woman who wants to deny the inevitability of the life cycle:

"I got involved with a younger woman, twenty-seven years younger than me. At first it was great and, of course, I was walking on cloud nine. Then, it hit me (after three years!) that I had no one to talk with who understood the things I was talking about. I was constantly supporting her ego and providing the support that she needed. I did not receive this from her, and it was many days that I would look at her, and wish I had someone who knew what I was talking about."

I couldn't summarize the main point of Stupid Mismatch better than that: "someone who knows what you're talking about." Whether it's children, religion, politics, sex, hobbies, love, family, morality, or decorating the living room, you need to make sure you're with someone who knows what you're talking about. It's not that you always have to agree. It is that you both have to understand, care, have compassion, be willing to compromise, determine to put the relationship first, admire each other's basic qualities, support each other's strong side, help with each other's weaker side, fix your own inadequacies, take responsibility for your actions, and respect your vows as sanctified by G-d.

10

Stupid Breakups

> *"I broke up with a guy once for snoring while watching TV. Now, I didn't tell him why—I just said I wanted to be friends.*
>
> *I also have had a guy with bad breath. That one I told why."*
>
> —A LISTENER

Another listener wrote to me about having asked her husband why, after twelve years and two children, he left her for another woman.

"He said he had to think about it. Two days later he called back to tell me his answer. He said, and I quote, 'I always wanted you to go to my mom's house and learn how to make jam, but you never did.' I was dumbfounded. All of this because I never learned how to can fruit? I said to him, 'Oh, okay . . . well, thanks.' I hung up the phone and sat there for a few minutes. Then it hit me. All of this was not because of the me that I was. It was because of the him that he was. It gave me a great tool in getting the closure I needed. There was no abuse in the marriage, no arguments . . . just not enough 'jam.' "
We'll never know if he meant that figuratively or literally; probably a bit 'o both.

Fortunately, I don't get many such calls, e-mails or letters from folks whose reasons for breaking up sound quite that stupid, but I am deeply concerned by the growing number of unnecessary and unwarranted relationship breakups based on "modern" notions of rights and happiness.

About two-thirds of divorces currently are sought by women, and my male callers tell me that their wives left because of "growing apart," "not happy," "feeling underappreciated," "needs not being met," "differences in changing goals or lifestyle," "boredom," and the old favorite, "find myself."

It is important to note that violence, drug and alcohol abuse, neglect and abandonment, and promiscuous infidelity, which used to be the areas of complaint that women had about their husbands, are rarely the motivation for the wife to call it quits. In fact, it is usually the opposite. Some women seem willing to be more patient with these behaviors than to sustain themselves through the growth and effort needed for the maintenance and nurturance of a marriage when the only issue is moon spots or boredom.

I *dis*-credit feminism for this sad and sorry, embarrassing development in gender relations. Remember Gloria Steinem's proclamation that, "A woman without a man is like a fish without a bicycle"? What the heck was that about? Feminists have emphasized men as the "evil empire," oppressing their women with sex (one other prominent feminist called all sex "rape"), child-bearing and child-rearing (that's being remedied by abortions, day care, and surrogate mothering), and marriage itself (subservient, second-class citizenry). When women become "enlighted," they leave. To what?

One listener, a grandmother and recovered feminist wrote to me:

"Back in the seventies, I read The Feminine Mystique, *about*

the housewife's 'problem with no name.' I promptly left my husband all three beautiful daughters and went back to college looking for that elusive 'something' that would make me whole.

"Raised in the 'Birthplace of Women's Rights,' I quickly became a vocal feminist. It took me years to figure out what a sham the women's rights movement really is. The horrific results are all around us. The goal of feminists was, and is, destruction of the family. To that end, they have been very successful.

"I'm a grandmother now, and I try every day to correct the wrongs I've committed on my children."

Every so often I find myself going on a tear on my radio program about this very issue. I rant about the obvious negative impact on women, not to mention men, children, and society, by the warped notions of what feminists support. How does aborting babies from their bodies for reasons no more important than timing elevate a woman's consciousness? How does shacking-up with some guy(s), becoming sexually intimate in a noncommitted relationship, elevate a woman's spirituality? How does having babies out-of-wedlock, with the concomitant problems with poverty, child care, and isolation elevate a woman's status? Obviously, it doesn't. And, as I've asked time and again on my radio program, "How have you women allowed such a stupid philosophy to destroy your lives, and that of your children and society?"

Another listener wrote in with her complaint about the warnings she got from her liberal, feminist, college friends about what kind of a man she should avoid. She now believes that by listening to that, she jumped right into Stupid Breakups:

"When I was a senior in college I decided to break off my relationship with my boyfriend of two years. He was an intelligent, affectionate, religious man, who had a promising career as an attorney ahead of him and a deep, loving relationship

with his parents and five siblings. He expressed to me a desire to marry and assured me that when we had children, I would not have to work and would be able to raise our children at home.

"I was mortified! Appalled! He thinks women should stay home and raise their kids! 'What a jerk!' I explained to my equally liberal, feminist friends. Of course, they agreed. 'What year does he think this is! It's men like that who keep us down!,' one friend said.

"Well, I broke it off with him and made a 'better choice,' according to my friend. A twenty-nine-year-old college senior, with a drinking problem, who smoked, covered in shall-we-say body art, and a shaved head. He lived at home and, of course, had no job and no money."

According to her letter, her father went out and bought her my first book, *Ten Stupid Things Women Do to Mess Up Their Lives*, and is happy to report that her eyes are now open, and she is married to a wonderful man (with a job and no body art). One of the main issues of that book was my restating the obvious, which is that women want love, attachment, family, and children. Though choosing to have a major career instead is a reasonable, personal choice for some women, diminishing the value of motherhood and marriage by outright denial and attack or by relegating them to the edge of a woman's more important worker existence is cruel, because it denies the basic psychological and biological truth of women to bond and nurture; and that of men to provide and protect.

Be Wary!

Young women, brought up on all this feminist propaganda, are wary about marriage. Young men, brought up on all this feminist propaganda, are wary about women. Try being a young man in college these days, exposed to the feminist dominated reeducation process going on under the guise of neutral academics in courses in psychology, sociology, and even history! I have had innumerable men write to me about their growing fears in being able to find a nice girl who will get married and not soon after walk away with his kids and his home.

Men and women are being programmed to be wary and be careful about not getting used. Unfortunately, for too many folks, having to provide for his family, or having to raise children, is now being viewed as in that category of "being used."

In addition to the destructiveness of feminism has been the overall shifting of a society from the nobility of obligations and commitments to an emphasis on rights without a balanced emphasis on "responsibilities." Without a firm sense of responsibility to others and their needs and rights, we are a group of neurotic ants, each with our own selfish mission—and you can pretty well visualize that state of chaos!

This listener certainly could:

"There was a time I let the word divorce *into my vocabulary, and once you say it, it becomes a part of you and suddenly it consumes you. I was very close to divorce, and I was sure I no longer loved my husband. All I could think of was ME, and what I deserved, and everything I gave to him was attached to the condition that I get something in return. I am not sure that is the reason it wasn't returned—no one likes to receive with expectations. Every moment at home, all I did was complain of not having enough. I spent so much time wondering what was in it for me, that I didn't see just how much I already had! Lose yourself in SERVICE, and it is then that you will find yourself."*

Bow to the All-Important MEEE!

Face it, it's a fact, you cannot have in life, or from another person, all that you imagine you should, could, or would. Real life simply has more texture than that. Additionally, can you really imagine being all of what another person imagines they should, could, or would have? No, of course not. Spending one's time in coveting is to lose the moment of appreciation of what you do have—which generally includes many blessings and advantages. For example, though my husband can't dance to save his life (something I've always loved to do), he would give his life to save mine or our son's. Somehow, I think that's a pretty good trade-off. And, I'll bet, you could look at your relationship in the same way, once you threw away the notion that G-d put you here to gratify every desire or fantasy that plunked into your awareness.

It's that ugly movement toward self-fulfillment, with its protection of the self against the "destructive" needs of another, be it spouse or children, that has caused the largest number of Stupid Breakups.

"I believe in thinking about yourself before others—but only to an extent. If you are in a relationship it is your right to take care of yourself and put yourself before the relationship . . . but not selfishly."

Oh yeah? How do you figure that?

"For example," she continued, *"I am a college student and I will always put my education before my relationship, because it is the education that I will have forever, the guy might not be there forever."*

Now, why might the guy not be there forever? Death in the service of his country? Death by natural causes? Probably not what she is thinking. She's probably thinking about how many of her closest friends and relatives have been in and out, in and out, in and out, of various pseudo-commitments and she is worried.

As another listener wrote:

"I have talked to many of my friends whose parents are divorced. They tell me they feel personally flawed because the legacy of their parents' divorce scars them in some way that says they are part of a lineage of people who can't follow through, are capable of making huge mistakes, and who walk out when things get tough. They all doubt their ability to spot and maintain love, because they see that their parents thought they were in love, and it didn't 'work out' for them."

Interestingly, this letter was written by a young woman who says that she is part of an unusual and unfortunately small segment of the public in which her parents are still married—yet, by today's reckoning, should have been divorced.

"Did the fighting, yelling, un-child centered living make me a little neurotic and make it hard for me to become a well-adjusted adult? Yes! But one thing I could always hold on to was that my parents never divorced. I had to work through a lot of bad habits and personality flaws, but I never doubted that I would be able to be committed to someone, that I could carry though with a promise, or that I would ever marry until I was completely ready. I know my parents were not in love for most of their married life, and yet they still stayed in it. Did I see my mom as a wimp? No way. She is the strongest person I know, and I admire her greatly. My dad has had my respect from day one."

The argument is often made, in cases like this listener, that all she has learned is how to have a bad relationship. Wrong. She doesn't want the same marriage her parents had in terms of how they behaved toward each other, but she does want the same marriage, in terms of the ultimate commitment they had to family and to vows.

Ideally, they would have used their determination to commitment to improve their behavior, or become more compassionate about each other's shortcomings. Though that is not the ultimate point of commitment, it is the ultimate opportunity within commitment.

People Need to Work Harder at Marriage

One of the reasons I keep reminding people that "love is not enough" for a quality marriage is that emotions are labile, vulnerable, situational, unpredictable, and without an IQ. Commitment and respect for vows, promises, obligations, and tradition are much more worthy and predictable building blocks for a good relationship. You may get your "jollies" fantasizing about some movie star or neighbor, but nothing fills your heart with deeper affection (and perhaps passion) than watching the tenderness of your spouse with the children, having your spouse be compassionate and noncombative when you're in a mood, or having your spouse be solicitous when you feel (and look) like garbage.

If you really think there is anyone who can sustain a happy, fulfilled state all the time, you're wrong. You're also wrong if you think there is some one person out there with whom you certainly would sustain a perpetual happy, fulfilled state. You're also wrong if you think that the best of relationships don't go through stages, and phases, and problems, some seemingly insurmountable:

"My Stupid Breakup was from my second marriage. I was 'unhappy.' I've been married three times. My Priest finally explained the five Stages of Marriage to me. Stage 1: Falling in love. Stage 2: Discovering the foibles, faults, etc. Stage 3: Deciding what to do about this new knowledge. Stage 4: (If you reach it) Is the hard work involved in getting through the realities of Stage 2. Stage 5: Is the glorious falling in love at a whole new level of intimacy and commitment.

"A light went on! Now I know that when the going got tough, I got going. WOW! What a revelation. The stupid comes in when I consider the harm to my children and the pain I caused my ex-spouse. If we had known that relationships go through these stages, I think we would have been able to work through the problems."

I believe that millions of people would be able to work through their problems if they had that knowledge and support from their families, friends, and society at large. Unfortunately, there have been studies showing that even the so-called Marriage Education courses at high schools and colleges, according to current research, are negative and hostile to the institution. Ironically, those who are married are happier, healthier, and wealthier. Go figure.

In most cases, couples don't try hard enough to stay together. They don't talk about the problems, try to identify the issues, or work them out. And they don't take the time to remember what made them fall in love with each other. One listener added:

"I believe that most divorces are caused by materialism. In a way, our society is becoming corrupted by materialism. There is competition about having the best car, the biggest house, the nicest clothes—but no one seems to care about having the closest family, the most dinners together as a family, and ongoing friendships with family members."

I have written in many of my books, and reminded people on my radio program, that though divorce has been used as the easy way out of the challenges of marriage and family, the three A's—addiction, adultery, and abuse—justify divorce as a valid consideration. Nonetheless, that doesn't mean that there is never a way back from even these travesties and tragedies.

One listener wrote to me of her alcoholism and her loss of faith in marriage, G-d, and herself. She spent a year in AA, with a growing realization that she might lose her daughter.

"I knew that I did not have feelings of love for my husband, so it was a big struggle, and I knew the only way to get the feelings back,

was to have faith, pray, go to church, and get help. It was not easy, and there were times where I wanted to give up, because it is very hard living with someone you do not love, but I knew G-d wanted us to make it work. If I could just keep the faith in G-d, I knew he would give me my feelings back for my husband, and He did, indeed. We now have a five-month-old son, and we are very happy."

She went on to say that she is disgusted with what she put her daughter through and believes that parents should think more about their children than themselves and the world would be a better place. That means making your marriage work—and it does take work!

When there are terrible problems, like the three A's, it becomes a major challenge to consider whether or not to stay. When there is repentance (responsibility taken, true remorse, behaviors to repair and not repeat), there is hope. When there is no repentance, the hope is just postponed disappointment.

One listener wrote that he was still hopeful in spite of his wife's continued shack-up affair and her abandonment of the children, whom he raises alone,

"I think that people give up too easily on marriage when love, understanding, and forgiveness can help your partner remember what it was that caused them to commit to you in the first place. . . . Giving up on a marriage without attempting to prove your love and worth is a stupid reason for a breakup."

I wish him well, although reuniting with a woman who would abandon her children is nothing I can get too excited about.

I'm Finding Myself

I'm always amused by this expression, "I have to find myself." First, there is the notion of being somewhere other than where you are (some kind of cosmic lost-and-found), then there is the idea that you can't find yourself under the present circumstances of marriage and children, and finally there is the epiphany that you can't simply find yourself in the bed of someone new.

Truly, you find yourself in your commitments; you find yourself in the eyes of people who depend on you; you find yourself in your noble responses to life's challenges; you find yourself in your actions and decisions; you find yourself right where you are now.

This notion of "finding oneself" is an intellectually dishonest approach to frustration, a pouty reaction to obligations and routine, and a bratty manipulation of another's compassion and understanding.

"I dated a guy for two and a half years in college and found my true love in him. He was and is everything that I could ever want from a man. I knew in my heart that he would be a decent husband and father. A few weeks after I returned from a study-abroad trip through our school, I called off the relationship, because I felt I needed to find myself as an individual. That was the worst decision of my life. I will forever regret that breakup," writes a listener.

Why does finding oneself as an individual seem to imply that you must unload significant people from your life like your spouse, boy/girl friend, and/or parents? The answer is that the most immature part of yourself has reverted back to infanthood—wanting to be the center of the universe without obligations: You get to have, you don't have to give.

With that attitude, you will either end up alone, or with superficial escapades, and regrets for a Stupid Breakup.

Don't lie to yourself or anyone else. When you feel like it's time to get going, stay put and face whatever it is that worries or frightens you.

Welcome to Fantasy Land

What must you be thinking when you put a fantasy aside your reality and believe that the fantasy will have more depth, longevity, satisfaction, respect, promise, and meaning? The answer is that you don't think—you just imagine.

One of the newest and most destructive forces on marriage today is the Internet. Cyber-affairs are costing too many children and innocent spouses the warmth and comfort of an intact home. Both men and women are carrying on in chatrooms and develop "feelings" sufficient to propel them out of their homes and families to be with someone they "know will be everything that's missing in their lives." Everything, of course, other than a brain!

"My wife and I have been married for twenty-seven years. I thought we had a good relationship. We have had our problems, but we always seemed to work them out. To make a long story short, I bought my wife a computer two years ago, and it seemed to make her happy, because she always said she was bored. She had fun in the chatrooms, flirting and having a good time. I thought it was harmless. But, as time went on she spent more and more time on the computer. Well, seven months ago I found out that she is in love with a man that lives eleven hours away from her, whom she's never met. She lies in her bed and cries for him. She still talks to him every day and tells him she really loves him and is going to marry him.

"I love this lady with all my heart. I really don't know what to do. I know in my heart she still loves him—she tells him all the things she once told me."

I mean, really, how insensitive and cruel can one be to someone she once thought she couldn't live without? And why is anyone bored? The answer is, only because he or she is boring. Bored people rarely think of anything or anyone besides themselves and being entertained, thrilled, titillated, excited, distracted, or being the center of attention.

When people call and tell me that they're bored in their lives, or bored in their marriage, I jump on them to admit that they don't do anything to add to the well-being of themselves or their family—they just want to feel a certain feeling and, in that laziness, think that there is just some other guy or gal who'll just make it happen. Good luck.

The Grass Is Greener

"I left my husband of five years for a much younger man, hoping that the spice would reenter my life. WRONG!!! I thought I could find happiness in someone else. WRONG!!! I left my husband and hurt my three children very badly. Nine months later I realized that a lot of things were wrong . . . but with ME. I had just turned thirty, went back to work full-time, exhausted from the kids, and wanted out, yet realizing that what I was feeling was totally normal, and by leaving my husband the stress was still there because it was me!!!

"I strongly urge people to get help for themselves first and take some accountability for their actions and stay AWAY from temptation because now I realize I may have lost the best husband and father in the world all because of my self-centeredness."

This listener hit the main point of my argument, which is that when you imagine improving your life by simple demolition is to miss the truth. The truth is that you are largely the architect of the quality of your life. Therefore, begin first with renovation—of yourself: your attitudes, your reactions, your expectations, and your actions. Only then can you hope to have any credibility or power in your determination to make improvements in your relationship, marriage, and family.

Another important issue brought up by this listener, is the idea of avoiding temptation. Unfortunately, between the Internet and the workplace, a lot of temptation presents itself.

"I thought I had to go to work to get a life and get away from the kids. The money was nice, but it only caused me to feel I didn't need my husband anymore. I divorced my husband."

Well, nothing but bad things followed. At work she got lots of attention from men, and liked it. As she started to become more aware, she began to appreciate that her husband was faithful and considerate. She ended up marrying some guy who molested two of her three children. After two decades of therapy for her children and herself, she reports that they are doing better. Based on her experiences she had this closing message:

"Stay home with your kids. It keeps away so many problems. So much temptation. Stay married because, believe me, no matter how nice a guy he is or how much he loves your kids, it is never the same as their real dad."

The temptation issue is one that is too often, and inappropriately, scoffed at. It is not fashionable to say that people should not be alone with members of the opposite sex. It is not fashionable to say that married folks should not carry on solo "friendships" with members of the opposite sex. It is not popular to suggest that people avoid even the appearance of wrongdoing so as not to cause pain to their spouse. Yet, sensitivity to these behaviors strongly adds to the value of your relationship and your partner. All actions taken to preserve and protect your commitment—do just that!

Let Me Try One From Column A . . . and One From Column B

"Before my husband and I got married, I broke up with him several times and caused us both (moreso to him) a lot of pain. I broke up because I felt that it was important to try different people so I could develop an idea of what I wanted. Please tell your lis-

teners and readers that it is not necessary to try different people on like clothing. The more times you give your heart away, the more scars you carry and the less innocent devotion you have to give your spouse."

These words from a listener are most profound. There is a big difference between dating someone to determine whether or not he or she is a keeper, and dating around, as in sampling jellies, ostensibly to get a better view of what's out there.

Where young people are brought up in a loving and intact home, where religion is a significant part of their lives, when they have allowed themselves to mature to the degree of knowing what is meaningful in life, there is only the need to join with someone with whom you can celebrate these values together.

Unfortunately in our society these days, those factors are generally not the ones which function to guide people in their choices. Instead, they look around, try things to see how they work, and see if one style works better.

"When I was in university, my friends all told me that I couldn't stay with my high-school girlfriend permanently, because we would both lack the experience of the greater world out there— with other possibilities. I almost listened to them and would have lost the marriage and baby daughter that I now enjoy fifteen years later. You can have the life of adventure and wandering or life of depth and security. I prefer the latter."

The sad thing is that most people prefer the former. It is sad, because we have a society that doesn't train or support people to search and settle for depth and security. Instead, we urge people to experience, not settle, look for better, get something different; never be satisfied.

I have challenged many men and women on my radio program, who have cycled in and out of many stupid relationships, if they really thought their lives would be worse off with an arranged marriage. After some silliness, almost all of them said, "Yes, maybe if someone who knew me and knew what was good for me, and would match me with a good woman/man, my life would be better." Then they wonder about the excitement lost in the search, and the difficulties with learning to love someone from scratch. I then point out that the excitement would come from learning to love someone from scratch—someone with similar values, morals, ideals, goals, lifestyle, and life's plans. Talk about learning in safety!

"There Shalt Be No Gods Before Me," Say Mommy and Daddy

"We were married for eleven years with three small children. Our marriage was wrought with in-law problems from the beginning. We both saw how his mother despised me from the onset of our engagement. We loved each other deeply, and thought that our love would conquer all of life's adversities. My husband saw what was ongoing (insults, snubs, slams) yet was torn over his loyalties . . . his wife, should he defend her? . . . or his family, should he support them?"

I am flabbergasted by how many people are absolutely tyrannized by a clearly disturbed parent—to the extent that they will jeopardize, disrupt, or abandon their healthy, happy relationships. When they call me, they ask if they can dishonor their parents by not listening to their choice in a spouse, reprimand a destructive parent, or disconnect with a parent who is blatantly attempting to destroy their marriage. There are parents who are so insecure, mentally ill, or downright evil, that they will even sink to undermining their children's lives to feel alive, in control, powerful, and important.

Sometimes these parents will operate indirectly: offering

money with conditions, pleading desperation (illness or upset) for visits and support, virtually turning their adult, married children into their own parents, or by being punitive when their child even plants the lawn with grass that isn't the parent's preference.

I've heard it all. Recently, a male caller told me that his mother-in-law-to-be offered to give his fiancée a quarter of a million dollars if she would make him sign a prenup specifying that his name would be on nothing (like their own home). I told him not to sign and not to comment to his girlfriend about the money and to wait to see if she takes the money. I told him that if she took the money, she was not a candidate for marriage because he'd be marrying her mother. Several days later, he called back. She had, on her own, decided not to take her mother's money. Wonderful. Because if she had broken up with him because she catered to her mother's neurotic need to control and her hatred of men, that would have been a Stupid Breakup.

Since young people today seem to be more geared to "have it" than to "earn it," they find themselves obligated to their parents in the most unhealthy ways. If they live in their parents' homes, or on parental property, or in a house paid for by their parents, or live on income supplied by their parents, they seem to revert to their child-parent behaviors as though they had to be careful not to lose an allowance this week.

As I tell folks, "If you can't afford the wedding, and your own place to live, or the clothes on your back—you're not ready to get married. If you can't afford the car you'd like to have, or the neighborhood you'd like to live in, or the toys and jewelry you fantasize about, earn them. If you stay attached to your parents in an infantile manner, it will probably destroy your adult relationship."

Unresolved Personal Psychological and Emotional Issues

➤ *"I came from a broken home, my mom married a man who beat and molested me, and the only consistent support I got was from this guy who was very nice. I suggested that we see other people because I was bored and confused. I know I let a good man go and broke a heart that didn't deserve it just for novelty and insecurity."*

➤ *"My self-esteem used to be so low, that when I would be in a great relationship, and the guy started to really care, I would do anything to make things bad so that he would break up with me."*

➤ *"I broke up with her that night for no better reason than for not wanting her to ever break up with me. The saddest part was that she had no intention of doing that. I had dated a [girlfriend of mine] who cheated on me, and it broke my heart really bad since she was my first love. I guess I just didn't want to get dumped again, so I took the initiative and broke it off first. To this day I miss that girl. I guess you could say that in not wanting to be hurt by her, I hurt myself."*

➤ *"I grew up in a very dysfunctional home where my father molested me in front of my entire family, so I did not know what true love was—that is, until Ronnie and I came together. I was able to be myself and still have his love. When we became engaged my parents sat me down at the kitchen table and told me that Ronnie was controlling and brainwashing me. They told me that my mom was so upset about our relationship that it would make her lose the baby she was carrying, and if she did, it would be my fault. So, I broke off a relationship with a man whom I was crazy about and was perfect for me. My parents abused my trust in them, so they could keep me in the house to care for their kids.*

*It was stupid to ignore my own instincts. I take responsibility for
my actions by continuing to attend therapy. But, there will always
be that part of me asking how I could be so stupid."*

These are a few of the thousands of letters, faxes, and e-
mails I've gotten from folks suffering from real and serious
problems, stemming anywhere from simple immaturity, to
painful reactions to the abuse and insanity of their original
homes, to mental illness. When I talk to some of these folks
on the air I remind them that everybody is capable of loving
and worthy of being loved. How we all differ is in our ability
to come out of ourselves to sacrifice for another, and our
willingness to become vulnerable and open to somebody
else.

Those qualities are sometimes not easy to come by, and for
some people, quite damaged and frightened by their
upbringing, it becomes a serious challenge. This is the area of
searching for oneself that does have merit: *becoming* the kind
of human being who can be of open heart with wisdom, not
cynicism. For those of you for whom this is a challenge,
promiscuity, substance abuse, and workaholism are not the
solutions. Soul-searching, therapy, spiritual development,
and risking are the solutions.

All these considerations are why I beg clergy to refuse to
marry people who are unwilling to undergo at least six
months of premarital counseling. This is the most wonderful opportunity for you to do something scary (face truths
about yourself) and wonderful (become a more loving, open
person).

Consider yourself an artist. As talented and creative as you
are, without good tools, your best work will never be
expressed. As a human being in a loving relationship, wishing to create a happy home, you are your tools; therefore,

you are your own limitations. Please put aside your ego and face-saving notions to get the kind of education or therapeutic assistance you need to become the best tool you can be.

Stupid Breakups are caused by your not wanting to see the worst in yourself—and if you choose to stay blind, you will never have the love you want:

"One mistake was never taking responsibility for my own short-comings. When I got in trouble I always expected someone to bail me out—including God. And most of the time that is what happened. I was a dreamer who never had the intestinal fortitude to stick it out until my dreams came true.

"I married two times, and did the same stupid things again, and then something happened. I was flying mining equipment into old Mexico and crashed a plane into a mountain. It should have killed me, but by the grace of God, it didn't. Two days later, I was sitting by myself on the side of the mountain, my life devastated, and said to myself that I know someone else who can do a better job with my life than I have. I had no idea why I was saying that or to whom I was talking, but I strangely felt that 2000 lbs. was lifted from my shoulders and peace and joy came upon me and everything was okay, even though I had gone broke in business, lost my second marriage, and just crashed a plane.

"With a relationship with God, and the teachings of the Bible, I got married for the third time. This marriage will work because I finally realized that love is a decision, not a feeling (commitment, covenant), and that feelings come later. We fuss and argue, but never let it interfere with our marriage covenant."

From all the correspondence I receive, it would seem true that the single most impressive tome for helping people get focused on a purposeful life and a satisfying relationship is Scripture. I believe that's because people who open themselves up to G-d are already in the mode of thinking beyond themselves, more charitable of heart and action, more resolute in their intent to "work it out," and more savvy about the deeper levels of satisfaction.

So, in conclusion, to avoid Stupid Breakups, now that you've read this book, open up the Bible.